MW01014155

An **Unconventional**
Introduction to the **Greatest**
Little Town in America
and the **Monumental**
Battle that Made It Famous

Discovering
Gettysburg

W. Stephen Coleman

Illustrations and Maps by Tim Hartman

SB

Savas Beatie
California

For Marilyn
and Diana

© 2017 by W. Stephen Coleman and Tim Hartman

All rights reserved. No part of this publication may be reproduced, stored in a retrieval system, or transmitted, in any form or by any means, electronic, mechanical, photocopying, recording, or otherwise, without the prior written permission of the publisher.

First edition, first printing

Library of Congress Cataloging-in-Publication Data

Names: Coleman, W. Stephen, author.
Title: Discovering Gettysburg : an unconventional introduction to the greatest little town in America and the monumental battle that made it famous / by W. Stephen Coleman ; illustrations and maps by Tim Hartman.
Description: First edition. | El Dorado Hills, California : Savas Beatie LLC, 2017. | Includes bibliographical references and index.
Identifiers: LCCN 2017017815 | ISBN 9781611213539 (alk. paper) | ISBN 9781611213546 (ebk.)
Subjects: LCSH: Gettysburg, Battle of, Gettysburg, Pa., 1863.
Classification: LCC E475.53 .C746 2017 | DDC 973.7/349—dc23
LC record available at https://lccn.loc.gov/2017017815

SB

Savas Beatie LLC
989 Governor Drive, Suite 102
El Dorado Hills, CA 95762

Phone: 916-941-6896
(web) www.savasbeatie.com
(E-mail) sales@savasbeatie.com

Savas Beatie titles are available at special discounts for bulk purchases in the United States by corporations, institutions, and other organizations. For more details, please contact Savas Beatie, P.O. Box 4527, El Dorado Hills, CA 95762, or you may e-mail us at sales@savasbeatie.com, or visit our website at www.savasbeatie.com for additional information.

Proudly published, printed, and warehoused in the United States of America.

Table of Contents

Table of Contents (continued)

List of Maps

List of Caricatures (by page number)

List of Caricatures (continued)

Preface

This book is very unconventional. Let's get that out of the way up front.

Discovering Gettysburg is an account—quirky on occasion, serious when it needs to be—of my "discovery" of one of the most unique places in America and its profound importance to our nation: Gettysburg, Pennsylvania.

It is a snapshot in time of a timeless place; a journey from ignorance to understanding. Part history, part personal memoir, and part travelogue, it aims at making the reader more familiar with Gettysburg through a rather unconventional, and very personal, approach.

In it, I explore the modern community, discuss the famous battle and walk and describe the ground over which it was fought—including some "hidden" or off-the-beaten-path places most visitors to Gettysburg never see. Along the way I highlight some little-known facts about both the town, the people who live and work there, and the battle that made it all famous.

During this journey I met and discussed the town itself with many people, and consulted historians, authors, administrators, rangers, and Licensed Battlefield Guides at the Gettysburg National Military Park about the battle. These conversational "sidebars" are spread throughout the historical chapters. What they have to say is fascinating and insightful—including some of the questions they have been asked over the years.

The artwork is also unconventional. My illustrator-partner in this endeavor, Tim Hartman, is one of the finest illustrators in Pennsylvania. Early on we decided to limit the number of photos and emphasize instead the people, both living and dead, who are forever associated with this remarkable place. Tim has a special talent for capturing in caricature the essence of the "particular look" of an individual through his charming artistic style. (Being the author, I reserved the right to appear in a few "unusual" photographs, along with an occasional friend—actually there's only one of Enis—no "photo" of me, just caricatures.)

Tim's maps, while historically accurate, take on a different quality than the ones you'll find elsewhere. Erring on the side of less detail, we have attempted to make ours accessible, understandable, and frankly, a bit more entertaining, striving for a better understanding of the overall picture. Tim has even created the occasional "cartoon" of a small number of subjects that lend themselves to a lighter approach, but always good-naturedly. Most of the photos in this book were taken by me or my best friend, Enis Koral. In only a few cases have we used an archival photograph, with permissions acknowledged, and I wish to extend my sincerest thanks to the organizations that provided them.

More has been written on Gettysburg than any other battle. Much of it, especially its broader outlines, has become common knowledge. Of course, there are still new diaries and letter collections waiting to be discovered, a hitherto unknown official document shedding light on something, or a historian who simply puts two and two together to come up with a richer four. I am not a trained historian of the Civil War or of the battle itself, so I have relied on a variety of sources to help me in the writing of this book.

It takes a while to get a book finished, submitted, and published, so some things changed since I conducted the research and interviews. Sadly, several of the people have died, and others have retired from key positions. Despite these changes, I have decided to leave the text pretty much intact—my conversations with these wonderful people, and the information and insights they shared with me during our meetings have not diminished because an occasional detail has changed here or there. These conversations were at the very core of my journey of discovery of this little town where ten roads meet. Moreover, it was especially important for me to capture the impressions and feelings of these people during this special period in Gettysburg's history: the period leading up to and following the celebrations of the Sesquicentennial—the 150th Anniversary of both the Battle of Gettysburg and the Commemoration of Lincoln's Gettysburg Address. In a few cases, however, where the information I initially garnered was overtaken by events, I have taken the liberty of updating it.

This book is intended for two audiences: general readers who are not very familiar with Gettysburg and what happened there, and more knowledgeable readers already familiar with the subject matter. How does that work? For the former, it allows the reader to accompany me on my journey of discovery, learning and understanding as much as I did about it; for the latter, it provides the opportunity to renew their excitement at being there, and perhaps even gain a few new insights and discoveries about a favored place.

It is my hope everyone who reads this is rewarded by my experience of this extraordinary place and what it represents in our history. At the least, Tim and I sincerely hope you enjoy our book as much as we enjoyed creating it.

W. Stephen Coleman
Pittsburgh, Pennsylvania

Introduction

The best place to begin is the beginning.

Several years ago, my wife Marilyn and I, along with our dear friends Mimi and Enis Koral, sat musing over a few glasses of wine and bourbon about a long weekend getaway to enjoy the beautiful fall foliage in our home state of Pennsylvania. After much discussion we decided on a trip to the iconic little town of Gettysburg in the south-central part of the state. We all knew some Civil War altercation had taken place there, and thought it might be fun to see just what it was all about.

We had all been there before. Marilyn was there as an attendee at the Governor's Awards for the Arts (she is a consultant for non-profits). The Korals spent several days in the area in the late 1980s, which included a short visit to Gettysburg and the battlefield. My Gettysburg connection came during a childhood trip (I was about seven) with a Baltimore-based uncle and his sons, my fraternal twin cousins. I even remember buying a minié ball—long since lost along with less significant youthful detritus. I found it all fascinating at the time, and two weeks later forgot the whole thing. But none of us had been back since those first visits, and certainly none of us had spent any time examining the Civil War set-to for which it was known. We thought it would be interesting to find out if there really was something special about the little town, or was it just one of those places that has enjoyed some arcane historical notoriety and had, in fact, been passed over by time?

I've always had an avocational interest in history in general, and especially military history, but have made my living teaching and exercising my talents as a theatre artist—all-consuming, enervating, time-intensive theatre! Indeed, I've spent most of my adult life in large darkened buildings looking evermore like some reclusive, pale-complexioned cave dweller who never saw the light of day. Fifty years of switching back and forth between being a professor, an actor, a director, and back again . . . and again . . . and again . . . (the schizophrenic nature of the changes sometimes reminding me of that wonderful scene in the film Chinatown: ". . . my daughter, my sister, my daughter, my sister!"). But perhaps my attraction to history, and especially military history, is quite understandable given that as a theatre practitioner my focus had always been on

Shakespeare—his people, drama, history, battles, and all that swordplay. (I am a specialist in stage dueling.)

As I edged closer to retirement, however, I could feel my interests changing. The theatre no longer held the allure for me that it once did. Oh, I still enjoyed performing, and even teaching to a degree, but I had to be dragged kicking and screaming to the theatre to see other productions. It felt more and more like the proverbial "busman's holiday"—doing on vacation what you do at work—and I'd had enough. (I won't even tell you how I felt about faculty meetings—one is not supposed to use that sort of language in polite company.) I yearned for another milieu in which to immerse myself; as the (Monty) Pythons once said, maybe it was time for "something completely different."

Discussing the possibility of our trip, Marilyn mentioned that when she was in Gettysburg she had stayed at a nice little boutique hotel just a half-block from Lincoln Square, the center of the town. We all decided to give it a try. Mimi added that she had heard about a sort of "guide service" that provided "in-car" guides to tour the battlefield. That sounded great; you could probably even ask them questions. We decided to look into arranging one of those. Finally, given our separate work schedules, we decided to take our own cars and meet there. What the hell, we all thought, it should make for a nice quiet weekend.

Who knew?

So we took that fall trip. Indeed, I have now been to Gettysburg more than forty times since that gorgeous fall, and have taken another twenty-five or so trips to other Civil War sites. You remember that old maxim about "old dogs and new tricks?"—don't believe a word of it. As I quickly discovered, the Civil War was the most significant event in the history of the United States, and the Battle of Gettysburg the largest engagement ever fought on American soil, probably the most important of the war, and I wanted to know more about it.

My interest could not have begun at a better time, for the Sesquicentennial was approaching. The planning for this book began in 2011—exactly 150 years after the beginning of the war. Thus I have found many insights into the conflict I would not have had during non-anniversary periods. The Civil War Sites Advisory Commission study in the early 1990s designated 384 battle sites for preservation (out of 10,500 where fighting took place). It appeared there would not only be a lot for me to see, but that I would enjoy the added advantage of watching them prepare for their respective anniversaries.

I'm very pleased to report that my concern about finding a new avocation has been met—in spades. Studying the Civil War provides something of interest for everyone: from its historical significance and the prejudices and politics that got us into it; the culture, mores, and values of the time; the experiences of its people—both men and women—and the artifacts they left behind; to simply being outdoors enjoying breathtaking landscapes while getting in touch with nature. This hobby allows one to marvel at the magnificent job being done by the National Park Service (NPS)—which, incidentally, celebrated its 100th Anniversary in 2016—and the many concerned citizens that lend their time and talents to the preservation of historic sites. Following the Revolution, the Civil War was the defining struggle of our Republic.

A fascinating conversation with an actor colleague brought this into the clearest possible focus. Douglas Harmsen, a Canadian actor with whom I once shared a dressing room, observed that when he first visited this country, it struck him "the only way you could truly understand modern America was if you understood the Civil War." His comment was revelatory. It helped me understand, at least in part, why my new interest was becoming a passion. I'm glad to say Doug has since emigrated to the United States and has become an avid student of the conflict and its effects on our culture. I envy his youth and that he was smart enough to begin his journey so much earlier than I did.

Understanding the Civil War helps us define who we are as a people, who we were as a people, and who we would become. Consciously or unconsciously, we live with its effects almost every day of our lives. That conflict in which, according to the most recent scholarship, at least 750,000 Americans lost their lives, along with hundreds of thousands more wounded or maimed for life, is a significant part of the foundation of modern America.

Beyond merely reading about the Civil War, it is wonderful to be able to discover and explore the hundreds of small towns, villages, and crossroads where these battles were fought. Usually peaceful, frequently charming, and often idyllic, these communities were torn asunder as thousands of men bent on each other's destruction descended upon them. And while not all of them can recapture their original cachet, many have struggled to restore a sense of what they were like before the Civil War changed them forever. I like visiting during the "off-season"—it is less busy and easier to really experience what you want at your own pace.

Gettysburg is among the finest examples of a Civil War town that not only preserves and honors its history, but has managed to grow into a small modern metropolis. Considering the scope and significance of the monumental struggle that took place there, what the town itself endured and witnessed, and how it has evolved into the living testimony of the greatest test of our survival as a nation, may actually qualify it as (to quote my publisher Theodore P. Savas) "the most unique community in America."

If you haven't been, now is the time to go.

Each of us has an opportunity to discover this unique place in his or her own way. So what might that be for you? For me the choice is easy: I love discovering new places. I enjoy learning what makes a community like modern Gettysburg tick. By far the most fascinating and intriguing part of encountering a piece of history like this little "town where ten roads meet" is to experience it by walking those sacred pieces of ground where the events took place—touching history, ex post facto as it were, firsthand. As the great novelist and travel writer Paul Theroux observed in The Long Way Home: "No history book can equal the experience of walking those battlefields." I could not agree with him more.

With that behind us, please join me on a journey to the little town in south-central Pennsylvania where 51,000 men were killed, captured, or wounded in just three days . . . the Adams County seat, named after tavern-keeper Samuel Gettys . . . that little place called Gettysburg.

Chapter 1

Why Gettysburg?
The Civil War in 1863

ay 1863.

Once again, victorious Confederate General Robert E. Lee and his Army of Northern Virginia have handed the Union cause another major defeat at Chancellorsville. And that's a good place to start understanding how Gettysburg came about.

Considered by many to be Lee's tactical masterpiece, the Chancellorsville campaign began in late April and would not end until May 6, when the Army of the Potomac under Maj. Gen. Joseph Hooker retreated after being repeatedly attacked and outgeneraled.

"Fighting Joe" Hooker was but one of the many Union generals who suffered at the hands of Lee. The last Union debacle occurred at Fredericksburg the previous December, where Maj. Gen. Ambrose E. Burnside (notable for his prominent sideburns) led the Army of the Potomac to a bloody defeat with his series of headlong attacks against an impregnable Rebel position. The final straw for President Abraham Lincoln arrived a few weeks later in January when Burnside's army bogged down in the the winter mud in yet another failed effort to get at Lee's Virginia army. Burnside was out.

In his ongoing search for a general who could win against Lee, Lincoln decided on Joe Hooker, a bachelor with a penchant for the ladies and a host of

GENERAL
ROBERT EDWARD
LEE

vices—swearing, gambling, and alcohol among them. (While "hooker" is much older than our general's taste for the companionship of females of questionable character, the term is still frequently associated with his name.) The origin of his appellation "Fighting Joe" was the result of a bad pick-up by a typesetter of a newspaper reporter's dispatch that read: "Fighting—Joe Hooker . . ." The Northern press, naturally enough, seized upon the nickname "Fighting Joe" and ran with it. It is said Hooker disliked it, though that seems doubtful. General Lee—a man not widely known for his sense of humor—took a malicious delight in referring to his opponent as "Mr. F. J. Hooker."

MAJOR GENERAL AMBROSE BURNSIDE

In the spring of 1863, Hooker led an army of some 130,000 men against Lee's roughly 60,000 strong. (Much of Lee's First Corps under James Longstreet was away in southeastern Virginia, leaving Lee to operate solely on the defensive.) When Hooker stole a wide march around the Confederate left flank, Lee boldly divided his army to meet him. He left a small part at Fredericksburg to watch Federals hovering there and marched westward to confront the bulk of Hooker's command in the tangles of the Wilderness around Chancellorsville Inn, a crossroads with little more than the brick mansion.

Lee seized the initiative and sent Lt. Gen. Thomas "Stonewall" Jackson's corps marching around Hooker's exposed right flank. Jackson attacked and crushed Maj. Gen. Oliver O. Howard's XI Corps in a bold surprise attack, but was accidentally wounded by his own men on the evening of his greatest triumph. During ferocious fighting the next day, Hooker was knocked temporarily senseless by a cannonball that smashed into the porch upon which he was standing. When Federals broke through at Fredericksburg and marched against Lee's rear, the Southern general split his army yet again and turned to meet the new threat at Salem Church. The heavy fighting killed and wounded thousands across the sprawling front. With his confidence shattered, Hooker—even though a large portion of his army had yet to fire a

MAJOR GENERAL
JOSEPH "FIGHTING JOE"
HOOKER

shot—withdrew across the Rappahannock River, giving Lee what many consider to this day to have been his most spectacular victory.

Lee's victory at Chancellorsville, however, was costly for the South. At the height of his greatest success, Stonewall Jackson was wounded by friendly fire.

Stonewall Jackson's Appendage

His arm was amputated (and buried on a farm near the battlefield), and it appeared as though he would make a full recovery. Pneumonia set in, however, and he died just one week later. When he learned of Jackson's wounds, Lee lamented, "Jackson has lost his left arm, but I have lost my right." Stonewall's death was an irreparable loss to the Confederate cause.

LIEUTENANT GENERAL THOMAS "STONEWALL" JACKSON

Late May 1863. Lee has reorganized his army from two corps into three, and reinforcements have swelled his ranks. Despite the loss of Stonewall, he decides for the second time to invade Union territory. The first thrust north, undertaken after Second Manassas in September 1862, ended in the bloodbath in Maryland known in the North as Antietam and in the South as Sharpsburg. (It was the general practice for the Union to name battles after a geographic feature—usually a river—near where the battle was fought, while the Confederates named battles after communities closest to the fighting. Thus the Union battles of First and Second Bull Run (a stream) are the same as the

Confederacy's First and Second Manassas (a community). Occasionally, however, the warring sides settled on the same name— like Gettysburg.)

By mid-1863, the South is seriously feeling the strain of the war. A long war it is not equipped to fight and win. As far as Lee is concerned, only a battlefield triumph on Northern soil will quickly bring it to a close. This time around Lee's goal is to move through Maryland and into

MAJOR GENERAL J.E.B. "Jeb" STUART

Pennsylvania, where he hopes to threaten its capital Harrisburg, as well as Philadelphia, Baltimore, and perhaps even Washington itself. Lee expects one or two more major victories— especially on Northern soil—to finally swing European support behind the Confederacy.

Strategically, he hopes to draw the Army of the Potomac into a tiring pursuit and turn and defeat it piece-by-piece on favorable terrain of his choosing. Despite a steady

MAJOR GENERAL ALFRED PLEASONTON

LIEUTENANT GENERAL RICHARD STODDERT EWELL

string of Union victories in the Western Theater (that area of the country between the Appalachian Mountains and the Mississippi River), enthusiasm for the conflict is waning in the North. The numerous defeats at the hands of Lee's army and growing casualty lists are exhausting Lincoln's people. Lee's confident troops believe they can whip the Army of the Potomac anywhere they meet it. Even without a major battle, the invasion will give the Confederates access to the lush and prosperous Pennsylvania farms while relieving the pressure on hard-pressed Virginia, which has known firsthand two long years of war.

Hooker, meanwhile, remains in command of the army. He does his best to keep it between Lee and Washington, DC and Baltimore. If either of those cities is successfully attacked, the results would be disastrous. The first clash of the campaign arrives early—even before Lee's army steps northward—in the form of a large cavalry engagement at Brandy Station, Virginia, on June 9. Union troopers under Maj. Gen. Alfred Pleasonton surprise their Confederate counterparts under Maj. Gen. James Ewell Brown "Jeb" Stuart, the storied Confederate cavalier. The clash is the largest cavalry battle of the war, though of course no one knew that at the time. According to noted Civil War cavalry historian Eric Wittenberg, "Pleasonton had been charged with catching Stuart, and destroying the Confederate cavalry as an effective force. He failed to achieve his objective." However, the battle is a coming-of-age event for the Union troopers, who discover something within them that day that remains until Appomattox. At the end of the battle, Union forces withdraw back across the Rappahannock River and rejoin their main

LIEUTENANT GENERAL A.P. HILL

force en route to Manassas Junction. Lee's move north is delayed by at least a full day.

Ewell's corps leads the way west into the Shenandoah Valley and then north. Up near the Potomac River, Ewell strikes like lightning at the Second Battle of Winchester (June 13-15), clearing the path for the invasion to proceed across the Potomac River, into and through Maryland, and into Pennsylvania. Some whisper that it is as if Stonewall Jackson is still leading the corps.

Cavalry skirmishes throughout the middle days of June keep the Federals from discovering Lee's large movement north; the cavalry are the eyes and ears of any army, and Stuart's troopers kept the passes in Rebel hands and Hooker's troopers at bay. As a result, Lee's forces begin crossing the Potomac on June 15, and enter Pennsylvania on June 22. Hooker has no idea.

Shortly after Confederate troops begin crossing the river, Lee approves Jeb Stuart's plan to cut behind Hooker's army, ride around it as circumstances dictate, and create as much distraction and damage as possible while threatening Washington, DC. Lee's orders are vague—an object of deep controversy ever since. The one thing he insists upon is that Stuart shield Lt. Gen. Richard Ewell's Second Corps once it is deep into Pennsylvania and meet up with it there. As we will see, Stuart's raid removes him from the Army of Northern Virginia for a full week, during which the Battle of Gettysburg commences without him. Lee will enter Pennsylvania and fight nearly all of the battle without his "eyes and ears."

Meantime, Hill's Third Corps follows Ewell, with James Longstreet's Corps bringing up the rear. Against all prevailing military theory of the day, Lee has again divided his forces by sending off Stuart and letting Ewell operate well

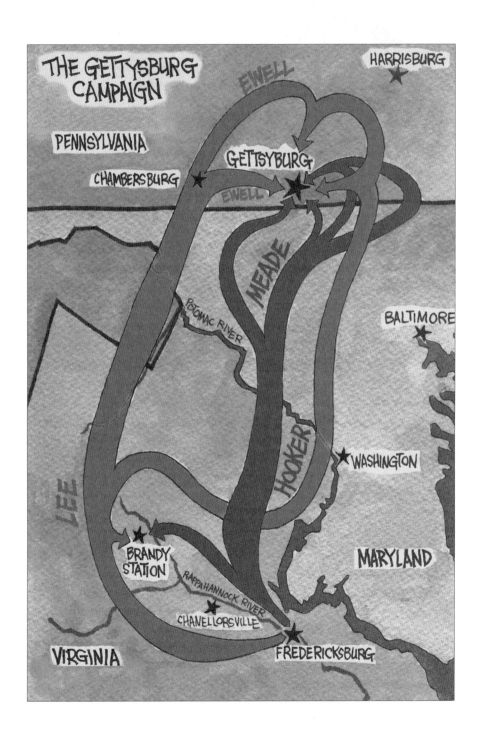

MAJOR GENERAL JUBAL A. EARLY.

away from his other two corps. His plan calls for a pincer-like movement toward the Susquehanna Valley. Meanwhile, Hooker—still trying to figure out what Lee is up to—proceeds cautiously north in an effort to locate the Virginia army while shielding Washington and Baltimore.

Ewell Progresses — But Where is Stuart?

By June 28, Ewell's Corps is just north of Carlisle—not far from Harrisburg. One of his divisions under Maj. Gen. Jubal A. Early (whom Lee calls his "bad old man") has arrived in the York-Dover area. Rebel cavalry operating with Early passes through Gettysburg on the 26th, as does a 2,000- man infantry brigade under Brig. Gen. John B. Gordon. Historian Scott L. Mingus, Sr. sets the stage:

One of Early's main goals was York, Pennsylvania. It was a significant town back then, with lots of industry, and of historic significance for the North—did you know the Articles of Confederation were crafted there in the 1770s? It was also an important railhead. On the morning of June 26th, Early's Confederate forces brush aside the Union 26th PA Emergency Infantry, a militia unit, around Knoxlyn Ridge, and proceed to occupy Gettysburg. An urban myth suggested that Early's mission to Gettysburg was 'solely' (pun intended) to capture shoes for his barefoot troops. He's not looking for shoes. In fact, there were no shoe factories in Gettysburg, and Early, on that same day, had captured Union boxcars filled with 2,000 Springfield rifled muskets, and possibly even, some shoes; they also took shoes from the captured PA militiamen. Then, on the

27th, Early marches away to the east to prepare his march on York and possibly onto Harrisburg.

Stuart, meanwhile, captures a large train of Union supply wagons in the Rockville, Maryland, area. Instead of burning the heavy slow wagons he rides with them as a present for General Lee. The lumbering vehicles slow the cavalier's progress north. Hooker's army is now moving north and is

HENRY THOMAS HARRISON

between Stuart and the Confederate main body, even as pursuing Union cavalry are on his tail. Stuart, the "eyes and ears" of the Virginia army, is cut off from the Virginia army.

Lee, along with Hill's Corps and Longstreet's Corps, meanwhile, have reached Chambersburg. They have not heard from Stuart in a long while, and have no firm idea where Hooker's army is or what it is up to. Lee has some cavalry on hand, but without Stuart, upon whom he has come to rely, he is operating blind.

Late in the evening of the 28th, Henry Thomas Harrison, one of

LIEUTENANT GENERAL JAMES LONGSTREET

MAJOR GENERAL
GEORGE GORDON
MEADE

Longstreet's spies and a cloak and dagger sort of fellow, informs Old Pete (Longstreet) that the Army of the Potomac is no longer in Virginia as supposed, but has crossed the river, marched past Frederick, Maryland, and is just below the Pennsylvania border. There is more news: Hooker is no longer in command.

The news stuns Lee. Famous for improvisation, he now alters his plans once more, moving east with Hill's Corps. He sends word to Ewell to turn south, and orders Longstreet to follow Hill along the Chambersburg Pike through the South Mountain range toward Cashtown—a mere eight miles from Gettysburg.

Harrison's shocking news was the result of Hooker's impulsive request to be relieved of command. It is doubtful he really thought Lincoln would grant his "wish," but the president did just that, swapping Hooker on June 28 with V Corps leader Maj. Gen. George Gordon Meade. Changing commanders in the middle of a campaign—and on Northern soil, no less!—is a momentous decision. The first shots of Gettysburg are just three days away. When he heard the news, Lee is reported to have remarked, "Meade will commit no blunder in my front, and if I make one he will make haste to take advantage of it."

Meade—who is as surprised at his elevation to command as Hooker is at being fired—moves his large army north hoping to bring the Confederates to battle just north of Taneytown, Maryland. ("Tawney" town is named after Raphael Taney, a recipient of one of the first land grants in the area. Roger Brooke Taney, one of his descendants, served as the fifth Chief Justice of the United States, and is best known for delivering the majority opinion in the Dred Scott case.) Meade briefly establishes his headquarters here as part of his "Pipe Creek Plan," which calls for the Union army to engage the Confederates in this area along a defensive line running from just south of Taneytown through Middleburg and extending to Manchester, Maryland, along a snake-like curve that flattens as it heads east.

Meade's plan calls for Union three infantry corps under Generals John Reynolds, Henry W. Slocum, and John Sedgwick, all under the overall command of Maj. Gen. Winfield Scott Hancock, to be in position to confront the Army of Northern Virginia as it turns south to attack Baltimore. (Hancock, one of the finest generals in the entire Union army, picked up the sobriquet "Hancock the Superb" after the Battle of Williamsburg during the Peninsula Campaign outside Richmond, when Maj. Gen. George B. McClellan wrote to his wife, "Hancock was superb today." The appellation stuck with him throughout the war.)

Lee as we have seen, is not cooperating with Meade's plan. Instead, he is concentrating his scattered army east of the South Mountain Range in southern

The Shriver Home. *Union Mills Homestead Foundation*

Pennsylvania. In developing his plan, however, Meade is moving large elements of his army into positions in Maryland just a handful of miles below Gettysburg.

Every military campaign turns on small things, and Gettysburg is loaded with "what ifs." Just south of the Maryland-Pennsylvania border is the Union Mills Homestead Park. Located on Big Pipe Creek and the Baltimore Pike, this historic and beautiful home was owned by the Shriver Family of northern Maryland. Elements of Jeb Stuart's cavalry pass through early on the morning of June 30. General Stuart breakfasts there with the Southern sympathizers of the family just across the road from the main house and mill, but leaves early in his exhausting effort to locate Ewell's infantry corps near Harrisburg. Just four hours later, Brig. Gen. James Barnes, in command of the 1st Division of the Union's V Corps, arrives at the home and sets up his headquarters in the main house. He spends the night there with some of his officers sleeping on the porch, and departs early on July 1 on his way up to Gettysburg.

The Shriver family built the magnificent home and commercial gristmill in 1797. The property is now run by the Union Mills Homestead Foundation, with Jane Sewell as its executive director. During the summer season it is open to visitors and provides guided tours of both the house and the mill. The

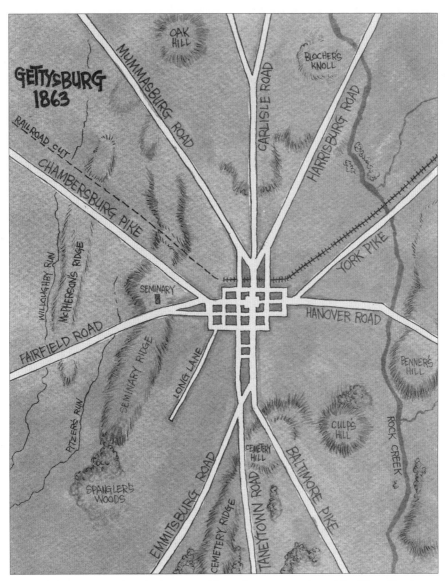

beautifully preserved main house, mill, and property along Big Pipe Creek are worth a visit.

As Confederate forces under Hill and Longstreet tramp eastward toward Cashtown, Meade, one of the ablest of the Union's generals, concludes a battle will soon be upon them. He sends a cavalry screening force under Brig. Gen. John Buford to Gettysburg to determine Lee's location—what is Lee up to and where does he intend to fight? Ewell and Early, meanwhile, have met up in Heidlersburg and been recalled south with orders to concentrate on Gettysburg or Cashtown, as circumstances dictate. Stuart can't find Ewell, who is now moving in a different direction because of Lee's altered plan. By the evening of June 30, as Confederate forces gather west and north of Gettysburg, a solitary Union cavalry brigade arrives to determine the enemy's intentions.

Gettysburg is a major logistics hub in this portion of the state. The thriving community is fed by ten roads and a railroad, includes a host of businesses, a college, and more. It is a thriving and prosperous community. Unbeknownst to its citizens, it will soon become the site of the largest battle ever fought in America.

Chapter 2

Cashtown—The Jumping-off Point for the Army of Northern Virginia

*C*ashtown rests just east of South Mountain where it merges with the top end of the Catoctin Range. Gettysburg is eight miles to the east.

Just a mile south of the current Route 30, the little village sits astride the road formerly known as the Chambersburg Pike, which leads eastward into Gettysburg. (The route is also a part of the original Lincoln Highway, the first "named trans-continental highway" that celebrated its 100th anniversary in 2013.) The road here is an idyllic two-lane blacktop whose simplicity lends itself to envisioning the tens of thousands of Confederate troops who once marched along it on their way to their individual fates at Gettysburg. It was here in the area of Cashtown that Robert E. Lee assembled most of two corps—the bulk of the Virginia army—for its coming confrontation with George Gordon Meade's Army of the Potomac.

To call Cashtown a village is to overstate its size, for it is little more than a crossroads with a few stores. Its main claim to fame is the Cashtown Inn, which stands next to the road like a silent sentinel observing history as it passes by. It was built in 1797, so the main building was a witness to 1863. Unwilling to merely observe the fateful events of that year, the Inn played an important role in the campaign. Today, the Inn boasts an outstanding restaurant, coupled with a cozy and utterly charming bed and breakfast featuring four rooms and three amazing suites.

The Cashtown Inn

Jack and Maria Paladino purchased the Inn in early 2006. They completely renovated the kitchen and made many other improvements. Today, it is apparent the business with pride in their accomplishments and a deep enthusiasm for the Inn's place in history. "Every day is a new day—it's always interesting," Jack explains. "The people who visit us are here because they want to be with us; they want to be at the Cashtown Inn, enjoying its history, enjoying its hospitality."

The Inn still has a few elements of the original 1797 building, but it is the red brick building of 1863 we might justly consider the "jumping off" point for the Virginia army and Gettysburg. A newer addition in the back, which now houses some of the rooms of the B&B, was built over one of the sections that had served as a Confederate field hospital during the battle.

The Paladinos' interest in the area was encouraged by Maria's sister, a confirmed Civil War buff. They were first attracted to Gettysburg because "The place was so calming, so relaxing; we'd just drop the top on the convertible, drive around, look at the monuments, and leave our hectic lives back in the 'Burgh [Pittsburgh, that is]." As a result, Jack and Maria were frequent guests at the Cashtown Inn before they were owners. Jack recalls telling the former owner to "call me" whenever he was ready to sell. To their delight, the former owner made the call, and the Paladinos bought the Inn.

They also soon discovered their fascination with the "ghosts of Gettysburg," and especially those who had taken up residence at the Inn, which is listed as one of "the ten most haunted buildings in America." Its basement, through which water ran at the time of the battle, served as an operating room. There was so much surgery and bleeding there, explained Jack, that "it took four days for the blood to dissipate." In 2008, after it was featured on the TV program *Ghost Hunters*, the Inn's website registered 252,000 hits in the next 24 hours. "For the next two years we were at 92% capacity—not just seasonally, but year-round!"

In addition to its tremendous business around the anniversary of the battle, the Paladinos put together special packages throughout the year featuring the Inn's history and the battle that erupted just a handful of miles to the east. "Lack of communication, lack of follow-through, lack of following orders lost Lee the battle, and maybe lost the war," opined Jack, who is very familiar with the history and can speak at length about the roles of Lee and many of the Confederate generals before the battle and after the battle—including A. P. Hill, Jubal Early, and Henry Heth.

According to Jack, Lee did not want a major engagement at Gettysburg. Several days before the fighting began, General Early had passed through on his way to Wrightsville on the Susquehanna River. General Heth suspected that "Old Jube" had not paused long enough in town to secure all its provisions, and offered to march to Gettysburg to find what he could. "None in the world" was how Heth's commanding officer, A. P. Hill, replied when asked if he had any objections to the idea. Lee met with Hill on the morning of July 1 as the sound of rolling gunfire eight miles east waved over them. Brig. Gen. J. Johnston Pettigrew had approached the town the previous afternoon only to return with a surprising tale: Union cavalry was in Gettysburg. Heth, who dismissed the warning, was convinced that if Pettigrew had seen enemy troops, they were only Pennsylvania militia and the not veteran cavalry from the Army of the Potomac. As history has come to know, Heth was wrong.

The historic Inn played itself in the 1993 film epic *Gettysburg*. Jack and Maria had heard stories about the movie experience from Bud Buckley, the Inn's former proprietor. Sam Elliott, the crusty actor with the voice like sandpaper who played Union cavalryman John Buford, spent three weeks in the beautiful General Robert E. Lee Suite on the Inn's top floor. He frequently mixed with other residents and by all accounts was a thoroughly pleasant and gracious guest. Before filming the well-documented meeting between Generals Lee and A. P. Hill on the very road where the event occurred, tons of dirt were hauled in by the truckload to give it a historic appearance.

In December of 2012, my wife and I returned to Cashtown and spent a night at the Inn. During a little exploring before dinner, we found a beautiful old stone farmhouse near a small intersection. That's the home of Henry Hahn, explained Jack, "the patriarch of a family of Pennsylvania farmers who were among the first Yankees in Pennsylvania to shoot at the advance elements of the Confederate army on its way to Gettysburg." Hopefully, they survived the decision to take pot-shots at more than 20,000 hardened Rebs.

Our room was the same room the ill A. P. Hill occupied just before the battle. It's on the Inn's second floor and overlooks the road. At night, it's probably as quiet now as it was back in 1863—at least in December. We can't speak for what it's like any given July. While most of the Inn has been renovated, graffiti on the walls of rooms left by "stage runners" going all the way back to the 1830s has been preserved. Notes about ghosts and "things that go bump in the night" have also been preserved in the form of guest registers left in the rooms. Many modern visitors recall seeing "glowing areas" or being "touched" or had something "moved" in their room. Alas, none of the ghosties paid us a visit that night. If you're into this sort of thing, you will definitely enjoy staying here. We recommend it.

Ready for dinner, we went downstairs to the tavern and enjoyed a delicious meal while sharing our experience with a few other customers and enjoying Jack's charm and their conversations with him, along with our delightful waitress Krystle Brough. The next morning we bid Jack and his staff farewell. We hope we will have the opportunity to make many return visits.

Gettysburg: Battlefield and Community

We drive east out of Cashtown and pass through the tiny village of McKnightstown and quickly rejoin modern Route 30. Inching ever closer to Gettysburg, we cross Marsh Creek, the little stream that witnessed a pre-battle skirmish between members of the Army of Northern Virginia and some brave but relatively ineffective Pennsylvania militia.

A little farther down on the left and opposite the Knoxlyn Road is an easily missed but very important historical monument. The "First Shot Marker" is a simple stone obelisk about five feet tall in what looks like someone's backyard, but sits on a patch of land now owned by the National Park Service. The brick house next to it was owned by Ephraim Wisler in 1863, and according to some accounts he was nearly killed by a Confederate artillery shell when he stepped outside to see what all the ruckus was about. Near the marker someone—a Union cavalryman by all accounts—leveled his weapon and fired at the Rebels approaching from the west. There are several claims as to who fired the "first shot" of Gettysburg, but a trio of troopers from the 8th Illinois Cavalry believed their claim to that honor was strong enough to produce their own monument in Naperville, Illinois, and haul it more than 600 miles to Wisler's yard.

Passing the intersection at Herr's Ridge with Herr's Tavern on the right, we come to historic Willoughby Run. A "run" is another term for a stream or creek, as in the more famous Bull Run in northern Virginia. Is there a difference between a "run" and a "stream" or "creek"? Tradition has it that a stream is larger than a creek, which is larger than a run—but between you and me, it's probably six of one, half a gallon of the other, or, as they should say, "just so much water over those rocks."

Finally, we see the sign welcoming us to the "Gettysburg National Military Park." About here the landscape begins to change. As you enter the battlefield itself, the vista opens rather dramatically. The view gives me a little chill when I realize what I am looking at. What had been a sort of rural suburbia that often surrounds small towns gives way to beautiful rolling fields edged with wooden fences—some straight, some in an odd zig-zag pattern. (These fences are sometimes called "snake-rail fences" or, more commonly, "Virginia worm fences.") Farther east the landscape is dotted with a large variety of stone and bronze monuments of all sizes and configurations. There are so many different kinds. A small stone building off to the right looks like an office and some restrooms, and a large old barn sits near the edge of one of the fields. In the distance on a spine of land we soon learn is called Seminary Ridge, is a tall building with a white cupola on top of of the Lutheran Theological Seminary.

Names soon to be very familiar label the streets: Reynolds Avenue, Doubleday Avenue, Seminary Ridge, and Buford Avenue (this section of Route 30, or the old Chambersburg Pike), along with many others. As we continue east it is impossible not to notice a small older building on the left. General Robert E. Lee's headquarters had been in private hands for a long while, but was recently purchased by the Civil War Trust and is now part of the

Lee's Headquarters—or, a nice place to have dinner.
Lynn Light Heller, The Civil War Trust.

Gettysburg National Military Park (GNMP). The Trust recently demolished an entire motel next door and transformed the area back to its 1863 appearance. We find out later that Lee's headquarters was in a tent just south across the pike, and that he probably only went into the little house for an occasional meeting or meal.

The downhill journey off Seminary Ridge leads to an intersection with West Street that boasts a bronze Civil War sentry where the road angles off to the left as we enter Gettysburg. The street name changes here to Chambersburg Street. In just a few blocks we arrive at Lincoln Square, and stop.

We are in the heart of Gettysburg.

Chapter 3

A First Look at the Town and the Gettysburg National Military Park

*G*ettysburg is a small town of some 8,000 residents, yet its history has made it one of the most important places in America. It regularly hosts well over a million visitors a year, with that number more than doubling in 2013—the Sesquicentennial Year of the Battle of Gettysburg. But I want to know more than just its history. I want to get to know the *modern* town and its people, and understand their take on life there today. I enjoy the feeling of almost being at home in a place that is not my home. According to the many people I've met researching this book, little Gettysburg is like a powerful magnet that attracts people from all over the world. What is it, exactly, that draw in so many people?

Noted historian and author J. David Petruzzi calls this phenomenon the "Gettysburg Addiction Syndrome," which boils down to the thoroughly entertaining acronym GAS! J.D. is onto something. One becomes addicted to the place, always craving a little more knowledge, a little more experience, a little more enjoyment of all the wonderful amenities and rewards it offers. It's about coming to understand not just the great battle and the people involved, but the "community" of Gettysburg—the way the disparate elements of the place come together to create a truly unique experience.

The village that came to be known as Gettysburg has its origins in 1761 when one of its early settlers, Samuel Gettys, established a tavern at the crossroads of the Shippensburg-Baltimore Road and the Philadelphia-Pittsburgh Road. Its clientele consisted mostly of traders and soldiers, along with the occasional traveler. In the mid-1780s Samuel's son James laid out a town of 210 lots with a central town square on the land surrounding the tavern. Gettysburg was originally part of York County, but by 1790 the growing population of the area decided to separate from York. The new county was approved by the state legislature in 1800 and was named after President John Adams. Gettysburg was chosen as the county seat of Adams County.

The exact location of that famous founding tavern is easy to find. Just look behind the historic downtown Gettysburg Hotel, parking plaza is a plaque that commemorates the Samuel Gettys' Tavern. The tavern also played a role in an even earlier altercation called the American Revolution, and Samuel gave money to the Continental Army.

By 1860 the tiny village of Gettysburg had grown to 2,400 citizens. Ten roads fed the town and helped created a thriving community. Approximately 450 buildings housed carriage manufacturing, cobblers, and tanneries, as well as the usual assortment of merchants, banks, taverns, and homes. A railroad line was completed from Hanover to Gettysburg in 1858, with the Gettysburg Train Station opening in 1859. There were also several educational institutions, most notably Pennsylvania College (known today as Gettysburg College) and the Lutheran Theological Seminary. It is generally felt these 10 roads are the primary reason why two great armies converged there in 1863.

Our "digs" on this, our first visit, are in the historic James Gettys Hotel at 27 Chambersburg Street, which was known as the Union Hotel back in 1863. Originally opened by John Troxell in 1804 as the "Sign of the Buck Tavern and Roadhouse" to accommodate travelers to the western frontier, it had grown into a flourishing business by the time of the war. It thrived until the 1950s, when the popularity of less expensive motels supplanted many of the smaller hotels forced the James Gettys Hotel to close its doors. It was used as an apartment building until the 1980s, when it became an American Youth Hostel for 10 years. In 1995, the building was purchased by its current owners and restored as a charming boutique hotel.

That charm is evident from the moment you step through the door. On our first visit in 2008 we were greeted by then-manager Stephanie Lower [today Stephanie Lower Shaara], accompanied by a massive black Labrador named Char. The dog almost always hangs out with his owner George Lower

STEPHANIE
LOWER SHAARA

(Stephanie's father) in Lord Nelson's Gallery. The lovely art gallery is on either side of the entrance to the hotel and is accessible from inside the lobby as well. In case you're wondering why an art gallery in historic Gettysburg is named after a British admiral from the Napoleonic era, take comfort in the fact that it is not: Lord Nelson was Stephanie's parents' black lab at the time, a forerunner, though not an ancestor, of Char. Char is the third such companion, preceded by yet another lab named Chief Logan. (The latest addition to our family is a black Lab named Jem, Scout's mischievous brother in *To Kill a Mockingbird*).

Lord Nelson's, one of the finest galleries in Gettysburg, is filled with art, sculptures, and a variety of treasures, not the least of which—I might humbly mention—is a framed print of Robert Griffings' painting "Wounding of General Braddock"—an event that occur- red during the French and Indian War. Griffings is a renowned artist who focuses on the American frontier, and I was honored to pose as Braddock when I played the ill-fated British general for the PBS four-part series *The War That Made America*. (During the filming I was "shot" off a horse and somehow managed to remain uninjured after performing the stunt myself.)

Stephanie possesses that deep sense of community I was talking about—she loves her town and its people. "It's an honor to live here knowing what sacrifices were made," She observes. "It's the civilian history that interests me most; the stories of the people who actually lived through the battle, who

GEORGE LOWER
AND
CHAR

The James Gettys Hotel.

tried to protect themselves and their animals—like the family that hid their cow in the parlor. To get a real sense of the civilian experience, you must visit the Shriver House Museum."

Stephanie had served as the hotel's manager since it reopened in 1996, but stepped down from that position in 2013. Born and raised in Gettysburg, she was unable to resist the lure of its history. She became a tourist guide at the age of 13 and moved on to the job of "Seasonal Ranger" at the GNMP, and its sister, the Eisenhower National Historic Site (ENHS). Stephanie attributes much of her love of history to her father, who was at one time one of the leading dealers of authentic Civil War memorabilia and accoutrements in America. Through his business, the "Gettysburg Sutler," he sold items to many of the best-known collectors throughout the world. Mr. Lower's interests changed in the late 1980s and he eventually sold his business. ("Sutlers," by the way, were the merchants who made available for sale items craved by soldiers to satisfy their many needs, like tobacco, specialized foods, shaving items, and other such things not provided by the military. Today, most sutlers are the source of authentic goods for the vast number of reenactors.)

Stephanie balances her love of history and community with her personal experiences guiding others to a better understanding of the "specialness" of the place. "I have seen people cry at our park," she explains, adding, "my grandparents are buried in the National Cemetery, and my entire life has revolved around the town and its history." She speaks of "the pleasure of raising a child here, and sharing the honor of being a part of this community."

For some of the town's residents there is a tension between the commercial and the historic. For them, every day is a struggle between history and the town. "Gettysburg," she adds, "is such a unique place, a modern working community with schools, businesses, a seminary, a college—and the Civil War and Abraham Lincoln. Strangely, it's not an easy place to be, caught between the community and history. No one wanted the Battle of Gettysburg to be here, but it happened. While the community deals with that every day, there is still a deep resentment among some about the tourism business that has grown up around the battle."

But there is no conflict as far as Stephanie is concerned, seeing as she does that tourism and history can be complementary to one another. "It gives me great joy watching people like yourself who come to love our community so much that you want to write a book. Not to mention people like Michael and Jeff Shaara, and Ken Burns—those men have done so much for our town and the people who visit. [Stephanie, by the way, is now Mrs. Jeff Shaara. Jeff is the son of Michael Shaara, the author of the Pulitzer Prize-winning novel *The Killer Angels*.] They have sparked the interest of so very many—how can we ever thank them?" Her pride clearly shows.

Michael Shaara's *The Killer Angels* (1974) is often cited as the book that started an interest in the Civil War. In it, Shaara tells the story of Gettysburg through the eyes of a host of characters. It was basis of the movie *Gettysburg* starring Martin Sheen, Tom Berenger, and Jeff Daniels. Jeff Shaara took up his father's mantle after Michael's death with the powerful prequel *Gods and Generals* (1998) and the equally engaging sequel *The Last Full Measure* (2000). Ken Burns, of course, produced the unforgettable ten-part documentary The Civil War for PBS in 1990—a work that has, and will, see frequent iterations.

The town, explains Stephanie has experienced "amazing growth . . . over the last twenty years," adding the little-known fact that "Route 30 through Gettysburg is one of the most heavily trafficked tractor/trailer roads in the US." While a bit odd for a town of such historical importance, unfortunately there is no viable way around it; a bypass was once proposed, but the idea was rejected.

On a lighter note, I inquire: "What's the silliest question you've ever been asked?" She replied with barely a hesitation: "I guess it would have to be the woman who asked me 'what do you do with the monuments in the winter?'" I laugh. "It must be monumental task keeping them all warm."

All twelve "rooms" of this wonderful hotel are suites. Over the years my wife and I have stayed at the James Gettys many times and always enjoy the hospitality of its outstanding staff, from Stephanie to current manager Tricia

Morrill. In a way it is technically a B&B, since breakfast is delivered to the room each day consisting of homemade pastry or muffins, with juice, coffee fixings, and fruit. There is also complimentary chocolate imprinted with the façade of the hotel—a tasty way to end your day. For location, comfort, hospitality, and service, this little bit of history can't be beat.

Our Exploration Begins: Gettysburg Today

As it's only mid-afternoon by the time our friends, the Korals, arrive, we decide to take a further look at the town. Our "platoon" heads out to reconnoiter the area—in this case, Marilyn, Mimi, Enis, and me. Lincoln Square is the center of town and the focal point of the ten roads that converge in Gettysburg (not all at that particular spot). You'll recall that Confederate cavalry zipped through here several days prior to the battle, scaring the bejesus out of the local residents. In fact, there are several historical markers around the Square picturing the event.

One cannot help but feel the history of the place which comes, to paraphrase Carl Sandburg, "creeping in on little cat's feet." This part of America's history helped determine the future of the nation. What would America be like if Lee had won this battle? Would the war really have ended? If half our country had remained slaveholders for a time, what would have been our fate? Was Gettysburg the turning point of the Civil War? Can there be a single turning point?

Look around Lincoln Square and take note of the notable—the highlights, as it were. The large hotel on the northeast corner is impossible to miss. Part of it was here in 1863. The two top stories were added later during restoration, and a remodeling of the building was performed after fire gutted it in 1990. The building underwent a complete renovation in 2013 and is now owned by Gettysburg College. It's an excellent hotel. The building that houses their restaurant, One Lincoln, was once an opera house adjacent to the hotel and was only recently connected to the hotel. I recommend the sixth floor for the views and relative silence compared to what you might hear at street level.

Across the street on the southeast corner is the David Wills House. This property, refurbished by the National Park Service, is a relatively recent addition to the historical sights open to the public. David Wills was a prominent lawyer (and later, judge) in Gettysburg who was instrumental in creating the Soldiers' National Cemetery. In addition to being the Wills' residence, its primary claim to fame is that Abraham Lincoln stayed here the night before he delivered the

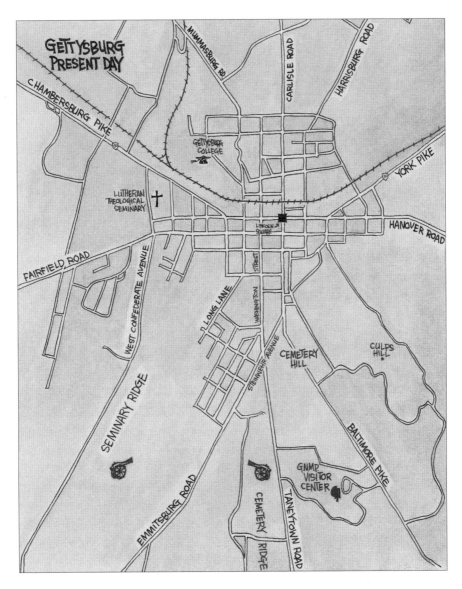

Gettysburg Address on November 19, 1863, at the dedication ceremony for the cemetery. Legend has it that he edited the speech during his stay, and the bedroom where he slept has been fully restored and is viewable. After the battle, Mr. Wills became a key player in organizing hospitals to deal with the wounded, Yankee and Rebel alike. There is an admission charge for entry but it is well worth it—Lincoln slept here!

Outside the building are two sidewalk-anchored, life-sized statues of President Lincoln and a "modern-man"—the so-called "Return Visit Statue." I

The "platoon" sets out.

don't like it. If you are inclined to have your picture taken with Lincoln, wait until you get to the Visitor Center and Museum at the Gettysburg National Military Park and sit down with the newer bronze statue of the seated Lincoln, who sits alone, just outside the entrance. He'll appreciate the company.

The rest of the square houses a variety of period buildings with the occasional modern structure thrown in—remember, it's been more than 150 years since the battle. There's a well-known B&B (the Inn at Lincoln Square), a variety of restaurants new and old, an old bank building, and a nice selection of stores. Most of this was here in 1863, although time and commerce have altered the look of much of it—and of course they've paved the damned roads! With some imagination and a squint of the eyes, however, it is not that tough to imagine what it looked like back in the day.

Our preliminary reconnaissance of the center of town over, it's time to start exploring farther afield. Parts of the battlefield are flat, but there are also lots of hills, valleys, and rocks to climb. The battle touched every part of this area—town, hill, and dale alike—so remember to wear comfortable shoes because you can and should, if able, do a lot of walking.

Gettysburg is laid out on a clear grid pattern, although many of the ten roads approach from a variety of directions. Look north and see a movie theatre across the street, more shops, and a small beautifully restored railway station. Originally owned by the Borough of Gettysburg, it was purchased by the

The Gettysburg Hotel

Gettysburg Foundation and placed under the stewardship of the GNMP/NPS. It was this station that welcomed the arrival of Abraham Lincoln on his way to dedicate the National Cemetery. On our side of the street is the Lincoln Diner—I confess, one of my favorite places in Gettysburg.

Despite my intent to identify some of our favorite eateries in a later chapter, I simply cannot help observing that the Lincoln Diner is a veritable treasure. Sheathed in the stainless steel of diners from the '50s, it possesses the same ambience and good food as the diners I remember from my childhood growing up in Long Island, New York. On those rare outings when we had to eat lunch away from home, when frugal Nana didn't pack our food, stopping at one of the many diners dotting the highways in those days that preceded fast-food joints was one of the highlights of my youth.

This little joint is a classic: traditional diner counter, booths, and décor, with a larger dining room in the back; great food at reasonable prices; and more personality per square waitress than one has a right to expect. As far as I'm concerned, unless you get a free breakfast where you're staying, this is the place to go! It is also a great spot for lunch or dinner if you're just looking for some basic fare (try the meatloaf). If you park in the little lot next to the diner, however, you take your chances—the wall of the building that borders the parking spaces could—as advertised—collapse! What's life without a little risk?

Gettysburg Railroad Station. Last stop on the train from Hanover.

Look east and see the other half of the main drag Route 30—now called York Street, and once the York Road. You will soon realize that all the roads that converge here were named for the towns they connected to Gettysburg. York Avenue splits a few blocks from the center of town, with Route 30 heading toward York and Route 116 to Hanover—thus the Hanover Road. There are more shops, restaurants, and B&Bs extending for another block.

Right next to the Wills House is the Cannonball Olde Tyme Malt Shop. It's an odd name and looks appealing enough. And then history smacks you right in the face just as surely as the "cannonball" (likely a shell from a Parrot Rifle) imbedded in the wall just below the window must have done in 1863. Given the direction it came from, it was almost surely a Confederate round. By now, you'll have noticed the number of "Civil War Building" signs that appear throughout the town—it helps get a little perspective on the 'Burg in 1863.

Looking back toward the west across the road we drove in on, is a large church across from our hotel. The Christ Lutheran Church served as a hospital during and after the battle, as did most of the buildings that were here then. All around are numerous shops and restaurants we overlooked in our excitement to get to the Square. (Never fear, we'll explore more later.)

For now, glancing south down Baltimore Street looks to be the most interesting direction. The route seems to extend "downtown" a bit farther than any other direction and is obviously filled with more shops, restaurants, and buildings that look old. On this first outing we decide that's the way to go. The Baltimore Pike once connected Gettysburg to Baltimore with some very interesting spots along the way. A short drive connects us with Steinwehr Avenue, the Evergreen Cemetery, and the entrance to the Soldiers' National Cemetery and, one mile from the Square, the entrance to the Gettysburg National Military Park. The downtown "business" district on the pike extends for only another block or so before giving way to what was once the closest residential area to the town itself. Even though Baltimore Street can be heavily trafficked, once you're away from the hubbub of Lincoln Square it feels just a bit quainter—at least, in mid-October when the place isn't mobbed with tourists.

Farther south the historic and the modern flow together. Park your car and walk. As you stroll down the street, keep a sharp eye out for the many interesting stores and museums behind often innocuous storefronts, important public buildings, and a few places offering "Ghost Tours." The Adams County Courthouse sits across from a rather large library, several more churches, something called the Gettysburg Museum of History, and on the corner of Wade Street, a charming little building claiming to be the birthplace of Jennie Wade. Then, after crossing Breckenridge Street, the Shriver House Museum, the rather imposing Farnsworth House (could those be bullet holes in that wall?), the Rupp House (also imposing and now the home of the Gettysburg Foundation), and farther down near the intersection with Steinwehr Avenue, the Virginia Wade House, another house related to Jennie Wade—the twenty-year-old girl who was the only civilian killed in during the battle when a bullet passed through the wall of the kitchen where she was baking. The home is now the Jennie Wade House Museum.

If you want evidence that the town of Gettysburg was a war zone in 1863, take a close look at the south wall of the Farnsworth House. In 1863, locals knew this building—parts of which date back to 1810 when it was part of an adjacent tannery—as the Harvey S. Sweney House. During the battle,

Confederate sharpshooters took up residence on the top floor and fired their rifled-muskets through the small window at Yankee troops off to the south on Cemetery Hill. (There was not much in the way of development between this and the Union soldiers reinforcing Cemetery Hill.) The Yankees returned fire, peppering the south wall with bullet. The holes remain.

Today, the Farnsworth House is the home of a lovely B&B, an outstanding restaurant and tavern with period fare and waitresses in period garb, a small bookstore, and ghost tours. (From what I have learned, the bookstore was once quite large and the place for bibliophiles to hang out and swap book-collecting stories.) Thanks to the efforts of the Shultz family, and particularly its patriarch Loring Shultz, the house in now on the National Register of Historic Places.

Loring, a robust bear of a man, is full of energy and humor despite his advanced years. Born and raised in the area, his great-grandfather, Jack Starkey, served in Company B of the 18th Virginia! Loring bought the house and property "for its history" in 1972 for $53,000. Three years later he managed to have it added to the National Register. In general, though, Loring feels Gettysburg hasn't done a very good job of preserving the town's historic buildings. "I'm a purist," he admits. "Take the town back to 1863." Loring has managed this business for forty years, so he's had more than his share of struggles—including some members with the borough council who resisted his efforts to expand his business. When Loring wanted to add a small theater to his property, for example, the council opposed it. "In a small town there are a lot of politics, some of it's jealousy, or resentment, or something," lamented Loring. Through the years he demonstrated his willingness to gamble on the success of

his business by investing more than one million dollars renovating and expanding, so he feels a bit frustrated when the council stands in his way.

On the other hand, Loring sings the praises of the National Park Service—"it's better than ever"—and former Superintendent Bob Kirby, though Loring remains a bit ambivalent about what he calls "the weeds" that grow around the Visitor Center in an

The Historic Farnsworth House

effort to capture the feeling of the battlefield in 1863. He likes the historical look—he just prefers it to be neat!

The issue of preservation versus commercialization is of real concern to the citizens of modern Gettysburg. Let's not forget that the *entire* town was part of the battlefield in 1863. The fighting on the First Day (July 1) began west and north of town, and, as the Confederates overpowered the defending Yankees, pursued the routing Unionists through the town until the Northern soldiers reached the newly fortified Union position on Cemetery Hill. Depending where you fall on the issue, Confederate General Ewell—who looked like the

LORING SHULTZ

second coming of Stonewall Jackson at Second Winchester two weeks earlier—did not think it was possible to drive the defeated bluecoats off the high ground. General Lee told him to take it "if practicable," but didn't attempt to do so. The Confederates remained in possession of the town for the next two days—a hub of activity that connected the Rebel left with the rest of the army. Given Gettysburg's central role in the battle, coupled with the fact that heavy fighting occurred all long its perimeter, the natural question arises: Where does the concern to preserve history give way to the need of a modern town to be economically viable? Ironically, most of the town's commercial success is a product of the momentous battle fought place here; without the battle, what would Gettysburg be? Overall, in my opinion Gettysburg has done a pretty good job of walking that fine line.

As I mentioned, just south of the Farnsworth House is the historic Rupp House, now the home of the Gettysburg Foundation. If they're open, go on in. It's a special and important organization. As we come to a fork in the road, Steinwehr Avenue (named for a Yankee German general) angles off to the right. A convenience store sits smack dab in the middle of the Y. A large hotel is off to the left, and a variety of interesting shops and eateries line the streets. We note that the ground is rising here. Cemetery Hill. Hallowed Ground. Commerce vs. history.

Proceeding along Steinwehr Avenue, we find a plethora of interesting shops and art galleries along with a concentration of stores advertising "Ghost Tours." On the right is the Historic Dobbin House. This longest-standing Gettysburg building goes all the way back to 1776, or as its website cleverly points out, "Four Score and Seven Years" before President Lincoln delivered the Gettysburg Address. Built by the Reverend Alexander Dobbin, one of Gettysburg's pioneers, it was intended as a dwelling for the Dobbin family as well as a "Classical School," a sort of combination seminary and liberal arts college. Dobbin was at the forefront of the movement to separate from York County and form the new Adams County, and subsequently became one of two appointed commissioners to choose Gettysburg as the county seat. In the 19th century, the Dobbin House became a station for hiding runaway slaves on the Underground Railroad. Like so many other structures here at the time of the battle, it served as a hospital for Union and Confederate soldiers alike.

Today the Dobbin House boasts two fine restaurants, a B&B known as the Gettystown Inn, and a gift shop. The restaurant is lovely and offers fine cuisine, but my favorite place to eat here is downstairs in the Springhouse Tavern, where good food, great period atmosphere, and lots of good brewskies await. (Try the Spit-Roasted Chicken.)

Rick Beamer, the Dobbin House manager since 1985, grew up in Gettysburg and started working for the Inn while still in college. "I wanted to raise my three children here," he explained, "in the best little town in America."

The Historic Dobbin House

Rick encounters "a sampling of the world's population. I meet famous people from presidents and world leaders to show biz types." He likes that "Gettysburg is near other larger cities, airports, the rest of the world—it's a beautiful area." And, he adds, "I'm a fan of history, especially American history, although not necessarily focusing on just the Civil War. Of course, I can tell you a lot about the battle."

Rick notes that growing up in Gettysburg was quite an experience. He attended the same Presbyterian Church as the Eisenhower family (who owned a farm just south of here). Dwight Eisenhower was posted to Camp Colt in Gettysburg in March 1918 and put in charge of training soldiers for the Army's fledging tank corps. Before the creation of the National Park Service, the United States War Department ran the Park.

RICK BEAMER

(There is even a rumor that those fledging tankers used Little Round Top, one of the most famous sites on the battlefield, for target practice.)

"In addition to the original Dobbin House," Rick points out, "we have the Little Round Top Farm within walking distance of the famous stand by the 20th Maine; you can rent the whole house." This property, built in 1858 by Jacob and Tillie Weikert, boasts five cozy bedrooms and the experience of living on the battlefield. Here is an interesting fact about the Dobbin House site on Steinwehr Avenue that few folks know about: The National Park Service wanted to buy the original part of the Leister Farm, which had served as Meade's headquarters but had been expanded in the years following the battle. The family agreed to sell the original building to the NPS and moved the addition—a two-story building—downtown. (That must have been quite a feat back in the 1890s.) The building is now part of the Gettystown Inn B&B. "This building has so much history to it. you've heard the term 'witness tree'? Well, this is a 'witness house.' You could have stood in the courtyard of the Dobbin House and heard Lincoln give his address in 1863." For just a moment, that realization takes my breath away.

The Dobbin House is one of the many properties thought to have ghosts. Rick observes that the "ghost tours" have changed the whole nighttime entertainment of the town. While he understands their role, he also wishes "for a little more historical accuracy." Most people who go on ghost tours, however, are probably not looking for historical accuracy but the thrill of exposure to the supernatural—if, of course, you believe in that sort of thing. Rick's "don't miss" list includes the Soldiers' National Cemetery, the Philippoteaux Cyclorama, and the Eisenhower Farm.

Getting tired after a full day of new sights, we take a quick glance across S. Washington Street. Farther down Steinwehr Avenue are all sorts of restaurants and bars, stores, antique shops, motels, additional tourist attractions, and even a gas station, and we can just make out where it begins to pass through the Gettysburg National Military Park. Recalling the restaurant right next to our hotel, a place called The Parrot, we certainly won't have far to go after our meal—we head back and enjoy a very nice dinner from its excellent menu. Full of satisfying food and drink, we bid Mimi and Enis goodnight, and have a relaxed evening in our very comfortable suite.

Our Introduction to the Gettysburg National Military Park

The next morning, having fortified ourselves with a good night's sleep, we drive down to the Gettysburg National Military Park Museum and Visitor Center to meet our Licensed Battlefield Guide (LBG) for our 10:00 tour of the battlefield. Not knowing what to expect, a first look at this relatively new facility is mind-blowing. But let me not get ahead of myself—a more detailed look is coming.

The procedure for these tours calls for the LBG to drive your car. By prearrangement, as we have cleverly made our reservation in advance, we await our guide's arrival at the "Will Call" desk at the far end of the ticket counter in the main lobby. Right on time, up strides Mr. George Symons, a large man just a bit stooped over with age. He is warm and friendly, complete with the hoped-for twinkle in his eye. Mr. Symons looks to be in his 70s and, as we soon discover, is sharp as a tack and full of wit. He has been an LBG since 1994, and I suspect we have found a winner.

As we head out to the car, several thoughts are running through my mind: "Will Mr. Symons fit in the Korals' Honda? (Damn, maybe I need to re-think my dislike of Hummers.) Yikes, I had three cups of coffee this morning; do we have any bathroom stops? How am I going to remember everything he tells us?

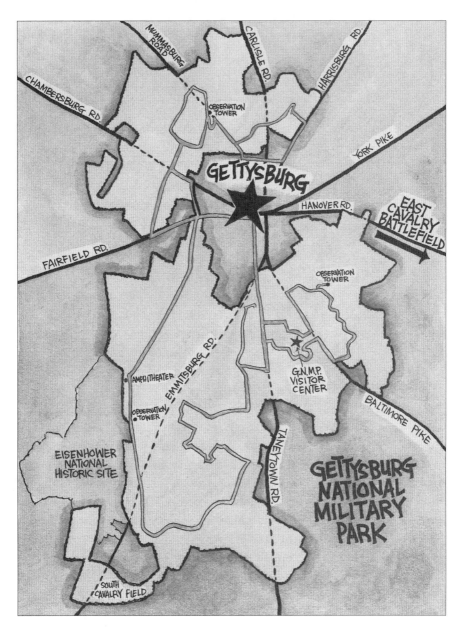

Do I need to take notes? I wonder if would be okay to take Mr. Symons' picture?"

We are each carrying one of the fold-up battlefield map/brochures found in large numbers at the Visitor Center. It contains a map of the battlefield and the directions for a "Self-Guiding Auto Tour," with a general description of the events that took place at each of the numbered stops. This will be the route Mr.

GEORGE SYMONS

Symons follows while providing additional information to complement the little pamphlet. If you prefer, you can also get a CD that will guide you through the tour on your own.

On the back of the map of the park are panels explaining the events of the "Three Days in July" (July 1–3, 1863), information on the "Gettysburg Address," a layout of the Soldiers' National Cemetery, and some additional advice for seeing the park and the battlefield, along with some regulations and safety tips. These pamphlets are invaluable, and are available at every National Park Service battlefield. Make it a priority to pick up a couple of these as a first order of business at each park; they are simply the best starting point.

Our tour begins just after 10:00 a.m. and is scheduled to last about two hours. Mr. Symons easily slides his large frame into the front seat. We leave the Visitors Center via the small road at the back of the Center, turning right onto the Taneytown Road. Heading north, back toward the town, we pass the entrance to the Soldiers' National Cemetery but do not stop. In addition to being the site of the Gettysburg Address, it is the final resting place for many valiant soldiers, and a place that warrants a separate and more comprehensive visit (see Chapter 7).

Ironically, the first stop on our tour turns out to be the area where we first encountered Gettysburg—Route 30 (the Chambersburg Pike). Mr. Symons confirms that this was where the battle started. One of the many things I find intriguing about the battle is the inadvertent way it developed. One unintended event leading to another until both armies were on the field and in the midst of a giant battle. Remember, neither Lee nor Meade intended to fight here.

Mr. Symons fills in the gaps with countless details of troop movements, commanders, units, and an endless variety of sidebars, including observations on the dozens of markers and unit monuments we pass along the route. Much to everyone's delight, he remembers to take three bathroom stops. Good man.

In fact, in the high season there are many restrooms, both in separate buildings and various locations for porta-pottis, many equipped for the handicapped. In the off-season, there are facilities in the Visitor Center, which is open year-round.

In a quick summary, we visit McPherson's Ridge, Oak Ridge, and the Eternal Light Peace Memorial, pass the first of three observation towers on the battlefield, and take a side trip over to Barlow's Knoll, all to the west, northwest, and north of town.

Proceeding back through downtown we next head for West Confederate Avenue, one of the earliest park roads that essentially defines the position of the Confederate army as it occupied Seminary Ridge on Day Two, but which was not here during the time of the battle. Heading south, we pass through the area of the greatest concentration of Confederate artillery, and from where the Pickett-Pettigrew-Trimble attack was launched on July 3. (Until very recently, history has referred to this attack as Pickett's Charge, but Pickett only led one of the three divisions involved.)

We next pass the second observation tower near the area occupied by Gen. Longstreet's corps, which saw especially heavy fighting on July 2 (and Pickett, of course, on July 3). The tower looks out over the battlefield and offers a beautiful view. Don't miss it. We keep driving around and pass Big Round Top on the way to Little Round Top, one of the two most visited sections of the battlefield, both for the events that took place here and its striking location. Overlooking the area of some of the most intense fighting on July 2 and 3, the vista from among the giant boulders is incredible.

Below us to the west is the Devil's Den, with its clump of gigantic boulders. The Slaughter Pen, an area near the base of Round Top, also witnessed heavy fighting. The view from Little Round Top (now that the NPS has cleared so many trees) is stunning. Looking west, we can see all the way to the Confederate lines. The Wheatfield is off to the northwest (it changed hands many times on July 2), and beyond that the Peach Orchard (which formed an angle in the Union line and was crushed by Longstreet's attack). The view to the northwest and northward is also lovely and encompasses the fields traversed during the Rebel attacks on July 2 and of course, on July 3 during "Pickett's Charge." Our guide pointed out the famous Copse of Tree on Cemetery Ridge, an area vigorously defended by Union infantry and artillery. Looking from this vantage point today one is awed by the sheer beauty of the landscape and the poignancy of the bloody struggle that occurred here.

Back in the car our tour continues passing through Devil's Den—even more remarkable now being down among the giant boulders—and then the Slaughter Pen, the Wheatfield, and the Peach Orchard. Heading north we come to the Pennsylvania Memorial, the largest and one of the most elaborate on the battlefield, before arriving at the Confederate "High-Water-Mark," as it is called, including the Copse of Trees. Some sources claim the trees were the target of the Pickett-Pettigrew-Trimble charge, along with the Angle—a right-angled stone wall that saw the culmination of the charge—the most frequently visited part of the battlefield.

Finally, we take the less-traveled route over to Culp's Hill in the northeast—an area that has become one of my favorites to visit, and one that historians continue to reconsider for its significant contribution to the Union victory. Here, too, is the last of the battlefield's three observation towers. After a short stay we return to the Visitors Center and give a fond farewell, along with a generous tip our very special LBG George Symons. (Don't be chintzy; the fee paid to the LBGs is comparatively small, so for many LBGs, it's the tip that makes it truly worthwhile.)

After this preliminary look, the power of Gettysburg is finally beginning to touch me in a visceral way—not just for its importance in American history, but for the sheer scope of its beauty and the aesthetic power of its setting. This includes, of course, the lightly sampled, but not yet fully explored, charms and treasures that await us in the town itself. I could have read 100 books on the battle but not understood it at the same gut level as I did now with just a two-hour tour. Truly the impact is astonishing. If you have not yet visited the field and town, do so as soon as possible—once you've finished this book, of course.

The Licensed Battlefield Guides

For us outdoor types, as amazing as the Visitor Center is (which we'll visit next), the battlefield is even more so. With approximately 25 miles of paved roads, numerous hiking and horse trails, beautiful woodlands and fields, and nearly 1,400 monuments and markers of every shape, size, and character imaginable, this park stands as the *pièce de résistance* of Civil War memorials. This isn't just history, and this place isn't just a shrine. It is a window on America and it is huge. Nothing can substitute for being here.

And with so much to see and understand, the way to go for your first encounter (as we did) is to hire a Licensed Battlefield Guide (LBG) to take you on a tour. Along with the Park Rangers, LBGs are the only individuals who are officially licensed by the National Park Service to conduct tours of the battlefield. They are an amazing group of men and women whose knowledge of the Civil War, and the individual battles they elucidate, is astounding.

The Licensed Battlefield Guide tours can be booked in advance or arranged on a first-come, first-served basis at the Visitor Center. The tours can even be tailored to your interests: information about a certain part of the battle, a specific state's participation, or even an individual regiment that fought here. Tours for special interests, however, must be booked in advance—indeed, I would recommend scheduling a guide in advance regardless of whether you have a particular interest or are just looking for an overview. You wouldn't want to travel to Gettysburg anticipating a guided tour only to be told that there are no guides available.

At the time of this writing, the man in charge of Gettysburg's Licensed Battlefield Guides was Supervisory Park Ranger Clyde R. Bell, who oversaw the licensing and day-to-day operation of the guides. Sadly, Clyde passed away unexpectedly in early 2013 at the age of 61. His duties have been assumed by Supervisory Park Ranger Angie Atkinson. LBGs provide 22,000 tours annually, serving more than 220,000 people. As Clyde told me, "National Park Service staff would be overwhelmed trying to provide this level of service."

To become a LBG you must both prove your in-depth knowledge and pass a test of your ability "to communicate not just the factual, but the emotional and spiritual connection to what occurred here, as well." The test is in two parts: a three-hour written exam followed by an oral exam consisting of conducting a vehicular "tour" with Angie and another LBG as your examiners. Questions during this phase can include information on the battle, the Civil War, and the monuments and markers on the battlefield. All this, of course, is in addition to providing a two-hour overview of the battle. About 200 people express an interest in taking the test, which on average is offered once every other December, and between 130 and 140 come to Gettysburg to take it. Out of that number, only the top 20 or so pass and move on to the oral exam. For those of you who are interested in becoming a guide, my sincerest wishes for the best of luck—you're going to need it. The Association of Licensed Battlefield Guides maintains a website with lots of information about becoming a guide. It is very interesting, and more than a little daunting.

With about 150 active LBGs, Gettysburg is foremost among the parks offering guide services. Antietam, Vicksburg, and other parks also provide guides, and each park establishes its own testing process. For all the obvious reasons, no other park has nearly as many guides as does Gettysburg.

**THE LATE
CLYDE R. BELL**

Former Supervisor Clyde Bell was a man of great knowledge. He pointed out that he often had to explain the military tactics of the 1860s for people to understand why "anyone would march across an open field, shoulder to shoulder, against fortified positions!" The Civil War was a turning point in the way wars were fought. The war started as the last vestige of the Napoleonic tradition of warfare, and ended as a precursor of the terrible trench warfare of World War I (and also introduced submarines, fighting iron ships, and much more).

Understandably, Clyde was deeply concerned about the amount of damage that is done annually to the park, some through thoughtlessly innocent souvenir hunters, but "too much by people purposely searching for artifacts, malicious vandalism, or drivers who can't control their cars and slam into the monuments and markers on the narrow roads." I personally don't know what the fines are for such behavior; I just hope they're severe. What sort of person would steal from a national park that is also a memorial for the dead? I would point out that alcohol and drug use are forbidden in national parks, and searching for artifacts is a criminal offense. Having enjoyed the magnificent resources of the Gettysburg National Military Park to the extent I have, I wish people were just a little smarter or more aware about preserving our heritage. It was a great pleasure meeting and talking with Clyde. His early death was a profound loss to the National Park Service and the GNMP.

The Personal Perspective of an LBG

Joanne Lewis, who has been a Licensed Battlefield Guide since 2004, feels "some sort of connection to this battlefield when I'm standing on it. I've been to many others and it's just not the same. She quotes Joshua Chamberlain, who commanded the fabled 20th Maine Infantry during its fight for Little Round Top. When he returned here for a reunion in the 1890s, she explains,

Chamberlain called Gettysburg a "vision place of souls . . . and what glorious company it is!"

Joanne, who traces her interest in history to an eighth-grade teacher, visited Gettysburg on one of her first vacations after her marriage. She simply got hooked. Today, she is one of a select few guides who is also a Licensed Town Guide—in fact, she is the program supervisor. Her primary focus is the "social history" surrounding the battle. Why did the soldiers fight? How did the town react to being occupied for three days? As she says, the people of Gettysburg lived between "valor and sacrifice." She is especially fascinated by the fact that nine women disguised as men fought in the ranks on both sides. One woman, Rebecca Peterman, fought with the famous Iron Brigade for three years before she was discovered.

"This time is a growing period for our country, and we should honor the people who did this—who shaped our nation—honor the soldiers," she continues. And the way to do this is by remembering them. She also tells me about the time a five-year-old girl on one of her tours asked, "Was slavery really the cause of the Civil War?" Taken aback, Joanne asked the girl's mother, "Should I really go into this?" The mother nodded yes. On a lighter note, the young girl also asked, "Why didn't the soldiers just hide behind the monuments?"

"Every man, woman, and child should go to Gettysburg," says Joanne, and visitors should not forget the town itself. She points out that people are mistaken if they think Gettysburg in 1863 was just a sleepy little village in south-central Pennsylvania. "The town of Gettysburg was a prosperous, thriving place with 2,400 citizens; it was the Adams County Seat; it was a trading center; the nexus of ten roads connecting it to other important towns and cities."

I am continually struck by the passion of the people who have committed themselves to helping others fully understand Gettysburg's significance, and,

JOANNE LEWIS

1,400 Monuments? A Conversation with an Expert

Before we examine in more detail the greatest battle ever fought on American soil, and head out onto the field where it took place, we need to learn a bit more about the hundreds upon hundreds of monuments dotting the sprawling landscape. As one might expect, there are several experts available on this subject, and it was my good fortune to find one of the best.

Sue Boardman was born and raised in central Pennsylvania, the land of the Pennsylvania German (often called "Dutch") community. "A hot time on a Saturday night was going to an estate sale!" she explains. Sue spent 23 years as an Emergency Room RN, but one of her other interests was history, especially that of the Holocaust. On one of her many excursions to estate sales throughout north-central Pennsylvania, she discovered and bought a Civil War diary by Michael Schroyer of Company G, 147th Pennsylvania, XII Corps, who recorded his war experiences from 1862 to the end of the war. Sue made a map of his journey and followed it through a dozen states. And that was the hook that got Sue involved with the Civil War.

Sue became a Licensed Battlefield Guide (she is a two-time winner of the Superintendent's Award for Excellence in Guiding) and an expert on the Philippoteaux Cyclorama painting. She discovered a deep attraction to the stone testaments erected to the bravery and heroism of the men who fought here.

SUE BOARDMAN

"The monuments are the key to understanding not just the battle but who the veterans were—you can't hug a veteran today, but you can hug a monument! The sad thing," she continues, "is that people don't really look at the monuments, they look around them." Sue fills in some of the historical background to these testaments in stone. "As early as 1864, the Gettysburg Battlefield Memorial Association (GBMA) is incorporated. Then, in 1878, the Grand Army of the Republic [Union veterans] takes over the GBMA, and it marks the Union positions during the battle and begins erecting monuments. By 1895, the Gettysburg Battlefield Park Commission of the War Department is marking

Confederate positions during the battle, facilitating the erection of Confederate monuments. In 1933, the National Park Service is charged with the preservation and interpretation of the Gettysburg National Military Park, which, of course, includes these many stone sentinels."

Lest you think the placement of monuments is arbitrary, Sue gives me a "Summary of the Rules Governing Monuments" created by the GBMA:

- Primary monument to be placed in the position the regiment held in line of battle.
- Monuments must have suitable inscription showing its historical relation to battle regarding time and service.
- Monuments must be made of only granite or bronze, or a combination of these materials.
- On front must appear the number of the regiment, state, brigade, division, and corps in letters not less than 4".
- Any statue or figure of a soldier must face the enemy.
- Effective strength and casualty figures if actively engaged must conform to the Official Records of the War Department.
- Location of monument and inscription thereon must be approved by the GBMA before erection takes place.

I am curious about a rumor that exists that each equestrian statue reveals the fate of its rider depending upon the positioning of the legs of the horse. Is this true? Sue is familiar with the myth of the position of the horses' hooves on the equestrian statues—all four settled on the ground meant the rider survived unscathed; one hoof up, the rider was wounded; two hooves up, the rider was killed. However, one sculptor who had produced three of the equestrian monuments at Gettysburg, denied the claim and called it "a coincidence." With a glint in her eye, Sue informs me that there is an unauthorized account of a symbol on the equestrian statues as told among the guides: "The position of the horses' tail is very important: if the horses' tail is down, the horse is about to charge; if the horses' tail is up, the horse is about to discharge." We both laugh.

especially in Joanne's case, the profound impact it made on the surrounding community.

There are several kinds of markers. Headquarters Markers consist of upright cannon tubes denoting the headquarters locations of the commanding generals and corps for each army. Battery Tablets, as one might expect, describe the role of each artillery battery at Gettysburg. Corps Markers locate the general position of the various corps, while Division Markers do the same for each division, and Brigade Markers indicate the positions and describe the actions of each brigade. A square base indicates a Union brigade, while a round base indicates a Confederate one. In addition, you'll find many black iron information tablets originally put in place by the War Department. And, of course, there are the beautiful Regimental Monuments, State Memorials, and bronze statues of various generals and key figures, as well as the hundreds of unit and regimental flank markers.

I would recommend the purchase of the *Battlefield America Topographic Map of the Gettysburg National Military Park*, which provides a cornucopia of information. In addition to the map itself, it includes the location and identity of every monument and marker on the battlefield, as well as the many farms and other historically significant buildings. It also shows you the location of footpaths and horse trails, and points out many of the geographic features of the land that affected the way the battle was fought. It does not, however, include the location of the War Department's black iron information tablets. You can find this at the Visitor Center Bookstore.

Chapter 4

Day One: An Accidental Engagement Evolves into a Confederate Victory

radition has it that the fighting at Gettysburg began about 7:30 a.m. on July 1, 1863. Privates Benton Kelly and James Hall of the 8th Illinois Cavalry in Brig. Gen. John Buford's division had been sent west of town to Knoxlyn Ridge (then known as Wisler Ridge) to keep an eye out for advancing Rebels. When several thousand were spotted tramping their way along the Chambersburg Pike from the direction of Cashtown, Kelly galloped east to Herr's Tavern to warn his cousin Lt. Marcellus E. Jones, who was in command of the picket posts in the area. Jones and Kelly galloped back to Knoxlyn Ridge, where Jones borrowed Sgt. Levi S. Shafer's Sharps carbine, propped it on a fence, leveled it at the head of the distant column—and pulled the trigger. He didn't hit anything of note, but some of Jones' fellow cavalrymen rode like hell to tell Buford that a significant portion of the Confederate army was coming down the road straight at them!

I wonder what was going through the mind of Lt. Jones when he decided to take a potshot at the approaching Confederates. Did he have any sense of what might follow? Rather than taking note of the approaching enemy and reporting it to Buford, this young man decides instead to make his own statement and squeeze a trigger. The echo still rings today.

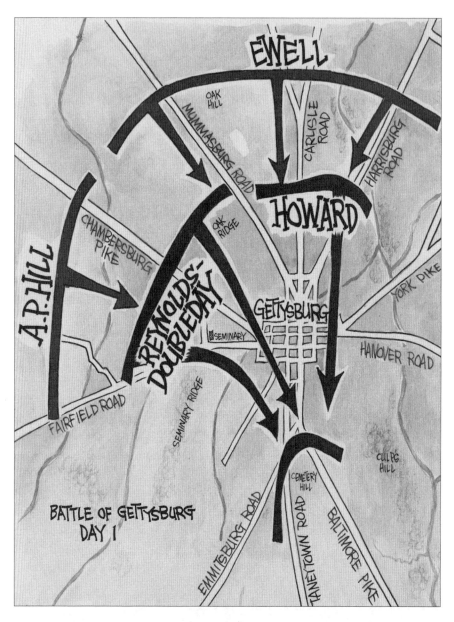

"Beginnings" fascinate me. Etiology is the study of causes—how things get started and what events set something in motion. Day One of Gettysburg offers a perfect example of a beginning that unfolded through a series of small actions and reactions, setting the stage for the larger combat that day, and the "set-piece" fighting that would follow on Days Two and Three. Seasonal Ranger Chuck Teague explained it to me this way: "This was a 'meeting

The First-Shot Marker

engagement'—two armies colliding in conflict. This was really confusing: fighting erupting without a fixed defensive position on either side. It's fascinating to see how Lee and Meade, arriving belatedly, sorted out what was happening here and what to do. Then by 6:00 p.m. on July 1 they have a whole other battle on their hands, having to change plans on the fly, and fight this battle."

General Lee wants the fight farther north closer to Harrisburg,

BRIGADIER GENERAL JOHN BUFORD

hopefully on ground of his choosing, and General Meade hopes to make his defensive stand along Big Pipe Creek in Maryland. Lee carefully instructed his army not to bring on a "general engagement." His army is spread out and he doesn't want to risk the same fate he intends to inflict on Meade's army—catch it tired and strung out as it is racing north to find the Rebels and defeat it one fragment at a time. General Heth is approaching town under the same restriction.

Many believed (and still do) the myth that division commander Heth—who was new to the Virginia army—was looking for shoes when he

MAJOR GENERAL HENRY HETH

marched his entire division along the old pike toward Gettysburg. We know for sure he was looking for Yankees, but more interested in scrounging up supplies of all kinds, shoes included. Lee's instructions were clear, and General Hill (Heth's commander) told Heth the same thing: Do not bring on a general engagement. It couldn't be much plainer than that. As a poet once wrote, "The best laid schemes of mice and men often go awry." Perhaps he should have added "generals" to that list.

On the fateful morning of July 1, however, Lee still had significantly more men at his disposal than Meade. Heth's division and that of Maj. Gen. William Dorsey Pender's, which was right behind Heth, totaled about 14,000 men, with Hill's third division under Maj. Gen. Richard Anderson not far behind Pender. The forces with Lee included Hill's Third Corps and James Longstreet's First Corps *en route* from Chambersburg. Lee has already recalled Ewell's dispersed Second Corps operating well north of Gettysburg. Buford's Federal cavalry, on the other hand, consisted of only two brigades and a battery of horse artillery, about 2,900 men.

Let's keep in mind how difficult it was to gather information back in 1863. Reconnaissance mostly relied upon cavalry, spies, and sympathetic civilians, with occasional outdated newspaper accounts and captured documents. As noted earlier, the usually reliable Jeb Stuart was absent—Lee won't reunite with Stuart until late on July 2, when the second day of the battle is well underway. Spies were (and are) deceitful and as a breed generally not trusted, and there were few civilians sympathetic to the Confederate cause in south-central Pennsylvania. As to our own senses, eyes are limited to line-of-sight, and from a distance it was easy to confuse thunder for cannon fire. West of Gettysburg, the Confederate commanders held differing opinions of exactly who they were

facing. Pettigrew was sure Union cavalry was in the town, while Heth and Hill scoffed at the idea. A few brief encounters at the end of June saw Confederate veterans routing poorly trained Pennsylvania militia. The trained soldiers of the Army of the Potomac under a capable Union commander were a completely different matter.

And so Heth marched eastward with his full division led, oddly enough, by a battery of artillery under Maj. Willie Pegram. Behind the gunner tramped a

MAJOR GENERAL WILLIAM RANSOM JOHNSON PEGRAM

small brigade of just 1,200 infantry under Gen. James J. Archer. Remember, neither side was looking to trigger a battle. If Heth knew his actions were about to precipitate the largest battle of the war, he almost certainly would have acted differently. (Buford was fighting a delaying action to keep the town and good ground in Union hands, so he may well have done the same thing.) Likely, Heth would have fallen back at the first sign of any serious defensive effort. But he didn't. Instead, when Buford's troopers offered resistance, and it became clear Union cavalry was in his front

MAJOR GENERAL WILLIAM DORSEY PENDER

BRIGADIER GENERAL JAMES J. ARCHER

(not militia), Heth deployed his front into line of battle perpendicular to the Chambersburg Pike and pushed forward until the bluecoats melted away over the next ridge, where they would form once more. Each effort drained precious minutes away from Heth's advance and gave time for more Union infantry to reach the area. Eventually, Archer's men assumed positions south of the pike and Brig. Gen. Joseph R. Davis' men formed north of it.

Buford's men had been sent

BRIGADIER GENERAL JOSEPH R. DAVIS

ahead with orders "to cover and protect the front," while other Union corps march northward via the Baltimore Pike and both the Emmitsburg and Taneytown roads, some utilizing the "most historic bridge" in Pennsylvania, the Sachs Covered Bridge.

A short side trip will take you over to the bridge, located just within the boundary of the Gettysburg National Military Park, halfway between the Emmitsburg and Fairfield roads. It's a little hard to find, but worth the effort.

The Sachs Covered Bridge. Legend has it that three Confederate soldiers
hung themselves from it; consequently, it's "haunted."

It's quite beautiful, and gives one a real sense of the limits of travel back in 1863. Back then it was called the Sauches Covered Bridge, and it remains a classic example of a "truss bridge" of the period. Built over Marsh Creek in 1854, two brigades of the Union I Corps used it heading to Gettysburg, and parts of the III Corps toward the Black Horse Tavern on the Fairfield Road. (Large numbers of Confederate troops used it during their retreat from Gettysburg on July 4 and 5).

A little less than three miles out of Gettysburg is the famed Black Horse Tavern, aka Bream's Tavern, built in 1812. After the Federal troops left the area, the intersection where it is located (Black Horse Tavern Road and the Fairfield Road today) was used by the Confederate artillery on July 2. A private home today, part of the original tavern survives. During and after the battle it served as a Confederate field hospital.

John Buford, the general opposing Heth west of town, was a tough and capable leader. An experienced no-nonsense cavalryman, he had been in the thick of combat and was not prone to mistakes. Once in the Gettysburg area, he dispatched his troopers forward as vedettes (mounted sentinels) to watch for the Confederates. A skirmish line of about 550 men dismounted and formed on Knoxlyn Ridge, stretching from the Fairfield Road in the south all the way north of town and to the east at the Hanover Road. Buford also placed a stronger and wider line of defense on Herr's Ridge, closer to town. Buford intended for his dismounted cavalrymen to fight as infantry, with every fourth trooper remaining behind holding the horses. This tactic is called a "covering force action" according to cavalry expert Eric Wittenberg, a technical term meaning trading ground for time and space.

Another noted expert on cavalry, J. D. Petruzzi, points out that Buford's brigades rode through Fairfield, southwest of Gettysburg, just before the big battle: "The troopers were exhausted, many falling to the ground while still holding the reins of their horses—most of the horses stood there sleeping on their feet." J. D. adds, "I was very impressed by the way Buford set up his vedettes north and west of Gettysburg. He has his men interview the locals and sends scouts out: by the time of nightfall on June 30, he knows the location of every Confederate corps and, in fact, predicted that the battle would begin the next day. I think that Buford's intelligence gathering was equal to or even better than Jeb Stuart's," continued Petruzzi. "his troopers did a fantastic job slowing down the advance of Heth's larger force. Remember, it was Buford who initially identified Cemetery Hill as a good defensive position. It was Buford who saw the Battle of Gettysburg as unpredicted, yet predictable. This man was clearly a great leader in the field—he actually starts the fight at Brandy Station back in early June with Gregg showing up late with the other half of the Federal cavalry force."

Buford's troopers carry the new Sharps, Smith, or Merrill carbines. Although a single shot weapon, these breech-loaders are capable of firing at a much faster rate than the muzzle-loading muskets of the Confederates (about five shots per minute versus the two or three shots of the musket), making Buford's cavalry appear to be a much larger force than it is, and certainly a more effective one. Buford's tactics, which he directed from the cupola of the Lutheran Seminary west of town (with the unfortunate name of Schmucker Hall) would buy the Union two hours. His men, once engaged however, are driven slowly back by the larger force of Confederates and eventually fall back to the western bank of Willoughby Run, a stream which affords a natural, albeit small, barrier.

Schmucker Hall was the heart of the Lutheran Theological Seminary. It stands today as part of the much larger campus and has been extensively restored as the new Seminary Ridge Museum. Indeed, the entire Seminary campus sits astride the ridge that was the backbone of the Confederate position during much of the battle. (More on this amazing place in Chapter 6).

Civil War armies were organized, from the largest to the smallest units, like this: corps, divisions, brigades, regiments, and companies. Artillery units organized as battalions. For our purposes, an extensive description of the structure of these armies is unnecessary. Union corps were about half the size of Confederate corps, and there were more of them. At Gettysburg, for example, Lee's Army of Northern Virginia consisted of three corps of infantry and a cavalry division, along with artillery divided among the corps. Meade's Army of the Potomac was comprised of seven infantry corps that also incorporated artillery, a separate cavalry corps under Maj. Gen. Alfred Pleasonton, and an artillery reserve. Roughly speaking, Lee has about 70,100 men and Meade about 94,000.

MAJOR GENERAL OLIVER OTIS HOWARD

Moving with the troops as the morning unfolds, we cross Herr's Ridge Road where the expanded Herr Tavern (currently a fine restaurant and B&B) stands. Here, Buford's troopers continued fighting their delaying action before falling back all the way to Willoughby Run and Herbst Woods. Late in the morning the Union I Corps (including the Iron Brigade) under the command of Maj. Gen. John F. Reynolds, one of the Union's most able commanders, arrived on the field. Maj. Gen. Oliver Otis Howard—the "Oh, oh" Howard of Chancellorsville fame—and his XI Corps are not far right behind Reynolds.

The area east of Herr's Ridge has not been well preserved. Excepting reclamation of the land that was once the Emmanuel Harman Farm that had been turned into a golf course, and the Willoughby Run itself, this area has given way to modern homes and businesses to the point where it's hard to keep in mind that the same kind of fighting that occurred on the better-preserved areas of the battlefield also occurred here. Some would argue this fighting was even worse, as this was where Ranger John Heiser, historian Scott Hartwig, and

MAJOR GENERAL JOHN F. REYNOLDS

others pointed out to me that the 26th North Carolina and the 24th Michigan nearly annihilated one another.

The 24th Michigan was one of five regiments that comprised the Iron Brigade at Gettysburg, the others being the 19th Indiana, and the 2nd, 6th, and 7th Wisconsin. It was the only fully "Western" brigade in the Army of the Potomac. Most argue it got its famous nickname at the Battle of South Mountain, where General McClellan observed them fighting and commented, "They must be made of iron." Curiously, they wore the tall black Hardee Hat, an old-fashioned military hat that by 1863 had given way

BRIGADIER GENERAL SOLOMON "LONG SOL" MEREDITH

to a variety of alternates, the kepi and the forage cap being the most common. Tradition has it that the Rebels expected only to encounter Pennsylvania militiamen, but when they realized they were fighting the Iron Brigade, yelled: "There are them damned black hatted fellows again. Taint no militia, it's the Army of the Potomac!" The Iron Brigade would never fully recover as a fighting force after its bloody encounter that July 1.

Conversation with An Expert:
The Iron Brigade's Lance J. Herdegen

The foremost authority on the Iron Brigade, Lance tells me what he finds most fascinating about the brigade's role here at Gettysburg: "Let's start by acknowledging that the defensive fighting on McPherson's Ridge saved the Army of the Potomac in what may have been the heaviest musket fire of the war. The brigade suffered horrific losses that first day. Starting out with 1,883 men, official reports put the number they were able to muster out on the second day at 691—but the quartermaster of the brigade said that he only fed 450 men. Gettysburg is a pivotal moment in Iron Brigade history—many of the veterans felt neglected as more attention was paid to what went on at Little Round Top or Pickett's Charge rather than what they accomplished on Day One. But the men were proud of what they had done—for example, there were 45 first-person accounts of the charge on the Railroad Cut. They wanted people to know."

I asked Lance, "What motivated these men to get involved in the first place? I mean they were far removed from where the actual fighting was going on, coming from Wisconsin, Indiana and Michigan?"

"Don't forget there were a lot of men from the east who had moved out west. And, in fact, many were driven by patriotism—not wanting to see the Union come apart. On Day One their fame rests on McPherson's Ridge and the Railroad Cut, but what happened to them on Day Two and Day Three? They were sent to help fortify Culp's Hill after the first day's battle. They weren't very heavily engaged in the fighting on Day Two. On Day Three, they sent a messenger to Meade asking him if they were needed. He replied, 'No, you are not needed.' As a result, they watched Pickett's Charge from the heights of Culp's Hill."

"What's the best-kept secret of the Iron Brigade's participation in the battle?"

"My favorite story is that as the Confederate attack began to develop, a staff officer rode up and told them to hold Cemetery Hill, the rally point south of town, at all costs. Unfortunately, his German accent caused some profound confusion, as they thought he said Seminary Hill just behind them. And, indeed, that was the last place they fought before the end of the day. Gettysburg is a strange and interesting place—I get back there once or twice a year—and every time I go, often depending on the season, I see different aspects of it. I'm intrigued by the 'open' areas—the kind of land where most of the fight on Day One took place. I do my own 'ghost walks' there; the ground emotionally moves me."

"What about the town," I ask Lance.

"The town of Gettysburg is unique—no other place like it—a community completely taken by what went on there some 150 years ago. I'm not very fond

LANCE HERDEGEN

of some of the commercialism, though. In one context, after all, as someone once said, it's a town that lives off its dead."

When asked whether he had ever been a reenactor, Lance smiles and replies, "Oh, I've done it, but I enjoyed being a shooter more—competing with Civil War small arms. Very valuable for what you learn."

General Reynolds may have been offered command of the Army of the Potomac when Lincoln decided to fire Joseph Hooker, but turned it down. Accounts differ as to the reason: he was either nobly deferring to his older friend George Meade, or selfishly, perhaps wisely, refusing because Lincoln would not grant him enough autonomy. There are some who think he shared a caution similar to McClellan's, who was known as a great organizer but not for being very aggressive. (McClellan is, in fact, a story for another day, and a very interesting one. Apparently in 1862 Lincoln once remarked about the recalcitrant commander, "If General McClellan isn't going to use his army, I'd like to borrow it for a time.")

Once he reached the fields west of town and assessed the situation, Reynolds began hastening infantry into Herbst Woods and toward McPherson's barn in an effort to relieve the beleaguered and exhausted cavalrymen. I have always enjoyed the way Michael Shaara depicted the meeting between Reynolds and Buford at the Lutheran Theological Seminary in his compelling Pulitzer-Prize-winning novel *The Killer Angels*. He has the polite Reynolds greeting his old friend with a "Good morning, John," only to have the crusty Buford reply, "General, I'm damned glad to see you." As Reynolds rides back to his own lines toward the I Corps and XI Corps, he adds, "I think I'll move over and hurry the boys along."

But returning to actual history . . . Reynolds was hurrying the men of his I Corps into place—including those veteran fighters of the Iron Brigade under the command of Brig. Gen. Solomon Meredith—when he was shot in the back

The Reynold's Memorial Monument.

of the head by a Rebel soldier (probably by one of Archer's men) and died soon after he hit the ground. His loss was deeply felt. Just east of the thinly wooded area south of McPherson Barn is the memorial marker at the site of Reynolds' death. This general area is one of the most heavily trafficked areas of the park, but few enter the sparse woods where the monument sits. A visit here offers a gentle respite from the cars and other visitors, for relatively few people take a moment to stop and reflect here; they just drive past.

On my first visit I was quite taken by the beauty of the spot. On subsequent visits, reflecting on this place that saw the first major clash of this battle, I came to better understand the power of the Gettysburg experience. I don't want to overstate this, but tracking the battle on the ground, as I now was doing, was my first exposure to the personal cost of this epic clash. I would strongly recommend you take the time to visit this spot. Seasonal Ranger Chuck Teague adds another telling comment: "The absolute utter contrast between its pristine beauty and the horror of that battle. It's the most beautiful place on the planet; it feeds my soul, feeds my heart—but one must never forget what went on here."

In addition to the Reynolds' monument, don't miss the McPherson Barn on the left (we passed it earlier). It was right in the middle of the action. Edward McPherson owned the farm but was renting it to John Slentz at the time of the battle. The National Park Service and the Gettysburg Foundation have done a wonderful job in their maintenance and restoration of these structures. This open field is the place where two Union regiments of Wadsworth's division, the 95th New York and the 14th Brooklyn (aka the 84th New York) were thrown into the fight against the 7th Tennessee of Archer's brigade. Eventually, the Yankees were forced back. Farther south (to the left) was the Iron Brigade.

Before they left the area, these giants in black hats were joined by 69-year-old John Burns, the only civilian to fight at Gettysburg.

JOHN BURNS

John Burns, a former constable of Gettysburg and veteran of the War of 1812, insisted on joining the Union troops under Colonel Langhorne Wesley Wister of the 150th Pennsylvania. He came onto the battlefield with only a flintlock musket, but was given a percussion rifle. He blazed away at the Confederates until three wounds ended his voluntary military service. He enjoyed a mention in Maj. Gen. Abner Doubleday's report of the action, later met President Lincoln, and as a tribute to his bravery had a statue of himself erected at the western edge of the field containing McPherson's Barn, not too far from Willoughby Run, which he helped defend.

The fallen Reynolds left Maj. Gen. Abner Doubleday as the next senior officer in command of the I Corps (yes *that* Doubleday, but don't get out your baseball hats too soon; he apparently didn't really invent the game). Later in the day Meade replaced Doubleday with a general from the VI Corps (Newton). Doubleday didn't like that much, and neither did many of the men of the I Corps.

Picking up the fighting for McPherson's Ridge, Reynolds' timely arrival effectively rescued Buford's exhausted command, replacing the beleaguered cavalrymen with the vanguard of Brig. Gen. James S. Wadsworth's lead division (including the Iron Brigade as noted earlier). The infusion of Union infantry made for a more balanced fight—at least initially. Confederate forces quickly become aware who they are facing as I Corps bands and flag-bearers make their presence known.

South of the pike, Solomon Meredith's men were quickly fed into the battle, catching Archer's brigade by surprise and capturing more than 400 Confederates (including Archer). North of the pike, Brig. Gen. Lysander

Statue of John Burns

COLONEL
LANGHORNE
WESLEY
WISTER

Cutler's men ran into trouble against the Davis' larger Confederate brigade. Driven from their initial positions, Cutler's men retreated toward Seminary Ridge, while many of Davis' men filed into an unfinished Railroad Cut just north of the pike to use it as a natural trench for protection.

In July of 1863 the Pennsylvania Railroad line from Hanover only reached to the station downtown and remained unfinished west of town. Unfortunately for these Confederates, the 6th Wisconsin (left behind the balance of the Iron Brigade fighting mightily just to the west, turned north and, under the command of Lt. Col. Rufus R. Dawes, attacked the Confederates manning the Cut. The Wisconsin men trapped many in the deep part of the scarred ground, firing down into the 2nd Mississippi and the 55th North Carolina. The Rebs suffer grievously, with many dead and wounded and, eventually, captured. Those farther east where the cut was shallower escaped by running north. The Wisconsin boys shot many of them down from behind.

The day I first visited "the Cut" was clear and bright, a beautiful day in May. I recall thinking, "I'm standing on the very ground where men were killed and wounded by the hundreds." Of course, that happened in many places on the

MAJOR GENERAL ABNER DOUBLEDAY

battlefield—for example over at Willoughby Run, as we've seen. Being within the bounds of these earthen walls, having just an inkling of what those soldiers must have felt in this claustrophobic confine, knowing it happened right here, and not within some "general" vicinity, gave me a more vivid sense of the experience than standing in an open field or next to a bubbling brook. I urge you, if you are able, to get out of your car and walk down into the Cut. You won't regret it.

Across the expanse of a century and a half, I come to realize just how much I love being here in Gettysburg. I feel myself more and more drawn to this iconic place. Adjusting for the difference in context, of course, Lee's famous observation at the Battle of Fredericksburg passes fleetingly through my mind: "It is well that war is so terrible, lest we should grow too fond of it." Am I growing too fond of this place—this well-manicured shrine to death and destruction?

As things heated up in Gettysburg, on July 1, Meade ordered Slocum's XII Corps (mentioned by Mingus) up to Two Taverns, barely five miles from Gettysburg. Receiving no orders to proceed farther, however, and

LIEUTENANT COLONEL RUFUS R. DAWES

BRIGADIER GENERAL JAMES S. WADSWORTH

BRIGADIER GENERAL LYSANDER CUTLER

Conversation with an Expert:
Scott L. Mingus, Sr. Offers Observations on Day One:

Scott Mingus is an award-winning Civil War historian and author when he is not working full-time as a patent-holding executive and scientist in the paper industry. Some of Scott's forebears saw action in the Civil War. His great-great-grandfather on his mother's side was a 15-year-old drummer in the 51st Ohio Volunteers and fought under William Tecumseh Sherman. On his father's side, three great-great uncles served with the 7th West Virginia at both Antietam and Gettysburg. He fondly recalls hearing Civil War stories from his parents as they passed them on from stories they had heard in their youth from veterans.

"There is something about Gettysburg—almost like an aura. I know my ancestors fought here, and then coming here as a boy with my Dad—taking my children and grandchildren here—I fall victim to what a friend of mine [J. D.

Scott Mingus

Petruzzi] calls the Gettysburg Addiction Syndrome." [or as I fondly refer to it, GAS!]

I wonder aloud whether Early's brief visit to Gettysburg before the actual battle begins is not without consequence for the little town? Scott replies: "Jubal Early and his entire division, save a few deserters and one very ill soldier, marched out of Gettysburg on the morning of Saturday, June 27, using several parallel roads to reach York County, where Early planned to ransom the prosperous Borough of York for money, supplies, food, and, yes, shoes. His men, before leaving [Gettysburg], had on Friday night raided the town for supplies, burned a wooden railroad bridge over Rock Creek, torched several boxcars after emptying their contents of anything of value to his men, and seized every horse they could find."

Scott picks up the account of Early's movements: "Once in York on the 28th, Early demanded $100,000 in cash, plus his other requisitions. The town could only raise $28,610 from door-to-door collections, and Early implied that he might burn the town's railroad facilities unless he received the rest of the funds. But Lee recalled him to Heidlersburg as he concentrated the army, so Early did not have time to carry out his threat. He left a note for the town's newspaper editor, though, asking him to print a statement explaining his rationale for not applying the torch. Years later, well after the war, Early was fond of telling reporters that he wanted the rest of his money from York, with interest, else he would turn the town over to a collection agency!"

Following the thread of Confederate movement back to the town, I ask Scott about the events of Day One. "To me, the fascination of the first day is two-fold," he begins. "First, so much of the early action west of Gettysburg paralleled the smaller engagement on June 26 on the same ridges. Rebels traveling east on the Chambersburg Pike encounter blue-coated cavalry near Marsh Creek. They push forward, and the cavalry retires, revealing a line of infantry. That was the scenario on June 26 when John Gordon's force encountered Pennsylvania militia cavalry and then almost 750 militia infantrymen behind them. Harry Heth's actions on July 1 show many of the same characteristics, and many of his men and officers may have assumed they were again facing inexperienced state emergency troops, which would soon run away." (You'll recall, "T'aint no militia; it's them black-hatted fellows!")

Scott continues: "Another little-known fact is that the Rebels made an aborted, perhaps even half-hearted, attempt to take Culp's and Cemetery hills on the evening of July 1. Many people have seen the famous, but likely fictional, scene in the movie *Gettysburg* where General Trimble pleads with General Ewell to be given first a division, then a brigade, and finally a single regiment so he 'can take that hill.' Jubal Early sent out scouts and then pushed forward a North Carolina brigade to flank the position and probe the hills, but long-range Union artillery drove off the Tar Heels."

And this brings me to one of those questions that has always intrigued me: "What might have happened had Ewell followed Lee's 'suggestion' and allowed Early to attack both Cemetery and Culp's hills on the early evening of July 1?"

Scott smiles, as if he clearly knows something I do not. "Even if Early had succeeded," he explains, "which was unlikely, he would have run right into Slocum's Union XII Corps which had moved into position just east of Gettysburg at the small village of Two Taverns on the Baltimore Pike during the morning of July 1—about 10,000 nice, fresh troops."

Slocum's Corps did go on to play a key role in the defense of Culp's Hill when the Confederates assaulted it the next day. Just as I leave Scott he informs me that as I return to Gettysburg from Spring Grove, where we have had lunch, I'll be following in reverse the route Early's cavalry took when they left Gettysburg *en route* to Hanover. In fact, Scott points out, they camped for the night of June 27th on the very ground where we ate lunch, at Genova's Restaurant (a nice little eatery, by the way).

with his own lack of initiative, Slocum sat with his corps for several hours in the idyllic village while John Reynolds' I Corps and O. O. Howard's XI Corps (which had moved through town and into the fields north of it) were fighting for their existence just miles away. Eventually, the situation in Gettysburg having been clarified to his satisfaction, Slocum ordered the XII Corps to move north. Quoting Stephen Sears in his book, *Gettysburg*, "Major Charles H. Howard, General Howard's brother and aide-de-camp, remarked in exasperation that on July 1 General Slocum demonstrated 'the fitness of his name Slow come'."

Perhaps part of the appeal of Two Taverns is that it's exactly what it says: Two Taverns, sitting like sentinels, one on either side of the Baltimore Pike. It's so delightfully straightforward. It's not a village, but a place that saw almost 10,000 men sit idly by for crucial hours because Gen. Slocum didn't have the initiative to move them toward the sound of the guns. Across the road from the "tavern" is an interesting bit of history: one of the few remaining stone roadside markers from the 19th century designating the distance to Baltimore.

MAJOR GENERAL ROBERT E. RODES

As Heth's bungled attack sputters to a bloody standstill, the Union forces seem to be holding their own. Elements of Howard's XI Corps are arriving on the field from the south and moving northward into and through the town. Howard's men would settle in on Reynolds' right to extend the Union front. Abner Doubleday noted the arrival of Maj. Gen. Robert E. Rodes' Rebel division of Ewell's Corps along the Mummasburg Road and his subsequent occupation of Oak Hill and ordered Brig. Gen. Henry Baxter's brigade, with support from Lysander Cutler's brigade, to form a defensive position just north of the pike on a spur

of Seminary Ridge called Oak Ridge. As the four companies of the 45th New York moved into position, a Confederate artillery battery commanded by Captain R. C. M. Page revealed Rode's position on Oak Hill by opening fire. This set up one of the more famous artillery duels of Day One. Union Captain Hubert Dilger, German-born and trained, rushed his Ohio battery from Cemetery Hill into the fray. Sighting two of his guns himself, his accurate aim disabled a Confederate gun. Dilger's fame rests not only on his incredible marksmanship but on the heroic manner in

BRIGADIER GENERAL HENRY BAXTER

which he helped cover the retreat of the Union forces from this area later in the day.

On Oak Hill stands the Eternal Light Peace Memorial with its eternal flame, one of the most visited memorials in the park. It was built in 1938 for the 75th Anniversary of the battle, and dedicated by Franklin D. Roosevelt.

Some of Gettysburg's "old timers" witnessed the historic event. Jim Tate, an LBG in his 90s (he died just a few years ago), was there. "President Roosevelt passed me by and said 'Hello, James.' Between 250,000 and 300,000 people were here for it. After 1938, there were barnstormers and wing-walkers who regularly performed near the Peace Memorial. And they used to do airmail pick-ups the old-fashioned way: grabbing a bag

CAPTAIN HUBERT DILGER

suspended between two towers with a plane equipped with a hook. I can remember a dirigible anchored over at Long Lane, as well."

The Eternal Light Peace Memorial.

CHARLES BENDER

THE LATE GREAT JIM TATE

Charles Bender, merchant and owner of the House of Bender (now retired, and the business sold) on Lincoln Square added more information about the event: "Because the town lacked accommodations for that many people a giant 'tent city' was set up for the veterans. Boy Scouts were assigned to help them. The tent city included medical facilities. There was a big parade through town. I believe Gettysburg's becoming a tourist center really began in 1938 with the 75th Anniversary."

Former mayor, octogenarian William Troxell, a descendent of the first settler in Gettysburg, caps the story for me: "My brother was one of the Scouts. The average age of the veterans that were still able to attend was 94; the oldest was 109. I remember one of the veterans caused quite a commotion when he couldn't be found. He'd disappeared for a day having gone up to Philadelphia to see a baseball game."

The impressive Eternal Light Peace Memorial sits near the crest of Oak Hill, which was where Gen. Rodes of Ewell's Corps was aligning his division and its five infantry brigades. Fortuitously for the Rebels, Ewell arrived from the north on the Union right flank; the opportunity to unravel the Union line of battle was a rare one. The arrival of Howard's fresh XI Corps troops made the task much more difficult. The remaining members of the Union I Corps were still heavily engaged across the Chambersburg Pike in the fight for McPherson's Ridge and would soon be routed backward to Seminary Ridge. Early's division (also of Ewell's corps) was also arriving from north of town just east of Rodes' men near the Harrisburg Road. This area is the northernmost part of the battlefield. In fairness to Howard, the terrain was not favorable for him and he didn't have enough men to hold it. Despite valiant Union efforts the XI Corps was about to be overwhelmed.

Throughout the afternoon of July 1 the battle raged, its outcome uncertain. Lee was against a major engagement, but when Ewell arrived on the Union flank and Rodes launched his attack, Lee joined in against Seminary Ridge from the west. If he was hoping for a quick victory, he would be disappointed. Rodes opened his battle with a staggered weak punch that hit air. Today,

MAYOR WILLIAM "BILL" TROXELL

Forney's Field below Oak Hill is bathed in serenity—open fields with grasses gently moving in the light winds. It was not always so.

Two of Rodes' brigades under Col. Edward A. O'Neal and Brig. Gen. Alfred Iverson started their attack against Baxter's position around 2:30 p.m. The coordination was off. Iverson failed to post skirmishers well in advance of his line to prevent any unwelcome surprises and remained well behind his advancing men. Not far ahead, hiding behind a stone wall on Oak Ridge, was Baxter's Union brigade, which stood and delivered a killing volley that dropped hundreds of North Carolinians in a perfect line. Iverson's brigade was cut to pieces in the open field and suffered more than 800 casualties. (Iverson thought his men lying in a row were afraid to move ahead, but in fact they were mostly dead.) The hastily buried Confederates were buried in shallow but temporary graves in what will forever be remembered as "Iverson's Pits." General Lee would later remove Iverson from command. The unlucky and mostly unskilled general would later turn in a solid performance in Georgia during Sherman's Atlanta Campaign, but the stain of Gettysburg would haunt him to his grave.

Across the park road not far from Baxter's position on Oak Ridge and just northwest of town is the first of three observation towers on the battlefield. I love them, but as a man of somewhat advanced years I don't mind complaining a bit about their height. This one, for example, has 5,260 steps. (Well, it only feels like that.) Throughout the history of this magnificent park there have been

BRIGADIER GENERAL ALFRED IVERSON

numerous incarnations of these towers, though only three remain today. Along with the natural high ground at Oak Hill, Little Round Top, and to a degree, Culp's Hill, they provide good bird's eye views of the battlefield.

This first tower overlooking the Carlisle Road is the lowest of the three. It is 23 feet tall, with 39 steps and two landings. It's easy to climb, and affords a spectacular view of the areas I have been describing. Barlow's Knoll is to the east, Gettysburg College and the town to the southeast, McPherson's Ridge

COLONEL EDWARD A. O'NEAL

southwest, the Lutheran Seminary and Seminary Ridge to the south, and the Chambersburg Pike and the fields that saw much of the early fighting on the first day to the southwest and west. To the north, one can see the Mummasburg and Carlisle roads, which General Ewell's men used to reach their positions on the afternoon of the first day. Looking back toward the Peace Memorial is one of my favorite monuments: the "tree-trunk" shaped memorial to the 90th Pennsylvania Infantry.

The Gettysburg College of today—easily viewed from the Observation Tower—was known as Pennsylvania College in 1863. There were only three buildings, two of which are still in use: The President's House and Pennsylvania Hall, then called the College Building. While the battle swept over the campus, whose main claim to fame was the extensive use of the large College Building as first a signal station and later a hospital for both Confederate and Union wounded. A beautiful campus, it is today the home of the Civil War Institute and considered one of the best small liberal arts colleges in the nation.

Driving straight onto Doubleday Avenue, we find ourselves in a beautiful wooded area, and to our surprise discover a B&B called the Doubleday Inn right there in the middle of the area of the Day One fight. Beautifully set and exquisitely maintained, it provides a charming and tranquil respite from the hubbub of the town and most of the park, with unbeatable access for pedestrian exploration of this part of the battlefield. They serve a wonderful and plentiful breakfast, so you'll be well-fueled for your trekking.

Conversation with an Expert:
LBG George Newton — Observations on Day One

A native of Baltimore, LBG George Newton is an Air Force veteran and a retired executive from the insurance industry. George and his wife Jan moved to Gettysburg in 1998, having purchased the Tannery Bed and Breakfast Inn (whose name they changed to the Baltimore Street Bed and Breakfast. They ran it successfully until May of 2002, when they sold it to the Friends of the National Parks of Gettysburg. The Inn is now the Rupp House, the home of the Gettysburg Foundation. George has been an LBG since 2005.

"I became interested in the Civil War when I was eight years old!" begins George. "That year, 1956, my parents brought me to Gettysburg. The monuments, stone walls, and cannon impressed me greatly—I was hooked on the Civil War and then it became a life-long avocation. My interests, however, go beyond those things that 'go boom in the night.' I'm a student of Civil War infantry and their tactics, as well, and am fascinated by the events at Gettysburg during the first day of the battle."

"What is the best kept secret about that first day?" I ask. George is quick off the blocks with his answer: "Day One is much bigger and bloodier than many think. It was not just a skirmish but a full-blown battle with about 27,000 Confederates opposed by about 20,000 Union troops, and total casualties of about 16,000—a 34% casualty rate! Everyone should know that Day One was a 'movement to contact' in military terms—neither side had determined to fight here, but a big fight broke out. Once battle is joined, the commanders make decisions on the fly with little time to ponder—they did not have 150 years or

GEORGE NEWTON

more to figure things out! Of course, the next two days then become the 'set-piece' kind of battles that are so common in the war. The whole battlefield interests me," continues George, "not only the monuments and cannon that are those 'silent sentinels' now [he is the author of *Silent Sentinels*, a book on Gettysburg artillery], but the very terrain where so many fought and died for their beliefs. You can't come to the battlefield and not be absorbed in the knowledge of what went on between our ancestors."

Being here among the rocks and hills, the valleys and streams, standing on the very board upon which this horrific chess game was played is, indeed, physically tangible. George philosophizes about Gettysburg's role in the larger context of the War: "There were two more years to follow. Gettysburg was not the last battle, nor was 1863 the bloodiest year—that dubious distinction belongs to 1864. The war was far from over in July 1863, and I don't think our battle here was the turning point. Wars are too complicated to hinge on a single event, however important it might be, and certainly Gettysburg was among the most important in the Civil War; but there were others of equal importance."

As our conversation winds down, I can't resist asking him about questions he's received. "One of my favorites," he replies, "was the visitor who asked me if the South Mountain Range seen in the distance to the west was here at the time. Hmmmm."

Throughout the afternoon of July 1, we have seen Union forces rushing into Gettysburg from the south, and Confederate forces appearing in increasing numbers from the west and north. As Howard's XI Corps does its best to hold out against the much larger Confederate forces under Dick Ewell, the culmination of this final phase of the Day One battle occurs along what is now Howard Avenue, a park road connecting the Mummasburg Road and the Harrisburg Road (Business US15), There on Blocher's Knoll, more commonly referred to today as Barlow's Knoll, after Brig. Gen. Francis C. Barlow.

Unlike the heavily wooded or hilly terrain of much of the rest of the battlefield, this area is largely open farmland with gently rolling hills. To prevent Confederate forces from capturing this high ground as an artillery position, Barlow moved his division forward, thinning its connection to Maj. Gen. Carl Schurz's division to his left. (By the way, if you are interested, you may want to further study the number of German officers and men in the Army of the Potomac, and their concentration in O. O. Howard's XI Corps, which adopted as its emblem a crescent moon).

COLONEL LEOPOLD VON GILSA

BRIGADIER GENERAL FRANCIS C. BARLOW

My opportunity to visit this area came as part of attending one of Gettysburg College's Civil War Institute meetings. These five-day sessions are held every year in late June. Started almost 25 years ago by Professor Gabor Boritt, an Abraham Lincoln and Civil War scholar, they are now under the administration of the Fluhrer Professor of History at Gettysburg College, Peter Carmichael. Part of their programs include field trips—some are full-day trips at a distance from Gettysburg, and some are shorter trips to sites on the battlefield or nearby areas. In 2012, the Institute I attended focused

BRIGADIER GENERAL ADELBERT AMES

on the events of 1862. I took a fantastic full-day trip to Antietam (the bloodiest single day in American history, fought on September 17, 1862), which provided a War College-like Staff Ride around the battlefield conducted by Professor Christian Keller of the US Army War College, and a half-day trip called "July 1: The 11th Corps and the Fight For Blocher's Knoll," led by Gettysburg College alum Brian Jordan. Both were extraordinary. (Brian completed his studies at Harvard with honors and was, until recently, a member of the Gettysburg College faculty.)

Our excursion bus provided by the Institute took us to the parking lot of the Adams County Environmental Services complex on the Harrisburg Road. This was the site of the Adams County Almshouse in 1863, an area occupied by three brigades of Barlow's division under Wladimir Krzyzanowski, Leopold von Gilsa, and Adelbert Ames. When Barlow spotted Confederate forces moving toward his position, he sent von Gilsa's and Ames' brigades forward to occupy the high ground due north of his present position. We were standing at the edge of a large field and about to head over to Barlow's Knoll when Brian offered us the opportunity to traverse the same ground that was covered in this forward movement on foot. Everyone in the group under the age of 102 accepted his offer, while the others hop

COLONEL WLADIMIR KRZYZANOWSKI

BRIGADIER
GENERAL
ALEXANDER
SCHIMMELFENNIG

back onto the bus for the short ride over.

The land we crossed is flat, and I am struck by how open it is. Regardless of how high the corn may have been in 1863, this area would not have afforded much cover. One can understand Barlow's impulse to establish an artillery position here, even if he made the mistake of stretching the Union defensive line too thin. Whether this position could have been held with additional Union forces is the subject of historical conjecture. But it's instructive crossing it. (If you are walking, it's a good idea to check your pants, socks, and shoes for ticks, which

inhabit the fields around Gettysburg. Some varieties cause Lyme Disease, so it is always recommended that you wear long pants, and even long-sleeved shirts if you plan on doing much hiking.) Barlow's Knoll is a beautiful spot, all too often neglected by visitors to the battlefield who seem reluctant to spend a little extra time to take the drive or walk over here. But it's well worth it.

Despite reinforcements later in the afternoon from Alexander Schimmel- fennig's division, the position was eventually outflanked and overrun by Confederate brigades under George Doles and John B. Gordon. Barlow was critically

BRIGADIER
GENERAL
GEORGE DOLES

BRIGADIER GENERAL JOHN B. GORDON

wounded and taken prisoner. This fighting, along with the combat across Rock Creek just a few hundred yards from here, represents the northeastern-most part of the Union line on July 1. With its collapse around 4:00 p.m., the entire XI Corps was in full retreat back through the town. In this area alone, Union losses totaled around 3,200 men, with 1,400 taken prisoner. Confederate losses in Doles' and Gordon's brigades was about 750. To the west, Hill's Corps had collapsed the Union defenses on Seminary Ridge and driven thousands of Union men (including many of the Iron Brigade) eastward through the town and toward

Cemetery Hill and Cemetery Ridge.

Leaving Barlow's Knoll we cross Rock Creek and visit Benner's Farm, a fairly recent addition to the Civil War properties managed by the NPS, and yet another building which served as a hospital.

One of my favorite spots that is rarely visited by the average tourist is Brickyard Lane, aka Coster Avenue. Located in the northeast part of town, East Stevens Street after one block becomes Coster Avenue. Directly ahead of you, with its four monuments and famed mural, is "Brickyard Lane."

BRIGADIER GENERAL HARRY T. HAYS

The Brickyard Lane Mural.

This curious little spot is fewer than 100 yards long. I first discovered it through J. D. Petruzzi's and Steven Stanley's award-winning book *The Complete Gettysburg Guide*, a wonderful resource, and simply a must-have for anyone interested in Gettysburg. The small open field is bounded on the right with four monuments and markers. On the entire wall of the modern building behind the markers is a mural depicting the height of the fight on the evening of July 1. The painting was done by Mark Dunkelman and Johan Bjurman, and dedicated on July 1, 1988.

As Ewell's Confederates were sweeping southward late on the afternoon of July 1, Col. Charles Coster led three regiments of his Union brigade, approximately 920 men, to this spot to help in time for the rest of the XI Corps' escape southward through the town. Later reinforced by Capt. Lewis Heckman's Battery K, 1st Ohio Light, they held off the 2,500 veterans of Harry Hays' famed Louisiana Tigers, at least for a while. The Union position was eventually enveloped and collapsed with the loss of nearly 560 men and two guns from Heckman's Battery.

Before we leave Day One, I want to follow up on Ranger John Heiser's mention of the heroics of Capt. Francis Irsch of the 45th New York. Having led his men well throughout the fighting for, and retreat from, Oak Ridge, his 375-man strong regiment found itself trapped in a row of houses in the town. Successfully repelling several assaults, they held out until nearly sundown, when Irsch accepted an offer to "parley." Recognizing the complete control of Gettysburg by the Confederates, he accepted their demands to have his men throw down their arms and surrender. It should be noted that he was later awarded the Medal of Honor for his leadership on this fateful day.

Fortunately for the Union forces retreating through Gettysburg, by the end of the day Cemetery Hill had been heavily fortified. When he arrived at

Gettysburg many hours earlier, O. O. Howard had the presence of mind to drop off one of his brigades there as a reserve. The arrival of Maj. Gen. Winfield Scott Hancock in advance of his II Corps, along with the retreating remnants of Doubleday's I Corps and Howard's XI Corps, helped establish strong defensive positions bristling with artillery on the high ground south and slightly southeast of town.

Cemetery Hill, the site of the town's Evergreen Cemetery, and to the east Culp's Hill—actually a pair of wooded hills—become Union redoubts (though Culp's was at this time not occupied by Union troops). Hancock, one of the North's best generals, had been named after the former General in Chief of the Union Army, Winfield Scott. Hancock was a battle-tested veteran of the Army of the Potomac who somehow always managed to find a clean white shirt regardless of the circumstances. He had distinguished himself early (his nickname was "Hancock the Superb") and earned his right to lead the II Corps. Before it was all over, Hancock and his men would play a pivotal role in winning the battle.

With the Union in control of the high ground below town, the Confederate wave crested and stopped. The Rebels had also suffered heavy losses, and the town (which was a mess jammed with men, vehicles, and mass confusion) had disrupted the advance. Hill paused on Seminary Ridge, and Ewell struggled to shake out the chaos in town and prepare for further fighting. Both sides settled into an exchange of skirmish fire, but there was still daylight left. It was then that a major controversy erupted that still echoes today.

About this time, General Lee sent a message to Ewell that he "carry the hill occupied by the enemy, if he found it practicable, but to avoid a general engagement until the arrival of the other divisions of the army." Huh? Fight by carrying the hill, but don't bring on too big of a fight? How could any general do that? Ewell also wasn't sure exactly what to do, but in the end he deemed the high ground too strong, his own available force too weak, and he did not launch an attack.

Historians and students of Gettysburg continue to debate what might have happened had Ewell attacked Cemetery Hill that night. As noted in my conversation with Scott Mingus, it may be a good thing for the Confederates that Ewell didn't make the effort, although some of his officers, notably John Gordon (at least according to John B. Gordon) chafed at the bit to attack and begged Ewell to do so. Part of Ewell's hesitancy stemmed from the fact that A. P. Hill's Corps was not going to offer any assistance from the west. Ewell's last division under Edward "Allegheny" Johnson had not yet arrived, and some of

Early's division had been dispatched north and west to guard against Federals reported to be approaching the Confederate rear. He did not believe he had enough fresh men to make the effort.

Perhaps the most accurate assessment of the situation came from Hancock, who said that if the Rebels had rushed Cemetery Hill during the first hour after they swept through the town—when the survivors of the I and XI Corps were in headlong retreat up the hill—they might've succeeded. After that time the front had stabilized, with the benefit of stone walls and pre-positioned artillery, and any assault would likely have failed.

MAJOR GENERAL WINFIELD SCOTT HANCOCK

We will never know since Ewell did not make the attempt and the important high ground (as well as nearby Culp's Hill), remained in Union hands as the northern and northwestern anchors, respectively, of a formidable defensive position that would soon run south down Cemetery Ridge to form a giant "Fishhook."

Day One was a bloody affair for both combatants. On the Union side, 22,000 men took part and some 9,000 were killed, wounded, or captured. On the Confederate side, about

BREVET LIEUTENANT GENERAL WINFIELD SCOTT

27,000 men entered the fray and more than 6,000 became casualties.

In the interest of not overlooking one of the most important sites relevant to the fighting on Day One—recently bought and completely restored to its 1863 appearance by the Gettysburg Foundation—let's have a look at the George Spangler Farm at the south end of the main battlefield. On July 1, 1863 this farm and all its buildings became the field hospital for the 2nd Division of the Union's XI Corps, which had suffered so grievously. Once established, the hospital served some 1,900 soldiers from the beginning of the battle until the second week in August— approximately 1,800 Union, and 100 Confederate. The remaining patients were moved to other better-equipped hospitals, including the Union's giant field hospital Camp Letterman out on the York Pike.

Conversation with an Expert:
Supervisory Historian, Ranger D. Scott Hartwig—

Observations on Day One . . . and More:

Now retired, the former Gettysburg historian and noted Civil War author and speaker was once responsible for creating the work schedules for all the rangers in the Interpretive Division and planning the park's interpretive program—in other words, he determined who goes where and when, and what they talk about.

"What's your most lasting impression of Gettysburg?" I ask. His answer was quite moving.

"You have to think about the impact this place has on people. After nine-eleven, two people who had been in the Twin Towers came to Gettysburg and went on programs I conducted. I did not know who they were. They wrote me afterwards and told me, and how this place helped them understand what they had gone through." Scott paused a moment before continuing. "This is a profound place, and when someone is willing to poke below the surface, it yields insights into not only what went on here, but into yourself, as well."

Scott has a deep personal respect and appreciation for the sacrifices made here. Consequently, he has a little trouble with the ghost tours: "they've become too aggressive in their marketing." He talks of a ranger friend who, when asked by tourists about the ghosts of Gettysburg, responds with the question: "How would you like it if we did ghost tours over the USS *Arizona* . . . or at Ground Zero?"

Scott points out that Gettysburg was one of those places that tested what war is about. "Lincoln talks about this in his address here: 'Now we are engaged in a great civil war, testing whether that nation, or any nation so conceived and

D. SCOTT HARTWIG

so dedicated, can long endure.' Remember, seven states seceded before Lincoln even took office; four more after Fort Sumter— the convictions so strongly expressed in his Gettysburg Address were simply not shared by many Americans of the 1860s, or before. The Civil War shaped what we believe, and who we became as a nation."

Always on the lookout for insights into the battle itself, I ask Scott to focus on Day One. "Percentage-wise, Day One is the bloodiest of the three—for the number of troops committed, the casualties were the worst," he explains. "Look at the statistics for the 26th and 11th North Carolina on the Confederate side, and the 24th Michigan and 151st Pennsylvania on the Union side. Lt. Col. John R. Lane, of the 26th North Carolina wrote that 'the woods became as dark as night' . . . with smoke! This was in the middle of the afternoon of the 1st. This area, in and around Herbst Woods, was a slaughterhouse. The 26th North Carolina brought 800 men to the fields of Gettysburg; they left with 80."

Scott's comments echoing George Newton's observations of that horrible day and ram home the fact that Day One, so often seen as merely a prologue to what followed, was, on its own, of the most important clashes of the Civil War. Had either army withdrawn at the end of that day, it would merit significant study and analysis as a stand-alone battle.

Scott moves to a more personal observation as he muses about how this battle changed the attitude of the Confederate soldier. After the sacrifices they made here, they went away with nothing to show for it. He mentions his own son and his fellow officers, and what they may feel about their service in Iraq and Afghanistan. Our conversation takes a pause here. We both need a moment to let this point settle in before we can move on. Scott is extraordinarily eloquent, and I can see what must have been one of the many reasons for his achieving the status he had here at America's premier military park. As we near the end of our conversation, he adds a few perceptions: "Gettysburg is a unique little town. For most Americans Gettysburg is the Civil War. It is not something dormant in the past, but still living history, still, indeed, controversial. The Gettysburg Address brought it international fame. This place has become the focal point for what happened in that war—the symbolism of the place redounds throughout America."

Part of the farm's fame rests with the fact that both Gen. Hancock and Rebel Brig. Gen. Lewis A. Armistead, who had been close friends before the war, would be treated here after falling with wounds during the Pickett-Pettigrew-Trimble Charge on Day Three. Armistead's wounds would prove fatal. Hancock's were serious, and would bother him for the rest of his life. This special place is one of the most intact of the Civil War field hospitals, and the entire farm has been restored to its 1863 condition—a tremendous undertaking and achievement by the Gettysburg Foundation.

Like the Eisenhower National Historic Site, the farm is accessible only by bus tours from the Visitor Center. Once there, qualified guides explain its significance as well as how it functioned as a working farm in 1863. The self-guided walking tour of seven stops, if you prefer, takes about 45 minutes. It is open year round and well worth the effort.

If you're beginning to think this is a big battlefield, just wait until we add Day Two and Day Three. How can you handle it all? The answer is easy: move to Gettysburg, or, if you can't do that, visit as often as you can. If you can only visit once, however, hit the high points as indicated in the NPS Brochure's Auto Tour. If you can't visit at all, set aside a couple of nice winter afternoons for a little light reading. I know just the book you should start with (!)—and, if your interest is piqued, you can follow up with a little heavier reading, watch videos online, and so forth. However, I hope the reasons for visiting in person are becoming clear.

Chapter 5

The Armies Head-to-Head, Day Two —
The Biggest and the Bloodiest, and My
Second Personal Encounter with History

*I*f nothing had followed on July 2, Day One would stand as one of the major battles of the Civil War. But there was much to follow, and much to decide. Even before the sun set, the leaders of both armies had a major decision to make: Gather here and fight the decisive battle of the campaign, or retreat and/or maneuver elsewhere?

General Lee's confidence in his army remained high. He had crushed two full corps of the enemy and captured a large number of men and substantial supplies. He also knew he would soon be outnumbered, his men were exhausted, and his trusted and most capable lieutenant, James Longstreet, was more in favor of fighting a defensive battle like Fredericksburg than the offensive action Lee had in mind. Indeed, "Old Pete" was already arguing that Lee should move the army to a strong defensive position between Washington and the Army of the Potomac to force Meade to go on the attack. Lee told him he intended to strike the next morning if the Union army was still there. Longstreet abruptly replied, "If the enemy is still there it is because he wants you to strike him," or words to that effect.

The Leister Farmhouse, Meade's Headquarters.

Lee was also unsure where all of Meade's corps were located or what the Yankees were up to because Jeb Stuart was still out of touch. The arrival of Longstreet's Corps, which was en route from Chambersburg, together with Stuart's cavalry when it finally did arrive, would push the Army of Northern Virginia to nearly full strength, less the losses suffered during the first day's fight. Hill's Corps was in hand and mostly posted along Seminary Ridge facing the Union position, with Ewell's holding the town and the terrain north of the Union positions. Each corps had a fresh division that had not yet fired a shot, and several other brigades in good condition. Meade's corps were almost certainly rushing north after the Virginia army, strung out and tired. Lee's army was mostly together. This was the opportunity Lee had been seeking. He had the initiative and he was not about to give it up.

General Meade was not on the field for the first day's fight. He arrived early on the morning of July 2 after a tiring ride from Taneytown. The new army commander was greeted by corps commanders Howard (XI) Slocum (XII), and Dan Sickles (III), along with his chief engineer Gouverneur Warren. Meade convened a brief meeting in a room in the gatehouse of Evergreen Cemetery on Cemetery Hill.

The I Corps and XI corps had fought well, but circumstances of terrain and Ewell's unexpected arrival from the north had conspired against them. But the generals assured Meade the ground now in their possession was excellent for defensive purposes. "I am glad to hear you say so, for it is too late to leave

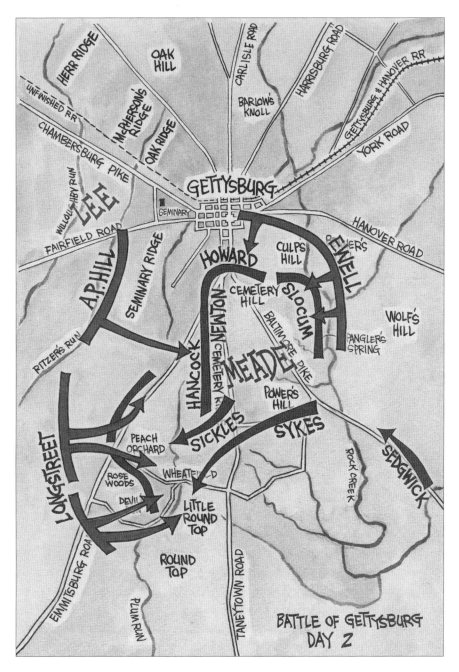

BATTLE OF GETTYSBURG
DAY 2

it," shot back the general some called "an old snapping turtle." The famous "Fishhook" defensive position was developing well, with the two crests of Culp's Hill anchoring it in the northeast (Culp's was not yet occupied by either side in strength), hooking up with the formidable infantry and artillery position on Cemetery Hill, and extending south down the length of Cemetery Ridge. In the distance off to the south was a pair of high rocky hills that would come to be known as Big and Little Round Top. "We may as well fight it out here just as well as anywhere else," Meade concluded. This was quite a burden for a man who had been in command for less than four days.

Meade selected the widow Lydia Leister's small farmhouse on the Taneytown Road, just south of Cemetery Hill and behind Cemetery Ridge, for use as his headquarters.

Should you desire to visit by car, there is a small parking lot across the Taneytown Road from the farmhouse at the intersection with Hunt Avenue. On foot, the Leister House can also be approached from the east along a new path from the Visitor Center, or from the west along a path from Cemetery Ridge. The first thing that will strike you is how tiny it is. (Lee, you'll recall, had established his headquarters in a tent just south of the Chambersburg Pike.)

Unlike much of Day One, which unfolded in a relatively straightforward, almost sequential fashion, the second day's battle was a complex multi-faceted affair across a much larger area, with almost as many miscues as there were actions and lots of simultaneous combat. Consequently, we'll need to jump around a bit.

Lee's Master Plan

Early on the morning of July 2, long before the sun was up, Lee dispatched Captain Samuel R. Johnston, an engineer on his staff, to reconnoiter the ground "along the enemy's left and return as soon as possible." The purpose was to determine where Meade's left flanked ended, and whether it could be attacked. It proved a fateful ride and one that still generates significant controversy to this day.

Johnston made his way west along the Fairfield Road and then south until he turned east, crossed the Emmitsburg Road, and continued on. He encountered two large hills. He later reported that he climbed the slopes of one of the hills, took note of only a few Union troops passing by, and that the hill appeared unoccupied. In other words, Johnston claimed to have gotten partway up the slope of Little Round Top, and had not seen any Yankee troop concentrations in the area. Exactly where he went remains something of a mystery, for a Union signal station was already in operation on Little Round Top, and large numbers of Union troops were camped nearby. Other Federals were marching northward up the Emmitsburg Road on the way to Gettysburg, although there were gaps between the columns.

As far as Lee was concerned, it looked as though Meade's left petered out somewhere on lower Cemetery Ridge. Using Johnston's report to help guide him, Lee decided to use Longstreet's arriving troops to march south, turn east, take up position and face generally north, and then drive up the Emmitsburg Road to crush Meade's exposed flank. Maj. Gen. George Pickett's division was still well behind the army with the wagons, leaving Longstreet with two divisions to call upon, one under Maj. Gen. John B. Hood and the other under Maj. Gen. Lafayette McLaws. The division holding the right flank of A.

MAJOR GENERAL LAFAYETTE McLAWS

BRIGADIER GENERAL EVANDER M. LAW

P. Hill's line on lower Seminary Ridge under Maj. Gen. Richard Anderson would cooperate with Longstreet to support his attack, an *en echelon* assault (one unit after another, right to left) that would move bit by bit northward up the line. Ewell's Corps, miles away to the northwest, was also to attack East Cemetery Hill and Culps' Hill to freeze those Union men in position, or break through. The major attack would be Longstreet's, but Lee was prepared to follow up success wherever it revealed itself. His ability to improvise was legendary.

Meade, meanwhile, had still not seen the ground with his own eyes in

MAJOR GENERAL JOHN B. HOOD

the sunlight. From what he understood, a Union attack on July 2 was impractical, so he fortified the Fishhook, feeding both present and arriving corps into what he hoped would be a nearly impregnable defensive line. Gen. Slocum's XII Corps, supported by remnants of the I Corps, would secure Culp's Hill, while the survivors of the XI Corps would hold Cemetery Hill. Next in line to the south was Hancock's II Corps, extending down the Fishhook shank (Cemetery Ridge). The final element was Maj. Gen. Daniel E. Sickles' III

Corps, which was ordered to take up a position beyond Hancock's left along the lower part of the ridge and anchor the Union line at Little Round Top. When the V Corps under Maj. Gen. George Sykes arrived later that morning, Meade placed it in reserve near the Baltimore Pike behind the Union right. The army's largest corps, the VI under Maj. Gen. John Sedgwick, had crossed into Pennsylvania and was still marching toward Gettysburg. Meade's army was not as dispersed as Lee hoped it might be.

MAJOR GENERAL JOHN SEDGWICK

The Day Begins

Early in the morning, skirmishers operating between the armies began a fitful exchange of gunfire. For the most part, these men were new to their positions, so when dawn broke it was important get a good grasp of the terrain and test the strength and intentions of the enemy. On the Union right, scattered skirmishers from Slocum's newly arrived XII Corps and Ed "Allegheny" Johnson's fresh division of Ewell's Corps begin testing each other around Culp's Hill. From the town itself and a lane below

MAJOR GENERAL GEORGE SYKES

MAJOR GENERAL HENRY W. SLOCUM

it, Confederate sharpshooters from Rodes' division poked at the Union lines on Cemetery Hill, and received fire from the defiant Federals in return. Farther south down Cemetery Ridge, John Buford's cavalry had originally picketed the sector but was ordered to withdraw from the field to rest and reorganize, and to guard the Union supply depot at Westminster. The Union left was suddenly stripped of its cavalry; ironically, this came about at a time when Jeb Stuart's Southern horsemen were on the verge of finding Lee's army.

On one of my excursions to the battlefield, I began the day on Seminary Ridge to find one of the hidden jewels of the battlefield. I love searching for those little secret places that abound on a battlefield like Gettysburg that most visitors never get to see. The key is doing a little fun research ahead of time to have some idea where these spots are before you arrive. Seen any dinosaur prints lately? No? Pictures and directions on how to find even those are included (with a host of other little-known gems scattered across this battlefield,) in the earlier mentioned Petruzzi-Stanley book *The Complete Gettysburg Guide.*

On this occasion, armed with only my battlefield America map, I find an opening in the stone wall on West Confederate Avenue just below McMillan Woods and trek eastward. The ground appears flat covered by tall grass and weeds, but the "trail" is not that easy to follow. The farther east I go, the less level the ground becomes, filled as it is with little hillocks and gullies.

Off to my right I spot a well-manicured piece of ground. As referenced on the map I carried, I had just come across the Bliss Farm—or at least where it once stood—along with several monuments to Union regiments that fought here. Serendipity strikes: I've found one of those "little secret places." No, the Bliss Farm itself is not a "secret," but few folks venture forth to tramp its soil.

Bloody skirmishing broke out over the farm about 9:00 a.m. on July 2. When you stand here and look around it is easy to see why. The farm was right in between the opposing lines, and Confederate sharpshooters were shooting at Union officers from windows and advanced positions. The Bliss land sits between McMillan Woods on Seminary Ridge and the Brian Farm on upper Cemetery Ridge. Its buildings and orchards provided good cover for whoever occupied it. The fighting would rise and fall here like so many tides and consume much of the day and precious resources the Rebels could ill-afford. It would also directly affect the battle to come later that day.

Rather than continue on all the way east to the Emmitsburg Road, I turn to my left to investigate Long Lane, a street I've often noted on battle maps of the area. This was a slightly sunken track during the battle, outside town, and usually filled with Confederate skirmishers and sharpshooters. Many died here from long-range fire and units that were never "directly" engaged suffered appalling losses by the time the battle ended. I walked along the sidewalk on Lost Lane, glanced to my right at the well-preserved battlefield, and to my left at the little suburban neighborhood there now. It was an odd feeling, this mixture of history and suburbia. I know towns must grow and people need places to live, but I also know that hundreds of Americans died or were wounded here. Frankly, my dear, I prefer the history.

This is a good time to distinguish between "skirmishers" and "sharpshooters." Skirmishers were soldiers pulled from the ranks and placed in front of the main body of troops. Their purpose was to harass the enemy, flush out their strength, and provide early warning of an attack or danger. They were usually sent forward spread out over a wide area. Sharpshooters, on the other hand, were specialists carefully chosen from the ranks for their outstanding marksmanship. Comparable to the more modern sniper, they were often equipped with specialized weapons capable of accurate fire over long distances. Confederate sharpshooters were drawn from each regiment, while Union sharpshooters, at least for the Army of the Potomac, generally formed a separate unit known colloquially as "Berdan's Sharpshooters," after Colonel Hiram Berdan, the guiding force and the commanding colonel of what would be the 1st and 2nd United States Volunteer Sharpshooter Regiments. His men wore distinctive green uniforms and belonged to Sickles' III Corps.

Farther east I encounter the ground along Cemetery Ridge between Ziegler's Grove, the scene of intense fighting on Day Two, toward the Confederate "High-Water Mark" and the Copse of Trees. This section of the battlefield has now been fully restored by the NPS, leaving only one small parking lot for the Soldiers' National Cemetery.

Until March 2013, part of this land was occupied by the former Visitor Center. The debate as to whether to preserve that VC as part of the history of the park finally gave way to the more important consideration of restoring the battlefield to its 1863 appearance. The building had been vacant since the new facility opened in 2008 and was becoming a bit of an eyesore. Its removal allowed for a better understanding of this part of the battlefield. I next pondered what was also taking place on the morning of July 2 farther south.

While the Bliss skirmish was underway Union sharpshooters and some II Corps infantry were advancing west across the Emmitsburg Road to see what is in the distant woods to their front. Gen. Sickles had sent them to find out because he disliked the position on lower Cemetery Ridge and was worried his III Corps was about to be attacked. The probe (partially conducted by members of Berdan's Sharpshooters) stumbled into part of Cadmus Wilcox's Alabama brigade of Anderson's division (part of A. P. Hill's Third Corps) in Pitzer's Woods. The fighting was brief, but heavy. Until then, few if any Union officers knew the Confederate left extended so far south. Longstreet's arrival later that afternoon would significantly alter that dynamic. The fighting, short as it was, disturbed Dan Sickles.

COLONEL HIRAM BERDAN

I have a confession to make. Two Union generals are at the top of my %#*@ list. The first is George McClellan for reasons I suggested earlier—he was arrogant, overly cautious, and seemed overly reluctant to take on Lee. The second is Maj. Gen. Daniel E. Sickles. What a character! Indeed, if you're interested let me strongly recommend *Sickles at Gettysburg,* by James A. Hessler. This even-handed and rather exciting treatment by a LBG will give you a full picture of the man. For our purposes, a quote from Hessler's book says it all:

No individual who fought at Gettysburg was more controversial, both personally and professionally,

A BERDAN SHARPSHOOTER

than Major General Daniel E. Sickles. By 1863, Sickles was notorious as a disgraced former Congressman who murdered his wife's lover on the streets of Washington and used America's first temporary insanity defense to escape justice. With his political career in ruins, Sickles used his connections to President Lincoln to obtain a prominent command in the Army of the Potomac's Third Corps—despite having no military experience. At Gettysburg, his unauthorized advance to the Peach Orchard was one of the most controversial decisions in military history.

Even though we are getting a bit ahead of ourselves, let's take a closer look at Sickles. Meade ordered him to place his III Corps on the left of Hancock's II Corps, extending the line along Cemetery Ridge to Little Round Top. Sickles did not like his position and thought the ground ahead along the Emmitsburg Road was higher. And what was in the distant woods? Sickles concern was partially justified, for the probe had discovered Rebels there. Were they gathering for a massive attack? He tried more than once to get Meade to visit, but was unsuccessful. Old Dan eventually made the decision early that afternoon to move his entire III Corps to the slightly higher ground along the Emmitsburg Road, about three quarters of a mile west of the position he was assigned to hold.

Sickles had two divisions. The first under Maj. Gen. David B. Birney stretched from Devil's Den northward and then northwest to the salient at the Sherfy Peach Orchard. It was a long, convoluted line over some bad terrain. The second division under Brig. Gen. Andrew A. Humphreys held part of the Peach Orchard position (the tip of the III Corps front) and stretched north along the Emmitsburg road on Birney's right. Behind Birney's left flank was nothing save one signal station on Little Round Top, and on Humphreys' right there was a three-quarter of a mile gap between his men and Hancock's II Corps, which was also farther east on Cemetery Ridge. Sickles had stretched his small corps, without immediate support, over an area it simply could not properly defend if heavily attacked.

Not only did Sickles disobey a direct order (for which some believe he should have been court-martialed), but he also failed to include the wagons with the necessary shot and powder to supply his artillery batteries in his supply train during his advance to Gettysburg. This oversight on Sickles' part, combined with the fact that both the I Corps and XI Corps had expended most of their supplies on July 1, could have been catastrophic for the Union army had not Brig. Gen. Henry J. Hunt, the army's chief of artillery, anticipated such a shortfall. Unbeknownst even to Meade himself, Hunt maintained a "ghost" ammunition train that would keep the army supplied through the three days. Hunt was an extraordinarily capable officer whose decisions not only preserved the power of the Union artillery on this second day of battle, but would also contribute significantly to the Union's success against the massed Confederate infantry charge and pre-attack bombardment on the battle's third day.

Sickles' decision to move his corps ahead shocked Meade when he discovered it just before Longstreet attacked. First, the move left a gaping hole in the shank of the Fishhook, breaking the connection to Hancock's corps.

Second, Sickles' left no longer touched upon Little Round Top, which was completely unprotected. Finally, and perhaps most important, his III Corps was too small to hold the meandering line running from near Devil's Den up through the Peach Orchard and then sharply northeast along the Emmitsburg Road, where his right flank simply . . . petered out. Sickles was now much closer to the enemy holding a very vulnerable salient (the Peach Orchard) susceptible to attack from two sides. His line was much too long and he had no reserves. As we will see, his arbitrary repositioning will compel Meade and Hancock to revise their battle plans later in the day to reinforce Sickles in what will become one of the bloodiest phases of the battle.

In all fairness, however, despite my admitted reluctance to be fair when it comes to Sickles, historians debate whether the repositioning of his III Corps helped the Union blunt Longstreet's assault. The presence of large numbers of Union men and artillery around the Peach Orchard surprised Lee (recall Johnston's scouting report?) and forced him and Longstreet to change how they would assault Meade's left. It placed significant Union forces closer to the Confederates, and it took advantage of terrain features that lent themselves to a strong defense. Some argue that the advance soaked up so much of Longstreet's strength that it prevented him from driving deeply into Meade's left-rear and even turning his entire position.

BRIGADIER GENERAL ANDREW A. HUMPHREYS

Meanwhile, on the Confederate side, the main event on the fight card for the day was getting underway. Around noon, McLaws' and Hood's divisions of Longstreet's Corps finally began marching to get below the left end of the Union line. Longstreet had insisted he be allowed to wait for the arrival of Evander Law's brigade before beginning his move to get into position, and Lee agreed. Some historians argue the delay was perfectly legitimate, while others fault Longstreet's wounded ego for having been overridden by Lee in having to attack at all.

Some say Longstreet sulked, dragging his feet to get into position because he was firmly against the assault. His third division under Pickett would not reach the field until late that afternoon, and would not be used. As we shall see on Day Three, Pickett's fresh troops were used as the spearhead for Lee's assault against the Union center.

The march southward was guided by the information gleaned from the reconnaissance of Captain Johnston. Not long after crossing the Fairfield Road, however, the Confederates realized they are in full view of the Union signal station on Little Round Top. Longstreet reversed course to find a new more protected route. It took several hours to cover some five miles before McLaws' division deployed in Biesecker's Woods behind the Snyder Farm. Across the Emmitsburg Road was the heavily manned Peach Orchard and the Rose Farm. Hood's division slid into place

BRIGADIER GENERAL HENRY J. HUNT

farther south on McLaws' right athwart the angling Emmitsburg Road, west of the Bushman and Slyder farms.

As noted above, the presence of the advanced Union III Corps—our dear friend General Sickles—caught the Rebel generals by surprise and forced a change of plans. Lee had originally ordered an attack "up the Emmitsburg Road." That was now clearly impossible for it would completely expose Longstreet's right flank to Sickles' artillery and infantry! McLaws was in position to attack directly across the Emmitsburg Road against the slightly elevated artillery platform of the Peach Orchard, and just below and above it, but Hood would need to swing a bit farther around the Union line to find its flank and perhaps, its rear. No one had any idea how rough the ground was beyond the timber and undulating terrain.

One final adjustment of the Union forces should be noted. Recognizing that it is too late to withdraw the III Corps to Cemetery Ridge, Meade ordered Sykes' reserve V Corps and a division from Hancock's II Corps to bolster Sickles' line. The forward elements of the huge VI Corps were now reaching Gettysburg and, and were available to replace the V Corps as the army's reserve.

MAJOR GENERAL DAVID B. BIRNEY

Hiking with My Friend Who Hates "Pollution"

On this visit to the Gettysburg, my friend Enis and I set out to explore the Day Two battlefield. After a hearty breakfast at the Lincoln Diner, we decide to begin our trek at the North Carolina Monument just below McMillan Woods on Seminary Ridge. The day is perfect: sunny, on the cool side, with just a little humidity.

We gather our supplies—water bottles, granola bars, maps, cameras, walking sticks, hiking boots, small daypacks to carry our gear, and for Enis, a complicated GPS device—and discuss our best route south. Our first objective is to hike the area of Longstreet's attack.

We drive south to the Virginia Monument on Seminary Ridge. The magnificent equestrian statue of Robert E. Lee mounted on his beloved horse Traveler towers over this part of the field. Virginia, you'll recall, was Lee's home state. One of the great ironies of the Civil War was that as hostilities were set to break out, then-Colonel Lee of the US Army was offered command of all Union forces. Declaring that he could not raise his hand against his native Virginia, which he suspected would secede, he turned the job down and eventually joined the army of the Confederate States of America.

We will pass a host of important monuments during our exploration of Day Two. Every monument on this battlefield is important in its own way. Each is a tribute to the men who fought here. The Virginia Monument has special significance as it is not only a tribute to Virginia and one of its most famous sons, but occupies the spot from which Lee is said to have watched the pageantry of the Pickett- Pettigrew-Trimble Charge, fol- lowed by its bloody collapse.

It is one of the largest monuments on the battlefield and truly beautiful. Sculpted by Frederick William Sievers, the granite pedestal was dedicated in

The Virginia Monument

1913 for the Great Reunion, and the entire monument, complete with the bronze figures, in 1917. Take a minute and walk around it to fully appreciate not only the Lee equestrian statue but the figures at the base. When you finish, come to the front, turn your back to the monument, and look out across the fields. The double line of fences in the distance is the Emmitsburg Road and, beyond that the "Copse of Trees" on Cemetery Ridge is clearly visible.

As we walk south down West Confederate Avenue, Enis informs me that he is not fond of "pollution" and asks if there are any roads-less-traveled we could take? I agree that I'm not particularly fond of pollution, either. I cast a furtive glance this way and that, but see nothing other than well-kept grassland, roads, paths, some cars, and other people walking. When I suggest we instead take the horse trail that parallels the road he is delighted—and notes once more that "there is far too much pollution around today." I am totally puzzled. What the hell is he talking about? Given the time of year, the battlefield is filled with more people than usual, but they seem a tidy lot, and no one seems to be littering. And then, I suddenly realize that he is referring to other people as "pollution." An odd thought. I suppress a chuckle when the famous movie line "Soylent Green is people!" leaped into my head.

Keep in mind that one of the hazards of visiting a place as famous as Gettysburg is that you are usually going to encounter lots of people. Some like crowds and others do not. I confess I am not overly fond of large crowds, especially the older I get, so I am always glad for an opportunity to get off the beaten track. Besides, it's much more adventurous. If you let your imagination run, it is not hard to imagine you are back in the day, watchful of where those enemy sharpshooters or skirmishers may be lurking.

Fortunately, any concern we have for the navigability of the horse trail is immediately ameliorated as we step through a slightly wooded area and pick up the trail itself, easily identifiable from the dotted line on our map (the NPS brochure), and the occasional fragrant detritus left by the horses. Yes, there are numerous riders out on this beautiful day, so if you choose to duplicate our route, watch where you step. Many of the horse trails are the remnants of the original farm roads. (Most of the paved roads through the park were added later for the convenience of the millions of visitors.) We are both happy to be on this road-less-traveled. As for the ease of walking it, however, don't count on that being true for the whole trail—just wait until we get to Big Round Top . . .

West Confederate Avenue is primarily intended for automobile traffic and is a part of the Self-Guiding Auto Tour route recommended by the National Park Service. Along the route, as is the case with all the roads throughout the battlefield, are numerous places to park your car. This road becomes one-way (as many of the park roads are), with designated parking areas on one side (and rarely both) so you can stop and see the monuments, read the historical tablets, and even better, get out on the battlefield itself. West Confederate Avenue runs along the spine of Seminary Ridge, the position occupied by the Confederates on Days Two and Three. It is an absolute "must-see" drive.

The NPS has placed numerous cannon along the road, most by far on the eastern side (the side closest to the Union line on Cemetery Ridge). Most are Civil War-era guns, though because of the expense of originals, a few copies can be found among them. (One gun on the field is known to have fired the first shot at Gettysburg. Cannon #233, now part of the monument to Brig. Gen. John Buford on the Chambersburg Pike, was the actual tube there during the battle.) Several types of cannon were used at Gettysburg, the most common being the 12-pounder bronze Napoleon (the pound designation is the weight of the cannon ball), 3-inch (iron) Ordnance Rifle (three inches being the width of the bore), and the 10-pounder Parrott Rifle (Captain Robert Parker Parrott was the designer of this rifled, long-range cannon). The Confederates also used some smaller howitzers (which by this time were not too effective), and British long-range Whitworths imported through the blockade were fired at Gettysburg.

It is very helpful to distinguish the various types of artillery ammunition. Shot are the all-too-familiar solid round balls (or when conically shaped, referred to as bolts). Shells were detonated by a fuse (there were different types of fuses) to explode and rain iron shards of shrapnel into the ranks of the enemy—the shrapnel either packed into the shell or fragments of the shell itself.

Canister is best likened to a shotgun shell filled with dozens of lead or iron balls ranging in size from ½ to a full inch in diameter. Shot and shell were used at longer distances to knock out enemy guns or break up infantry formations, while canister was reserved for close range to wipe out large swaths of approaching enemy infantry. It was strictly an anti-personnel weapon.

Back on the trail, we follow a jog to the right which reverses direction after a few hundred feet. We are very near the area where McLaws' and Hood's convoluted march on the hot afternoon of July 2 finally ended. As the trail straightens out, we find a small amphitheater off to our left, where several Boy Scouts are resting. We are now in Pitzer's Woods, where Longstreet anchored the left end of his line (the left side of McLaw's division) that would soon stretch down Warfield Ridge. The NPS, in cooperation with the Boy Scouts of America, has designated a number of trails of historic significance for Boy Scout outings. Interested parties should contact either the NPS or the Scouts for the specifics. This is also part of the area where some of the Confederate forces tapped to assault Cemetery Ridge assembled on July 3.

For something completely different, watch for the equestrian statue of James Longstreet designed by sculptor Gary Casteel. It's on your left, if you are on the horse trail, or on your right if you're on West Confederate Avenue. This modern statue was dedicated on July 3, 1998, and is the subject of some controversy. Instead of being elevated grandly on a pedestal, it is rather close to the ground. Some don't think the proportion is correct. As a result, many Longstreet admirers feel the general is being short-changed. I completely disagree and can honestly write that this statue is one of my favorites. The power of the man and his horse are not "inaccessible" or "static" as so many of the statues are—especially the equestrian variety. Compare this statue, for example, to the one of Lee on the top of the Virginia Monument we saw earlier. Lee's is grand, but somehow cold and aloof—like the man. General Longstreet's statue is *right there*, and feels almost lifelike in its scale and suggestion of motion, which is precisely what Mr. Casteel was going for.

When I spoke with him about the statue, he told me it is just five percent over life-size (the limit now set by the NPS) and Mr. Casteel has no problem with that. "I want people to know that they (the men and women of the Civil War) were just like us." The horse was modeled on "Summer," not a thoroughbred but a working animal on a farm near Gettysburg that would have had the stamina to carry the stocky well-built Longstreet who often spent long hours in the saddle. Indeed, horse tours that pass by the statue often must deal with the fact that their mounts get skittish reacting to the power and energy of

The Longstreet Monument

the general's mount. Most telling of all was when Jamie Longstreet, the general's grand-daughter, saw the statue as it was being sculpted and cried. This deeply concerned Gary, who later approached her to find out what was wrong. "I never thought I'd see him alive," was her moving reply. From the road, one must take a small turnout to access it.

Our trail continues south along the ridge and crosses the Millerstown Road, where we come face-to-face with a very tall and imposing Observation Tower. My initial hope is that it just looks gigantic because of my tri-focals, but I am quickly disappointed. It IS gigantic. I am with my "youngster" friend, so it is imperative that I put on a good show. Mustering up some courage, I march up to the bottom of what looked to be 565 steps and climb the tallest of the three remaining observation towers in the park. (The tower is 75 feet and has 110 steps.) I surprise even myself and accomplish my mission with only a few short pauses to catch my breatj—and at least one to check that my heart is still beating. It is quite a climb, but the views are so spectacular and it is worth every step!

Five observation towers were built by the War Department between 1895 and 1896 (remember, the War Department administered the Gettysburg National Military Park from 1895 to 1933). The three I've mentioned (Oak Ridge, Warfield Ridge, and Culp's Hill), survive, although the one on Culp's Hill was cut down to its present height as recently as 1968. The two towers since removed were located on Big Round Top and near Ziegler's Grove. There was an unofficial "sixth" tower—a 307-foot-tall commercially operated behemoth that stood for many years on private land adjacent to the battlefield. It was generally considered a blight on the landscape, seized by eminent domain, and demolished on July 3, 2000, when Union and Confederate re-enactors symbolically fired cannon at the structure (though actual explosives planted as part of a controlled demolition brought it down). The three remaining towers are simply designed, blend in fairly well, and do not detract from the surrounding beauty of the battlefield. Each affords breathtaking views of the battlefield. And (as you have certainly guessed by now), despite my grumblings I like them!

Warfield Ridge, and the continuation of West Confederate Avenue which turns into South Confederate Avenue once it crosses the Emmitsburg Road, mark generally speaking the positions taken up by McLaws' and Hood's divisions (eight brigades total) before they attacked. The Rebel artillery engaged in a bombardment for a time before Hood's division stepped out, charging essentially north by northeast. His attack and its command and control fell apart quickly for two main reasons: The undulating terrain covered with rocks, trees, and heavy vegetation (the Confederates had no idea how bad it was until they tried to cross it) broke apart formations, and Hood was badly wounded in the arm very early in the fighting by shrapnel. His men flooded around Devil's Den, died on the slopes of Little Round Top, and fought the battle without a guiding hand. McLaws was impatient to attack, but Longstreet held him back at least 30 minutes to determine how Hood was doing and how the Yankees were responding. When he let him go, McLaws attacked directly east across the Emmitsburg Road to engage Sickles' infantry and guns around the Peach Orchard and on either side. (More on this attack later.)

From the observation tower, with maps in hand, I soaked in the open fields in front. Facing east, the famous Peach Orchard was just several hundred yards to my front, and the Round Tops were clearly visible. It was easy to match everything to the maps. For the first time it really made sense to me. It was not hard at all to picture the long lines of men in gray, standing in battle order waiting for the order to go into action. Or across the way the boys in blue,

Conversation with an Expert:
Ranger Christopher Gwinn, Chief of Interpretation

Christopher Gwinn has the distinction of being one of the youngest rangers I've met at the GNMP, and despite his youth he has taken over as Ranger Historian, the position formerly held by Scott Hartwig. "I've wanted to be a Park Ranger at Gettysburg since I was 10 years old," he explains. "The whole thing fascinates me. When you visit and learn about the battle, you become part of it. It's an American epic—a massive story—running the whole spectrum of human emotion."

CHRISTOPHER GWINN

Each ranger has his or her own take on the battle. For Christopher, its best kept secret is sitting in plain sight. "George Meade!" he replies when I ask him. "He won the battle—it wasn't about Lee's mistakes—it was Meade. Meade had a huge responsibility and pressure thrust upon him in such a short time."

Chris sees a parallel to George Pickett who, also on very short notice, was charged with an awesome responsibility. Pickett arrived with his division late on July 2 and was dispatched by Longstreet, under orders from Lee, to assault the Union army that the rest of Lee's command had been fighting for two very long days. "After the war, when Pickett was questioned why the attack of July 3rd failed, he mused, 'The Union army had something to do with it.' The walk-away message about this battle is that people a century and a half ago—ordinary people—determined what kind of country we were going to have."

Chris is clearly affected by that thought. He remembers conducting a tour with a man who had attended the 1938 Reunion and had, as a Boy Scout, attended a Confederate veteran with a visible shrapnel scar. "I was in awe of the fact that I was, in effect," explains Chris, "separated from the actual battle by only one generation: the veteran, the Boy Scout, and me."

When I ask what aspects of Day Two fascinate him the most, he did not hesitate in his response: "I think the fighting on July 2nd is remarkable for many reasons. It was a day of superlatives, being the bloodiest day of the battle, and the day involving the largest number of men actually fighting on the battlefield. It remains the most difficult to understand—the most complex. It is also, even today, the single most 'controversy fraught' day of the battle, particularly regarding the actions of Dan Sickles and James Longstreet. July 2nd is also an example of how nothing goes as planned. Both Lee and Meade had, by midday, formulated some sense of how the day would go. Yet, because of time, terrain, the enemy, and their subordinates, nothing went exactly planned. It required a level of flexibility and adaptability."

Chris continues: "Meade, his officers and the army excelled that day; Lee and his, not so much. You can also look at July 2nd as proof that individuals can make a difference. Numerous times the actions of one or two men dramatically shifted and changed the outcome of the battle: Strong Vincent, Joshua Chamberlain, Samuel Johnston, David Ireland, John Bigelow, George Sears Greene—the list goes on and on." Chris adds: "I'm intrigued by what Chamberlain does after the battle at Little Round Top. He's charged with taking Big Round Top, agrees to do it, besides being completely exhausted from his fight at the head of the 20th Maine, and having just recovered from malarial fever, and proceeds to do so in the middle of the night with very few casualties. Numerous men of the 20th Maine recalled that the advance up Big Round Top was more frightening than the fight on Little Round Top. It was dark—too dark to see anything—the terrain was unknown. The last time they had seen the enemy they were retiring up the slopes of Big Round Top and they had just seen 130 of their number gunned down. Chamberlain receives the Medal of Honor for, not only his defense of Little Round Top, but also for carrying the Union advance up Big Round Top."

I close by asking Chris for two of the "best" questions he has been asked thus far in his young career. "Without doubt, one of my favorites was when I was asked, 'Where do you buy the tickets for the high-water mark cruise?' But, I also enjoyed a follow-up question from a visitor who had been here before: 'Has the Park Service shrunk the boulders in Devil's Den—they used to look bigger'."

It's a good thing both rangers and LBGs pride themselves on their cordiality and not their barbed rejoinders. Chris adds, "I love whenever I get a serious question I've never thought about before."

Chris leaves me with this: "Remember, every general was doing what he was doing for a good reason—or what he thinks is a good reason. No one wants to lose the battle."

I'm struck by this. It is so straightforwardly reasonable. For a moment it makes me wonder whether I should reassess my opinion of McClellan and Sickles? And then the moment passes.

artillery blazing as they gripped their rifles and steeled their nerves for the coming wave of bloodshed and death.

Climbing down the tower was a helluva lot easier than climbing up. Once back on terra firma, we resume our hike on the horse trail. After a short diversion through Biesecker's Woods the trail swings east and crosses West Confederate Avenue. Not too far away we take note of the Bushman Farm, through which our little trail passes before heading south toward South Confederate Avenue.

It was here Enis and I begin discussing Civil War horses and the time spent on the Bushman Farm. Shortly after I began my pedestrian explorations of the battlefield, I signed up for a Gettysburg Foundation Adams Seminar titled "'They Too Fought Here:' The Cavalry in the Gettysburg Campaign,"

conducted by LBG Andie Custer Donahue. We spent the morning in the large classroom on the first floor of the Visitor Center, and two hours of the afternoon at the Bushman Farm, where we learned the differences between the horses and equipment of both armies.

Most of the horses supplied to the Union were Morgan horses, bred for their stamina and agility, while many of the Confederate horses were farm animals brought by the soldiers themselves. Confederate officers, however, generally had more sophisticated mounts. Interestingly, Andie told us that cavalry for both armies had a weight limit of about 140 pounds, which along with sixty pounds of gear, uniforms, and equipment, held the burden on these amazing animals to about 200 pounds. Of course, that didn't apply to officers.

When I look at some of today's cavalry reenactors, I'm glad that the horses are usually only ridden for short periods of time and are well cared for by their owners. And while we're on the subject of *equus ferus caballus*, about 67,000 horses and mules were involved at Gettysburg and between 2,000 and 5,000 were killed or maimed. Ranger Christopher Gwinn, Chief of Interpretation at GNMP, cautioned that this subject has never been deeply researched [he has heard estimates ranging from 1,000 to as high as 9,000—a number he rejects outright]. What do you do with thousands of dead horses?

The four buildings dotting the Bushman Farm were there in 1863. Originally used by Union sharpshooters, the farm ended up behind Confederate lines once Longstreet launched his attack. The barn was used as a temporary field hospital for Confederate troops on the night of the 2nd, and the farm became the focal point of a doomed Union cavalry attack late in the day of the 3rd.

And of course, before we leave Andie and her wonderful presentation, I have to share with you what may be the best question ever asked of Andie, or anyone else: "Why were so many Civil War battles fought at National Parks?" [One reply I heard to this was, "That's where all the cannon were."]

We left the farm and walked directly south and across South Confederate Avenue. Off to the right, just before crossing Plum Run is a trail marker leading to a monument to the 4th United States Horse Artillery, Battery E. If this interests you, know ahead of time that this trail is long and steep, and the pay-off is on the small side.

When you arrive at the small bridge over Plum Run, pause for a moment and be transported back in time—not to 1863, but to the end of the Cretaceous Period 65 million years ago. When the bridge was built, several of the stones that went into its construction contained dinosaur tracks.

Shortly after crossing the bridge, off to the right is the continuation of the horse trail as it begins its ascent of Big Round Top. This was part of the route taken by the 15th and 47th Alabama regiments as they attempted to flank the left end of the Union line late on the afternoon of July 2. If you'll recall how gentle the horse trail was up to this point, it is now time to reconsider hiking the road-less-traveled. This trail is treacherous, filled with rocks and gullies and, strangely enough, bypasses the actual summit! Still, the trail is not without its rewards. Foremost is the sense of what it was like for those Confederates struggling up this hill. The terrain in 1863 was not that much different than it is today. After clawing our way to the top and, as we discovered later, missing the summit by a dozen yards, we begin our descent over a section of the trail that is much easier going.

Our descent of Big Round Top leads us to yet another discovery. We emerge in the very woods through which Colonel Oates' 15th Alabama repeatedly charged the south face of Little Round Top to engage Joshua Chamberlain and his 20th Maine. This area, where South Confederate Avenue turns into Sykes Avenue as it crosses Warren Avenue, is an idyllic wooded area today, and offers a moment's gentle respite before climbing up the steep grade to the top of the hill.

Before I move onto Little Round Top, I must share that the next day Enis and I returned to Big Round Top for another round. Beer? No. Another attempt to reach the actual summit. At the end of Day Two, Union troops, including the remnants of Chamberlain's 20th Maine, occupied the hill and held it for the Union on July 3. We just had to see the top. Fortunately, the NPS/GNMP provides a nice walking trail up the north face of the hill. The trail

The Peach Orchard (above) and the Round Tops (below).

is located directly opposite the most famous part of South Cavalry Field on South Confederate Avenue. Be advised the path to the summit is steep and meanders back and forth on itself a couple of times. It's not on the Top Ten List, but Big Round Top is a very pretty spot and well worth the hike if you have the time.

The Main Event

Although I already provided a rough overview of how the attack began, it is now time to go into more detail. The main event of Day Two got underway around 3:40 p.m. when Col. Edward Porter Alexander, Longstreet's acting chief of artillery, ordered his 54 guns to open fire on Sickles' advanced Union position. The 28-year-old colonel had proven himself to be one of the South's ablest artillerists, and he had Longstreet's complete confidence. The III Corps guns, supported by batteries from Hunt's Artillery Reserve, roar back. The artillery duel lasts about 30 minutes.

When Longstreet ordered the infantry in, Hood began his assault shouting, "Forward, my Texans, and win this battle or die in the effort!" His brigades swept ahead. The fighting was fierce within just a few minutes. His men moved northeast and north into Rose's Woods, flooded around Devil's Den, and later some reach the Wheatfield. Hood saw almost none of this because, as noted above, he was wounded within a few minutes and carried off the field. His senior brigadier, Evander Law, did not learn of Hood's fall for a long while, and never really assumed tactical command of the division. From that moment until the end of the battle, Hood's men fought a series of uncoordinated battles on their own.

About this time one of the legendary events of the battle took place. Brig. Gen. Gouverneur K. Warren, Chief Engineer of the Army of the Potomac, was surveying the area of the Union left flank when he arrived at Little Round Top (most likely riding up its northern slope). He quickly realized the vulnerability of the entire Union line if this sparsely defended hill was taken. He immediately sent aides in search of any available units to occupy it. After some initial confusion about who would go, the V Corps came through. Colonel Strong Vincent, whose brigade was standing by close to the George Weikert house on lower Cemetery Ridge, ordered his men to move up the slope of Little Round Top and take up defensive positions. Strong deployed the 20th Maine, the 83rd Pennsylvania, the 44th New York, and 16th Michigan into a line that will live on in the annals of military history. Later, Stephen Weed's V Corps brigade deployed on Vincent's right, and his friend Charles Hazlett's 5th US, Battery D, would unlimber to defend the hill. Both would die there. There is a reason the Warren statue sits atop this famous hill surveying the landscape.

Approaching from the southwest are their counterparts—the 47th and 15th Alabama, 4th Alabama, and 4th and 5th Texas—not as famous but just as courageous. (Note these regiments are from two different brigades with no overall commanding officer to coordinate their effort.) After sweeping over unoccupied Big Round Top, the Alabamians start up the southern slope of Little Round Top just as Colonel Chamberlain's Mainers rushed into place on the extreme left end of the entire Union line. The Texans struck up the rough western and southwestern slopes.

The Union defenders managed to hold onto the boulder-strewn Little Round Top. Strong Vincent was killed in the fighting. The struggle between the 20th Maine and the 47th and 15th Alabama earned its place as perhaps the second most famous fight during the battle. Remember, this action on the end of the line is occurring as a small part of the larger assault against Little Round Top, which in turn is part of the larger assault against Sickles' III Corps position by two divisions of Longstreet's Corps. To give it a little further context, the western and southwestern face of Little Round Top is assaulted by the 4th and

BRIGADIER
GENERAL
GOUVERNEUR
K. WARREN

5th Texas and the 4th Alabama. The men of the 16th Michigan, 44th New York, and 83rd Pennsylvania gallantly throw back attempt after attempt. Be sure you look for their monuments when you visit.

So, what happened on the southern extremity? Both the 47th and 15th Alabama had ascended Big Round Top and found no Union forces there. The 47th, first off the larger hill under the command of Lt. Col. Michael J. Bulger, engaged the left end of the 83rd Pennsylvania and the right of the 20th Maine. Fully prepared for the assault, the Union troops unleashed a murderous volley that stopped the assault in its tracks and seriously wounded Bulger. Meanwhile, the 15th Alabama swept down Big Round Top under its commander, Col. William C. Oates, who shifted his regiment farther east to "swing around, and drive the Federals from the ledge of rocks . . . gain the enemy's rear, and drive him from the hill." This decision set up the legendary head-to-head confrontation with the 20th Maine.

The Confederates charged up the southern spur of Little Round Top time and again, only to be repulsed by the smaller Union force. Endeavoring to flank the Union position, elements of the 15th Alabama moved farther right. Chamberlain, a former professor at Maine's Bowdoin College and not a professional soldier, adopted a complicated maneuver to defend his position by having his men spread out in a single line of battle (instead of the usual two-deep) and then "refused" his left, which bent back at nearly a right-angle from its previous position to make it harder for the enemy to get around. Earlier in the battle, Chamberlain had sent his Company B to reconnoiter beyond his left. When these men heard the fighting, they nestled down behind a stone wall between the Round Tops and waited to figure out what was going on.

The fight between the Alabamians and Mainers raged for 45 minutes until both sides were nearly out of ammo and fully exhausted. Depending on the account, Chamberlain either ordered his men forward shouting "Bayonet!", is overheard discussing the *possibility* of ordering his men forward, or for whatever reason, his men on the left suddenly swept ahead with a bayonet charge, swinging to their right like "a door on a hinge." Caught completely by surprise, Colonel Oates' Alabamians fled or surrendered. Many who fell back ran into the waiting muzzles of Company B and were captured or shot. Chamberlain policed his area, reorganized his battered regiment, and in the darkness that evening climbed to the summit of Big Round Top to act as a flank guard for

COLONEL STRONG VINCENT

the Union line.

The action on Little Round Top has long held the interest of visitors and students of the battle, but it was the publication of Shaara's *The Killer Angels* in the 1970s, with its focus on Chamberlain's defense, that seared that part of the battle into the public's consciousness and captured its collective imagination. You'll quickly discover the popularity of this rocky hill because it is usually filled with cars and tour buses full of visitors, especially in the high season. It also serves as its own tower and the views from atop the historic hill—especially now that the park has removed

COLONEL EDWARD PORTER ALEXANDER

COLONEL WILLIAM C. OATES

hundreds of trees to restore the battlefield to its 1863 appearance—are simply spectacular. It also helps make sense of why certain decisions were made when you see pretty much the same terrain the soldiers saw back then.

Before heading to the top, however, take that path to the right leading to the ridge defended by Chamberlain and the 20th Maine. Informative NPS information tablets explain the action that took place here. The first includes the desperate moment when Strong Vincent instructs Chamberlain to "Hold the ground at all hazards"; the second explains the 20th Maine regiment itself.

When I first arrived at the site of the fighting, I was struck by how small the area is: probably less than 250 feet wide by 75 feet deep. Filled with rocks and trees, its value as a defensive position is obvious. There is, however, not much room to maneuver. Chamberlain's small force rushed to the natural ridgeline at the lower end of this area before the ground drops away to the steeper cliff leading to the base of the hill. If the Confederates had taken this position, the Union line on Little Round Top would have been in danger of being rolled up.

Unlike many areas of the battlefield, this one is deep in the woods of southern Pennsylvania. An idyllic spot today, it echoes in the imagination with the gunfire and the screams of the dying and wounded late in the day of July 2, 1863. For a true sense of proportion, I took note of the flank markers of the 20th Maine—there was no place to run! Those men had to hold this ground or die there.

As famous as was the stand of Chamberlain and his 20th Maine, many visitors to Little Round Top don't take the extra minutes to walk out to where it actually took place. It is impossible to fully appreciate this patch of ground without seeing it. Sure, the western crest of Little Round Top is filled with beautiful monuments and spectacular views—and lots of "pollution"—but for a quieter, closer encounter with the agony and the ecstasy of the fighting, don't miss this quiet little spur or the monument to the 20th Maine. (If you are interested, there is also a monument to the regiment on Big Round Top, and another stone marking the position of Co. B near the stone wall off in the woods to the left.)

After taking in the 20th Maine position, we walk back along the path to Sykes Avenue—be careful to watch for passing cars during high-volume periods—which ascends to the summit of Little Round Top. Closer to the top of the hill, off to the left, are parking spaces for cars and, more importantly, several paths leading to the western face of the hill. A few moments later we are standing atop Little Round Top. Go ahead—it's okay to gasp as you take in the breathtaking view from this side of Little Round Top.

COLONEL
JOSHUA L.
CHAMBERLAIN

A few hundred yards ahead and below is Devil's Den and below it the area that earned the macabre sobriquet of "the Slaughter Pen." The Triangular Field (another place of slaughter shaped like a large perfect triangle) is just beyond Devil's Den, and farther out are the Slyder and Bushman farms. Just northwest of Little Round Top is the Valley of Death, between Houck's Ridge and Little Round Top, and farther northwest, the Wheatfield. Even the fields across which the Confederates charged on July 2 and 3 are visible. Once the view is absorbed it becomes obvious this was nearly an impregnable position. The thought of charging up that long difficult slope without anyone shooting at me is unnerving. Doing it while risking maiming or death is unthinkable. And yet…

Make sure and take a moment to realize the strategic importance of this hill. Once the Union established itself here, it became one of the key Yankee positions at the southern end of the Fishhook. This hill remained in Union hands throughout the battle. Although it was hard to get artillery up there, Union gunners who managed to unlimber there also fired the next day into

The 20th Maine.
Photo from one flank marker to the
other, just a stone's throw away.

Rebel infantry during Pickett's Charge. (The effect of that fire is apparently subject to debate.) If a picture is worth a thousand words, the following photos will give you an idea of the importance of Little Round Top.

The Slaughter Pen, just below Devil's Den, was crossed by different Confederate regiments in the assault against Little Round Top. Federal lead left this area between the base of Little Round Top and Plum Run strewn with the bodies of dead and wounded. Many were the subjects of photographs that give one pause. On the western face of the hill are numerous monuments, many of them quite beautiful. Don't rush; there's a lot to take in here. Its vistas alone make Little Round Top the most interesting place on the battlefield.

The fight for Little Round Top proper (the 20th Maine's battle was on a southern spur) seesawed back and forth but Confederate forces never seized the crest. The Rebel attack here eventually included the 4th, 47th, and 48th Alabama, and 4th and 5th Texas regiments, with the bulk of their weight falling against the 16th Michigan, 44th New York, and 83rd Pennsylvania of Vincent's brigade.

As the 4th and 5th Texas pressed the Union line, Strong Vincent was observed "Throwing himself in the breach he rallied his men, but gave up his own life." Mortally wounded in the groin, he was carried to the rear where he later died. The monument marking his wounding was the first erected on the battlefield (the current stone replaces the original). The unidentified soldier on top of the monument to the 83rd PA was likely modeled on the courageous colonel.

At one point, just as a Texas charge broke through the line of the 16th Michigan, help arrived in the form of the 140th New York commanded by Col.

Patrick O'Rorke (part of Weed's arriving brigade). Ordered into action, the men paused to load their weapons. Thinking the men were stopping to realign their formation, General Warren shouted at O'Rorke, "No time now, Paddy, for alignment. Take your men immediately into action!" O'Rorke was shot dead during the charge, but his men fought back the Texans and closed the breach. After this fight subsided, "one embittered man in the 5th Texas noted that the Federal position would have been 'impossible to take had the enemy only been armed with rocks.'" Meanwhile, more of Stephen Weed's V Corps brigade arrived, with some of its members helping manhandle to the crest the four guns of Hazlett's 5th US Artillery battery, which fired its iron into the Confederates. While standing near the guns, however, Weed was killed by a Rebel sharpshooter, and when Hazlett bent over to hear his friend's final words, Hazlett too was killed.

The Gouverneur Warren statue on Little Round Top is among the most impressive on the battlefield. Historian and author Thomas A. Desjardin, an expert on Little Round Top, notes that the Confederate fire upon the hill was incessant, and that if this idealized statue of Warren were depicted accurately, instead of calmly gazing out at the enemy he would be squatting down on the ground covering his head while Confederate artillery shells and small arms fire fell all around him.

For a closer look at the source of the incessant Confederate fire, we leave Little Round Top and descend into the Valley of Death via Sykes Avenue to the left, then Wheatfield Road and Crawford Avenue (you can also take a shorter route on Sykes Avenue to the right, then Warren Avenue and Crawford

The Devil's Den

Statue of Brig. Gen. Gouverneur Warren.

Avenue). Within a few minutes Little Round Top looms above us, and the less formidable Houck's Ridge running along Crawford Avenue.

Before long we enter Devil's Den and encounter its massive boulders up close. What struck us was just how big some of them are. The rocks were left here millions of years ago at the edge of a periglacial frost. Once over the little bridge on the road leading to the parking area, the Slaughter Pen sits off to your left. Approached by crossing a little wooden bridge, it's a beautiful spot today filled with an abundance of plants and birds. It almost feels like a nature preserve. But as I stood in the middle of it, looking up at the formidable heights of Little Round Top and back at the massive rock formation of the Devil's Den not far away, I began to come to terms with the sacrifice that occurred here. By the time the battle ended this small area of the field was covered with dead and wounded Rebels. What conviction they must have had, placing themselves in harm's way knowing the odds were high of being killed or wounded, and yet committing themselves to the fight without hesitation over and over again. So many diaries and letters speak of their hope of making it through alive and whole.

The Devil's Den was initially occupied by the far left end of Sickles' III Corps. Driven out by Alabama and Texas regiments, it fell into Confederate hands relatively early in the fighting.

Moving back across the little wooden bridge, we round the bottom end of Devil's Den and find one of the more interesting curiosities of the battlefield. There is a famous photo taken just after the battle by Alexander Gardner of the body and rifle of a Confederate "sharpshooter" in a "sharpshooter's nest" in

Devil's Den. It was sold to the public back then as an authentic image. William Frassanito, a Gettysburg historian and worldwide legend, discovered that the entire image was posed. The corpse was indeed a Confederate, but he had been killed elsewhere and moved to the "nest" to make for a more dramatic photo—history embellished. The same Confederate appears in more than one photo in different poses. Gardner even placed the rifle rather artfully, leaning it on the rocks as a prop. I am inclined to be a little forgiving of Gardner's impulse to enhance the effect. If ever there was an ideal spot for a sharpshooter to practice his craft, this stone enclosure qualified. Take a moment to read the information tablet just in front of it.

While I think of it . . . stopping on the little road that wraps around the southern end of Devil's Den can be very tricky because there is no place to park there. If you're lucky enough to find a parking place in the small area provided for cars around Devil's Den, take time to visit everything you can before heading back to your car. (This is another good reason for exploring on foot if you are able; you can go wherever you want and pause whenever you like.)

We walked along the winding road up the slight incline to a flat little piece of ground which, until it was driven off by the charging Confederates of Henry Benning's brigade, was the site of Smith's 4th New York Independent Battery. Silent cannons now mark the spot. If you have been hiking, as we were, it affords another nice place to pause and reflect on this tiny part of a vast battle. These guns used to be in woods, but the NPS has since PUT them back to their 1863 appearance. This effort helps makes sense of why a battery would be here in the first place.

Meade Musters

Despite capturing the imagination, the action on Little Round Top is relatively small compared to what is going on to the west and soon, to the northwest. Longstreet's powerful and determined attacks by Hood's four brigades are falling like hammer blows. Law strikes mostly at Little Round Top, while Robertson and Benning hit Devil's Den and Houck's Ridge, and Anderson fights across the Rose Farm to the Wheatfield.

The fighting for Devil's Den and Houck's Ridge is as ferocious as any. Initially defended by Brig. Gen. J. H. Hobart Ward's brigade and later supplemented by various brigades sent from farther north to bolster Sickles' collapsing front, Devil's Den is initially attacked by Confederate forces under Brig. Gens. Jerome B. Robertson and Henry Benning. For a while the Union defenders hold, but when additional Rebels attack from the east, the Yankees are driven out. This is the bottom end of Sickles' misplaced salient, and it is not well connected to the rest of his extended line that meanders northwest to the Peach Orchard. The inevitable collapse begins here.

The Wheatfield is north of Devil's Den, and the next point of confrontation we should discuss as the Confederates pour into the fight. By the end of the day, this infamous twenty acres will have changed hands at least six times and result in some 6,000 casualties on both sides. That number is staggering. Some of the wounded try to crawl off the field for Plum Run and water. The little creek runs red with their blood. History has come to see this patch of ground in the same way it remembers the Cornfield at Antietam, or Saunders Field at the Wilderness—an otherwise serene spot that hosted some of the most devastating fighting of the Civil War. And it was in this area that the Sons of Erin met a harsh fate. Or more accurately, another harsh fate.

As Noah Andre Trudeau notes in his brilliant and highly readable book Gettysburg: *A Testing of Courage*, "Of the fifty-one Union infantry brigades gathered at Gettysburg, few were more distinctive or more proudly conscious of their distinction than five regiments in Brig. Gen. John C. Caldwell's II Corps division, self-styled 'the Irish Brigade'." In addition to its original New York regiments, regiments from both Massachusetts and Pennsylvania augmented this famed brigade. Brig. Gen. Thomas Francis Meagher, however, the originator of the brigade, resigned his commission in May of 1863 and thus missed Gettysburg.

The men of the Irish Brigade enjoyed their reputation as fierce fighters and had lost heavily earning and maintaining it at Antietam and before the stone wall at Fredericksburg. With Meagher gone the outfit was tactically led by Col. Patrick Kelly, and spiritually guided by its famous adviser, Chaplain William Corby. The priest would gain additional fame this day for his blessing of the troops just before they went into battle. (We will meet up with Corby later when we reach his statue on Hancock Avenue just above the George Weikert Farm.)

His blessings comforted the men, but seemed to have done little to protect them. At Fredericksburg, their numbers were reduced from 1,600 men to 256. By July 1863, the brigade was only able to bring about 530 men into the fight at Gettysburg. Even with their reduced numbers, the Irish fighters once again distinguished themselves in the bloody Wheatfield, albeit at the cost of another 221 casualties.

With Hood's Confederates fully engaged, Longstreet unleashed McLaws' division of four brigades on Hood's left. Brig. Gen. Joseph B. Kershaw's large South Carolina brigade attacked just below the Sherfy Peach Orchard toward

The Gardner "posed" picture (above) and the same spot today (right), using Enis as my model.

the Rose property, supported by Brig. Gen. Paul J. Semmes' Georgians. Part of Kershaw's command breaks in half, one piece heading east and the other swinging north against the southern side of the orchard. The Peach Orchard is on the southeast corner of the intersection of the Emmitsburg Road and

BRIGADIER
GENERAL
JEROME B.
ROBERTSON

Wheatfield Road (today, a paved road that is part of the Gettysburg National Military Park). The southern half of Kershaw's formation mostly attacks the Stony Hill, where vicious back-and-forth fighting ensues.

The Sherfy Peach Orchard forms the tip of Sickles' misplaced salient, and so is vulnerable to attacks from the front and both sides. Its direct collapse was brought about by a large brigade of Mississippians straight to its front hidden in the woods only 600 yards away. William Barksdale's brigade was made famous by its fight in the streets of Fredericksburg. Its fiery leader was now chafing at the bit to be launched into the fray, but Longstreet held him back until the time was right. Barksdale was a renowned "fire-eater" in the US Congress prior to secession, and now a

COLONEL RÉGIS de TROBRIAND

proven combat leader who preferred to lead from the front. About 6:15 p.m. he finally got the go-ahead and his large well-formed brigade rushed ahead and crashed through the Peach Orchard held by the Union brigade of Charles K. Graham. The Georgians of Brig. Gen. William T. Wofford's brigade, McLaw's last brigade to engage, followed Barksdale and kept heading east driving deep into the Union lines and would only be thrown back at the end of the day. David Birney's III Corps division was collapsed and its pieces retreated toward Cemetery Ridge (where, of

BRIGADIER GENERAL HENRY L. BENNING

course, they should have been in the first place!)

General Meade recognized the potential disaster of the III Corps' position and has been mustering Union troops throughout that late afternoon and early evening to try and fill in the gaps and reinforce Sickles' overwhelmed command. Early on he pulled troops from George Sykes' V Corps—to both Little Round Top and to the ridges beyond Plum Run—and instructed General Hancock of the II Corps to send Caldwell's II Corps division to bolster Sickles along the Wheatfield area. The Peach Orchard could not be held, however, and one of Barksdale's regiments, the 21st Mississippi, began rampaging eastward up the Wheatfield Road, flanking Union battery after battery. In the orchard itself, Gen. Graham was wounded, pinned under his horse and captured by other charging Mississippians. After clearing the Peach Orchard of all but the Federal dead and wounded, Barksdale turned the bulk of his brigade north and northeast up the Emmitsburg Road to outflank Sickles' remaining troops under Brig. Gen. Andrew Humphreys.

BRIGADIER GENERAL THOMAS FRANCIS MEAGHER

CHAPLAIN WILLIAM CORBY

As Barksdale was hammering away at Humphreys' exposed left flank, Cadmus M. Wilcox's brigade of Maj. Gen. Richard H. Anderson's division (Hill's III Corps) entered the fight, charging the Emmitsburg Road head-on. The Union troops broke before the two-pronged assault and began streaming back to Cemetery Ridge. With the III Corps everywhere in retreat, Union commanders began to fear that the Taneytown Road, one of the only two roads into Gettysburg still in Union hands, might fall to the Confederates, effectively cutting the

BRIGADIER GENERAL JOHN C. CALDWELL

Army of the Potomac in two. Meade, Hancock, and other Union officers worked overtime to cobble together sufficient reinforcements to stop the Rebel onslaught somewhere. Hancock had taken over command of the left wing of the Union army, and gave his II Corps to Brig. Gen. John Gibbon, who was later wounded. The formation of an artillery position, about 15 guns under the leadership of Lt. Col. Freeman McGilvery just east of Plum Run, helped weaken the Rebel advance. Switching to canister shot, the guns blasted apart Barksdale's men and others, while a fresh infantry brigade under Colonel George L. Willard, comprised of New

York regiments, flung itself straight at the Mississippians, throwing them into disorder. Barksdale fell from his horse mortally wounded by lead and iron, while Willard had his face removed by a piece of shrapnel and died on the spot.

All this shifting of troops on the fly left holes in the Union defensive line elsewhere, and Wilcox's brigade appeared on the verge of overrunning a mostly undefended space on Cemetery Ridge. Hancock searched for a unit to throw into the gap. He found the small 1st Minnesota regiment supporting some artillery and ordered it to advance into

COLONEL PATRICK KELLY

Wilcox's brigade to stop it. Hancock shouted to Col. William Colvill, "Advance, Colonel, and take those colors!" The Minnesotans charged straight at the center of Wilcox's brigade and suffered 82% casualties in the process, a number that turned out to be the highest of any regiment in the entire war. But the bold advance stopped the onward rush of the exhausted Alabamians, and their heroic action of Colvill's men is often credited with saving the Union line.

Another significant casualty was suffered that day. Dan Sickles was sitting on his horse when a cannonball

COLONEL WILLIAM COLVILL, JR.

LIEUTENANT COLONEL FREEMAN McGILVERY

nearly severed one of legs (with a Union surgeon having the "final cut," as we say in the biz). Reportedly stoic throughout, Old Dan was reputed to have calmly smoked a cigar as he was carried from the field. Showman that he was, he also raised himself up from his stretcher so his men could see that he was not dead, and exhorted them to stand firm. Some of his biographers deem the story apocryphal. Still, it sounds like something Old Dan would have done.

If the story was true, many of the men and officers of Sickles' III Corps were, apparently, thankful that day for this one small favor. As for Sickles, he donated the bones of his severed limb

BRIGADIER GENERAL JOHN GIBBON

to the Army Medical Museum in Washington, DC, and visited them from time to time after the war! (The museum is now the National Museum of Health and Medicine in Silver Spring, MD, so if you want to visit the bones as well, along with a sample of the kind of cannon ball that took off his leg—do say hello to them for me.) Sickles' crippling injury may have saved him from being cashiered out of the army—that and the fact that he was the first general who fought at Gettysburg to speak directly to President Lincoln about the battle. Old Dan was well-connected and had well-connected cronies—ah, if he had only maneuvered that well on the battlefield.

As the early evening wore on, more brigades from Richard Anderson's Confederate division

THANKS, REX.

stepped off Seminary Ridge to make the long assault to Cemetery Ridge. The distance between Seminary Ridge and Cemetery Ridge in this area is something just less than a mile—quite a ways under a hot sun with people trying to kill you. After Wilcox entered the fight, General Perry's small Florida brigade under Col. David Lang followed on Wilcox's left, and as did another of Georgians under Brig. Gen. Ambrose Wright. And it was about that time that the grand effort to break Meade's center began to seriously bog down.

Remember the Bliss Farm? The heavy skirmishing had continued for hours and much of it had soaked up the attention of Brig. Gen. Carnot Posey's Mississippians, who were deployed just west of it. When it was his time to attack, his brigade fell apart—some of the men fighting around the Bliss farm, and others moving out late or even attaching themselves to Wright's line. It was a grand mess, and I have a hunch even worse than we think. And then it got messier and mysterious.

Anderson's final brigade under Brig. Gen. William Mahone didn't move at all. Mahone, whose entire campaign report is brief and not helpful on much of anything, stubbornly insisted he'd been ordered to "hold his position" when officers arrive begging him to attack. Mahone would later turn out too be one of Lee's hardest-hitting generals. But that was in 1864. In July of 1863 he was nothing more than a riddle, and a very skinny riddle at that. General Anderson is also something of a cipher that day. Where was he? Why didn't he ride along his front and order his brigades into action when needed? He never explained any of this to satisfaction, but the attack fell apart on his front. He had hours of notice of what was expected of him. A. P. Hill was nearly as invisible, likely ill again from the lingering effects of what we now know was a venereal disease caught during a youthful indiscretion.

The ridge south of the Copse of Trees on Cemetery Hill was under attack along much of its length. It was mostly defended by elements of the II Corps. Despite some heavy fighting the Federals hold on, repulsing the staggered Confederate assaults. Wilcox and Lang make deep inroads, but are repulsed. Ambrose Wright managed to reach the crest of Cemetery Ridge and perhaps deeper than that—or a least that is what he later claimed. There is a lot of controversy about just how far he advanced (and many interesting articles have been written about it.) Regardless of how far he got, with little support on his flanks he withdrew.

By the time darkness fell the Confederate attack against the Union center has been halted, preserving the Army of the Potomac to fight another day. It was a near-run thing. The Union troops had fought magnifi- cently, as had the Confederates once engaged. Meade was jubilant. At one point he had drawn his sword and started to lead a counterattack. In response to a fellow officers' observation of how desperate the fight had been, Meade replied, in his typically understated way, "Yes, but it is all right now, it is all right now."

BRIGADIER GENERAL CARNOT POSEY

A Visit to the Bloody Wheatfield and Sickles' Misplaced Salient

Continuing along the little paved road (Sickles' Avenue) that leads away from Devil's Den, we enter the Rose Woods. Suddenly, being in the shaded canopy of this forested area gives us an entirely different sense of the battle, which to this point has been mostly fought out in the open. As I discover it is also a false sense of security, for artillery air blasts not only sent iron splinters down through the branches but deadly wooden ones as well. Most visitors just pass through this quiet area on the way to the next "famous" spot. Don't make that mistake. Take the time and explore it.

Much happened here.

One of the early casualties of the fighting for the Wheatfield was Col. John Wheeler of the 20th Indiana Infantry. In 1885, an inscription on a large rock near where he fell was photographed by William H. Tipton. It read: "Col John Wheeler 20th Indiana Vols. Killed in Action July 2nd 1863." While the inscription, probably written in white paint, has long since faded, the rock is still there. It is not hard to find. First, locate the 20th Indiana Monument and then

COLONEL AMBROSE R. WRIGHT

look across the road about fifteen yards. Colonel Wheeler was riding his horse among his men, exhorting them to hold their ground in the face of the Confederate onslaught when a Rebel bullet hit him in the temple, killing him instantly.

Back on the field, meanwhile, we are presented with a choice: Turn to the right onto Ayres Avenue, or continue straight on our little road. Both will lead us to the infamous Wheatfield, but I prefer the latter as it parallels the approach the Confederates took as they attacked through this southern section of Rose's Woods. Shortly after emerging from the woods, we find ourselves in the southeastern corner of the Wheatfield. We look out across about twenty acres of ground. It looks so tranquil today, a phenomenon I've encountered many times on a variety of battlefields, but this one feels a little different. As Enis and I head out across it, I'm struck by the sheer magnitude of the struggle for this

---

Conversation with an Expert: James A. Hessler — Sickles Historian and Observations on Day Two

James A. Hessler works in the financial services industry and has spent his professional life in banking. He also happens to be a Licensed Battlefield Guide and joined the very elite club of applicants who passed that horrendous qualifying exam on the first try. An historian and author, Jim writes articles and books on Gettysburg, is both a popular speaker and teacher on the subject, and because of his brilliant and award-winning book *Sickles at Gettysburg*, is a recognized authority on the controversial general.

I got right to it by asking him how he became interested in Sickles.

JH: "He's an amazing character; I didn't think the story had properly been told before. But he's become the butt of so many jokes. I mean, stop and think about it. People find it acceptable to laugh at the fact that he lost a leg. How many other figures at Gettysburg can we say that about? None! People hate him. When I first started guiding, I really enjoyed talking about him: his prewar, colorful past, his insistence that he was the true hero of Gettysburg, and his interesting postwar activities. People forget, or refuse to acknowledge, that he was also at the forefront of advocacy for battlefield preservation. Because I wrote a book about him, some people assume I'm a Sickles supporter and thus anti-Meade. That is not the case. I try not to answer questions about Sickles' so-called blunder during the battle and intentionally take a middle-of-the-road approach. Some people have trouble separating their personal opinions from the historical facts. I only really wanted to put the facts on the page and let the readers draw their own conclusions." [Me, for example.]

JAMES HESSLER

Jim admits to being more than a little weary of the public's general perception that because he wrote about Sickles, he can somehow be equated with that eccentric general. He elaborated on that point.

JH: "Ninety-right percent of the attention from my Sickles book has been positive and I love meeting people, but I've really had it with drunken guys confronting me about why I abandoned Little Round Top. To be clear, I am not Dan Sickles. I think there is a minority of people who take their GAS way too seriously. The battle's over and those guys need to spend more time with their family." [On the other hand, Sickles later insisted that the first day was not really part of the battle. The man was truly a piece of work—my opinion.]

Wanting to tap Jim's expertise from a broader point of view, I ask what he finds the most interesting about Day Two?

JH: "That changes over time. I have always been into the strategy—of course, there is the sheer size and scale of Longstreet's attack, and his not wanting to make the attack as ordered. Day Two is chock full of blood and guts adventure stories. Getting back to Sickles, keep in mind that Sickles did what he did because he thought it was right, and not just to spite Meade. Several times that morning he communicated with headquarters that he really wasn't sure where he was supposed to be and had concerns about his position. So, he moved to what he thought was a better position. These men did what they did based on past experience—Gettysburg did not occur in a vacuum. Their actions grew out of the background of their entire careers. But I love all the big decisions that went into making what became the second day's battle."

little piece of flat ground—6,000 casualties! The Wheatfield itself contains only ten or so monuments. It is open ground, and so not dramatic in the way that Little Round Top or Devil's Den are. It is an easy stroll on this comfortable day in May.

The Wheatfield evokes an emotional response from me for its sheer simplicity. We're not struggling up hills here, or using the cover of woods, or hiding behind giant boulders as we try to shoot each other down. We are charging back and forth across open ground into the face of muskets and cannon with nothing to protect us but a few stalks of wheat—which of course are no protection at all. What sort of determination or passionate commitment to hold your ground or seize someone else's does it take to do such a thing?

[This is another good opportunity to note that the grass here, especially the higher sections off to the right and left of the path, are full of ticks. Please dress appropriately and check yourself often through the day. When Enis and I returned to our hotel room after this day's hike over almost nine miles of varied terrain, we found several of the little buggers on each of us; they enjoyed a nice swim down the toilet.]

The path across the Wheatfield veers to the right as you approach the northern end. It drops you off on Wheatfield Road near the intersection with Ayres Avenue. If we had taken that route, we would have walked along the eastern edge of the Wheatfield. In our case, once we emerged from the field, we turned left and headed over to the Peach Orchard.

If you've walked or driven along the Wheatfield Road, once you've looked at the Wheatfield you may want to make a small diversion and continue straight ahead on Sickles Avenue. The road will turn sharply left, and then to the right, making a tight loop of sorts. The area is filled with monuments. Among the many you will pass is another of my favorites. On your left, just before the sharp left turn, is one of the monuments to the famed Irish Brigade. The Irish are as much suckers for dogs as I am. When you see it, you will see what I mean.

Whether you've walked across the field or driven along Sickles' Avenue, we will meet at the Wheatfield Road en route to the Peach Orchard. That road, by the way, was here at the time of the battle as a dirt farm lane.

Just ahead of us, less than a quarter of a mile away, is the legendary Peach Orchard. Often spoken of in the same breath with the Wheatfield, this orchard belonged to the Reverend Joseph Sherfy, and formed the tip of Sickles' III Corps. Of course (and as explained), it received its fair share of attention from Longstreet's attacks before the Federals were finally driven out. The National Park Service has undertaken a project to restore it to its 1863 appearance.

Turning right on United States Avenue will take you to the Trostle Farm, which was used by Sickles as his headquarters during the battle. Evidence of the bombardment is still apparent in the upper part of the barn, and it was near here that Sickles was hit by the cannonball, and later Capt. John Bigelow's 9th Massachusetts Battery made its heroic stand. With Union formations fleeing all around him and the Confederates about to flow against Cemetery Ridge,

Bigelow's superior officer told him, "You must remain where you are—hold your position at all hazards." For about half an hour Bigelow held off the gray tide until his battery was finally overrun by the 21st Mississippi. It lost four of its six guns, 27 men, and 80 horses. Bigelow was wounded twice but a faithful sergeant threw him across his horse and carried him to safety.

Shortly after Sickles was wounded and Bigelow overrun, what was left of the Union III Corps fell back to Cemetery Ridge. The III Corps has fought remarkably well given its over-extended position, but now it was wrecked and no longer able to wage organized war.

A Little Cavalry Altercation at Hunterstown: The Site of Custer's First Stand

It was about this time that Enis and I began discussing Jeb Stuart's cavalry and how it was on July 2 that the gray cavalier met up with General Lee. This seems like a good opportunity to break in the action here and dash up to the little community of Hunterstown, just seven miles northeast of Gettysburg.

Jeb Stuart finally reconnected with the Army of Northern Virginia on July

BRIGADIER GENERAL WADE HAMPTON

2. He met with Lee and by most accounts got a real dressing down. If he did, he deserved it. (Although cavalry expert Eric Wittenberg disagrees, which we will see later, Jeb made up for any lapse by his magnificent handling of his troopers during the long retreat back to the river and beyond.) One of his brigades under Brig. Gen. Wade Hampton was passing through Hunterstown to join Lee in Gettysburg. (Stuart and his other two brigades traveled on other roads to reach the battlefield but did not engage any Union forces that day). Two Union cavalry brigades were probing the area looking for Confederates, one under Elon J. Farnsworth and the other under George Armstrong Custer—both

newly made brigadiers. It was Custer and his four Michigan regiments who encountered Hampton's troopers.

As was typical of Custer, he launched a bold attack against Hampton's greater numbers. Shouting "I'll lead you this time, boys. Come on!" Custer led about 50 Michigan cavalry into the charge. That decision almost ended his career, not to mention his life. Custer's horse was shot out from under him in the first Rebel volley. Stranded, he can do little more than await his fate as Confederate horsemen bore down on him. Fortunately for him, he was rescued by his orderly, Private Norvell

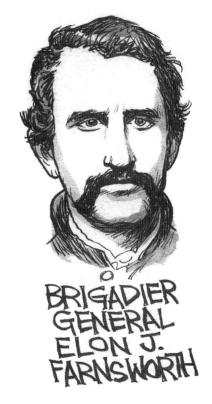

BRIGADIER GENERAL ELON J. FARNSWORTH

BRIGADIER GENERAL GEORGE ARMSTRONG CUSTER

F. Churchill, who got the better of a Confederate cavalryman either in a brief saber duel or by shooting the Reb with his pistol (accounts vary). Once the immediate threat was dealt with, the private pulled the beleaguered Custer up behind him and rode to safety. My, how history would have changed had Custer ended his fabled career on this, the second day of the great battle in a small fight outside Gettysburg at Hunterstown than on the lonely plains out west thirteen years later.

As the Michiganders withdraw, Hampton used two field artillery pieces to put an end to this cavalry

PRIVATE NORVELL F. CHURCHILL

skirmish, which discouraged any additional attacks. The Union troopers retreated toward their lines to the south. Hampton moved his men west to catch up with Stuart.

Hunterstown can better be described as a crossroads than a "town." Set in idyllic countryside, it requires something of a hunt to find the site of the skirmish between Custer and Hampton. Fortunately for me, I noticed a man raking leaves in the yard of a beautiful old home sitting on one corner of the main drag. I asked for information regarding the site of the skirmish, and we started chatting. Ron Myers proved to be one of the most cordial people it has been my pleasure to encounter. He not only gave me directions to the site of the skirmish (near the Felty Farm on the Hunterstown Road), but pointed out that his beautiful home, originally the Jacob Grass Hotel, served as a Confederate field hospital on July 2. Today it is fully restored and a charming B&B.

Enis and I continue our hike along the route of Sickles' III Corps' retreat. We soon cross Plum Run as it meanders through the Trostle Farm. Instead of rejoining the horse trail as it crosses United States Avenue, we decide to head over toward the next intersection where we find the well-preserved George Weikert Farm, one of several owned by various members of the Weikert family. Just under the lee of Cemetery Ridge, it was used extensively as a field hospital

Conversation with an Expert: J. David "J. D." Petruzzi — Cavalry Historian and Observations on Day Two

J. D. Petruzzi is a fascinating man. An insurance broker and owner of a small block of businesses in Brockway, PA, he is also a prolific award-winning author of cavalry topics relating to Gettysburg. Indeed, J. D.'s *The Complete*

Gettysburg Guide, co-authored with map designer and battlefield photographer Steven A. Stanley (winner of the US Army Historical Foundation's 2009 Distinguished Writing Award) is one of the most important books on Gettysburg available anywhere—simply a "must have" for any Gettysburg library.

J. D. was born in Erie, Pa, and was adopted as an infant from the St. Joseph's Home for Children. He tells of having been selected for his new family by his older "sister"—not his biological sister but another adoptee who had been adopted five years earlier. "She picked me," he explained. Although not formally trained as a historian, J.D. credits his interest with the Civil War by becoming "fascinated by the notion that this country fought itself."

"I always had an affinity for horses, they are such noble animals," J. D. says, carrying his love of them so far as to become a reenactor playing Col. Tom Devin of John Buford's Brigade in a variety of made-for-television movies and documentaries. He comments that he "sees them every day; my house is surrounded by Amish farms. You're more likely to see a horse and carriage go by than a car." He is continually researching his beloved avocation, writing, lecturing, and conducting tours about it. Indeed, he is one of the most sought-after speakers at Civil War gatherings. Whenever possible, he participates in tours with other Civil War historians.

After discussing Buford and Union cavalry—"On July 2, General Buford is eventually called off the field by Maj. Gen. Pleasonton, but leaves two companies of the 9th New York cavalry under Capt. Timothy Hanley. Sickles keeps them at his headquarters instead of using them for reconnaissance"— J.D. points out the significance of Hunterstown: "It was a 'side show' to the big show at Gettysburg," he insists, "but it was Custer's first mounted charge as a brigadier general—he leads the charge against the Confederates." As we shall see shortly, Custer, the most notorious of the Union's three "boy generals" [the others being Farnsworth and Merritt] would distinguish himself even more on Day Three during the fight on East Cavalry Field, which took place about the same time as the Pickett-Pettigrew-Trimble Charge.

Our general discussion of Day Two swings back around to the amazing story of Capt. John Bigelow, the Union artilleryman who helped cover Sickles' retreat.

J. D.: "Bigelow's battery is decimated—thousands of Confederates are coming at them. Many of their horses and mules are dead, they start 'firing by prolonge' at the advancing Rebs to buy time for the Federals retreating through the Trostle Farm. They are manhandling the guns while they are moving— without horses!"

"Firing by Prolonge" is an extraordinary maneuver: as the artillery piece is fired its recoil is used to initiate a movement to the rear. Once it has been reloaded on the run, it is stopped and fired again at the enemy, its recoil starting the process over again. "And don't forget the heroism of Union Col. Harrison Jeffords, who saves the colors of his regiment, the 4th Michigan Infantry while being repeatedly bayoneted in the bloody Wheatfield," notes the cavalry historian. [Jeffords' saving of the colors is depicted on the 4th Michigan's monument.] J. D. observes, "It isn't that Lee or the Confederates lost the battle, but that Meade's subordinates won it."

J. D. is a contemplative man; one might even say philosophical. Sensing that, and for reasons I cannot explain, I ask him, "How do you want to be remembered?" The question, I think, surprises him a bit. He smiles shyly for a few seconds as he contemplates his reply.

J. D.: "I'm hoping in some small way—I have no biological children of my own but I do have a stepson and stepdaughter whom I love—I create some permanent record, to be remembered. I'm fascinated by those obscure details, and want to record them, to keep them around." He smiles again: "I've asked my Cindy to put crossed sabers on my tombstone (the insignia of the cavalry), and somewhere the word 'author'." "Or maybe," he adds, just write on it, "I told you I wasn't feeling well"-a phrase borrowing Spike Milligan's famous epitaph. I love that; irony in the face of death.

J. DAVID PETRUZZI

during and after the battle. A gruesome account of what this little stone building witnessed includes the story of a pile of amputated arms and legs that had accumulated outside one of its windows, tossed there by the men operating inside. Apparently this was a common site outside buildings that doubled as Civil War medical centers.

We turned north onto Hancock Avenue and soon meet up with the statue of Father Corby himself, the famed chaplain of the Irish Brigade I referred to earlier.

Now on lower Cemetery Ridge, we pass numerous Union monuments, flank markers, and information tablets before finally arriving at the formidable Pennsylvania Monument. It is the largest monument on the entire battlefield.

The grand Pennsylvania Monument.

Designed by W. Liance Cottrell and sculpted by Samuel Murray at a cost of $240,000, it was dedicated in 1910 and rededicated for the 50th Anniversary of the battle in 1913. Internal stairs allow you to climb to the viewing platform just below the cupola, where fantastic views of much of the battlefield can be enjoyed.

Another of my favorite monuments near the "Copse of Trees," the generally accepted target of the Rebel charge on Day Three, and just beyond the spot that became the Confederate "High-Water Mark," is the monument to the 42nd NY Tammany Regiment. Atop the granite sits a bronze statue of the Delaware Indian Chief Tammany standing in front of a teepee. It's eye-catching and unique among the many monuments on the battlefield.

The fighting on Day Two didn't end on northern Cemetery Ridge when Mahone failed to move his brigade into the attack. General Lee had ordered General Ewell, who led the Second Corps, to commence his diversionary attack against the Union right to pin down the forces in his front so they couldn't be sent to reinforce the troops fighting against Longstreet on the southern end of

Conversation with an Expert:
Steven A. Stanley — Map Designer Extraordinaire:

Steven Stanley is perhaps the foremost map designer of Civil War battles working today. He has worked closely with J. David Petruzzi on some of the most important books about Gettysburg (as noted earlier, *The Complete Gettysburg Guide* being one). Steve is also an outstanding professional photographer, researcher, and writer. "J. D. and I have a great partnership," explains Steve. "He makes me sound smart and I make him look good."

STEVEN
STANLEY

Steven protests that he is not a cartographer, "I am a map designer." And, what a map designer he is! If you haven't seen his maps in one of the more than 40 books in which they're included, go online to the Civil War Trust website—he is their "map designer." When Steven first began working with the Trust, the organizations known as the Association for the Preservation of Civil War Sites and the Civil War Trust [CWT] had just merged. At that time, they commissioned him to do a map for one of their projects. Everything was well received by the Civil War public. On their next major project, however, they decided they didn't need one of Steve's maps. Oops! Bad idea! There were so many complaints that Steve was quickly put on as a regular. And so it remains to this day.

Steve has also worked on guide books for the Army War College, and produced 45 maps for their book on the Petersburg Campaign—the longest of the Civil War. He cautions, "Right now my brain jumps from battle to battle—preparing for the next thing I'll be working on. Doing what I do, you can't get too stuck in one place. In fact, three of my favorites other than Gettysburg are Malvern Hill, Cedar Mountain, and Williamsburg, all in Virginia."

Steve spent nine years in the Air Force working as a graphic designer, and completed his tour of duty as an E-5 working in the Graphics Dept. of the Chairman of the Joint Chiefs of Staff, where he got his start in map designing. When he ended his tour, he worked for a variety of printers as a graphic artist. In 1996, he moved to Fredericksburg, VA, went to an event for the Central Virginia Battlefields Trust, and volunteered to do any graphics work that might be needed. Steve ended up doing some very simple maps for them, and was eventually approached by the National Park Service, who commissioned him to do a 25-map set on the Battle of Spotsylvania Courthouse. That was followed by a set of maps for the Richmond National Battlefield Park. Initially, he used historic U.S Geological Maps as his primary-source base, but subsequently decided to start adding more modern elements to his creations, modifying these comparatively dry maps with colors and other features that make them so appealing.

I ask Steve about how his connection with the Civil War began.

SS: "As a teenager I picked up Bruce Catton's trilogy on the war and became more and more interested. I started visiting Civil War sites whenever possible." How about Gettysburg? "While living outside Fredericksburg, my girlfriend (and now wife) and I would visit Gettysburg often to ride our bikes—it's idyllic, as you know. We enjoyed it so much that we finally moved here in 2004. I don't really have a special deep affinity for Gettysburg except that I do feel attracted to it—it's a beautiful battlefield, anytime of the year. I tried to make that point, by the way, in *The Complete Gettysburg Guide*, purposely using photographs from all four seasons. When you're growing up your parents tell you where to live; in the service, it was the Air Force; when you're married, it's often your wife. This is the first time I got to choose. Gettysburg is the Mecca—for both reenactors and historians. I love the 'small-town' quality. If you don't believe we have one, just visit in the winter. You get to know a lot of people in a town like Gettysburg. I like that."

Given the fact that he knows the battle so well, I ask Steve if he has any favorite places? He thinks for a minute: "I really like Lost Avenue—Dean Shultz, who owns the property where it's located, is an amazing man—talk about someone who really knows the battle! Another favorite is the mural over on Costner Avenue. It could use some rehabilitation, but I really like it."

Given all the time Steve has spent in Gettysburg, I ask him about any of the interesting questions he had been asked. "I really hate those 'what if' questions—what if Jackson had still been alive—what if Longstreet had persuaded Lee not to attack. I never look at history that way. I look at what actually did happen. I love studying the Civil War, but I'm also interested in the Revolutionary War and the War of 1812. Lately I've become interested in World War I. I guess you could call me an amateur historian—I love studying the battles. And, that's true here! But get out of your car and walk the battlefield—walk Pickett's Charge—from the road or from your car it looks like a flat plain. It's not! Don't let your experience of these magnificent battlefields be limited to just 'drive-by' tours."

the field (or to score a breakthrough, if he could). Ewell spent most of the day moving troops into position as best he could to prepare for his part of the assault against wooded and rocky Culp's Hill. He was hampered by Union forces holding the high ground in his area, with their formidable array of artillery. Consequently, Ewell didn't order his men forward until almost four hours after Longstreet opened his attack. However, by that time most of Slocum's defending XII Corps troops on the Union right had been culled from the area to reinforce the crumbling Union front on the left, leaving Culp's Hill but sparsely guarded for Ewell's men to capture. It was a potential disaster for the North.

During the day, while Ewell was moving his men around, a Confederate search for a strong tactical position for artillery was made by Maj. Joseph White Latimer, the 19-year-old "Boy Major" who had been trained as an artillerist by none other than Stonewall Jackson when Latimer was his student at the Virginia

MAJOR
JOSEPH WHITE
LATIMER

Military Institute. His search led to a small rise just north of the Union line known as Benner's Hill. It seemed an ideal spot to deploy Latimer's four batteries of 16 guns. Reality was something altogether different. Benner's Hill was flat and treeless, so it afforded no cover for the Confederate gunners. There was little else to choose from, however. When Latimer opened fire, Federal batteries responded from Culp's Hill, Stevens' Knoll, and East Cemetery Hill. They smothered his position. Guns were lost, horses and men killed, and Latimer was mortally wounded when his injury turned gangrenous.

Most visitors do not take the time to stand on Benner's Hill. Don't make that mistake. It's about a mile from Lincoln Square, a right turn off the Hanover Road (PA Route 116) and well before you get to US 15. There are several markers on the other side of the road, and cannon on the right (as you head east). Route 116 can be busy, so be careful if you are crossing back and forth. It offers an entirely different view of the battlefield.

When Sickles' III Corps began collapsing, and as Longstreet's attack gained momentum, General Meade

BRIGADIER
GENERAL
GEORGE SEARS
"PAP" GREENE

transferred all but one brigade of Slocum's XII Corps to assist. The one brigade left to defend Culp's Hill was under the command of 62-year-old Brig. Gen. George Sears "Pap" Greene, the oldest general at Gettysburg North or South. His command consisted of five New York regiments, just over 1,400 men.

BRIGADIER GENERAL SILAS COLGROVE

The unwelcome task of capturing Culp's Hill fell to Maj. Gen. Edward ("Allegheny") Johnson's division. Greene's men, who were dug in on the summit, extended their line to the right to fill in for the departing XII Corps brigades (Colgrove's and McDougall's). Their line was stretched thin, but fortunately for the Union, Greene's men slipped into place just before the Confederates begin streaming up the hillside under growing evening shadows.

Pap Greene is one of my favorites. An 1823 graduate of West Point, he taught engineering at the academy before resigning his commission in 1836 to become a civil engineer. As such, he built railroads in six states, designed municipal sewage and water systems for Washington, DC, Detroit, and several other major cities, designed the Croton Aqueduct in New York's Central Park, and was a founding member of the American Society of Civil Engineers and Architects. Pap rejoined the army in January of 1862, was appointed colonel, and quickly rose to brigadier general.

Given Greene's background as a civil engineer, once assigned to protect Culp's Hill it is no surprise that he ordered his men to dig trenches and build breastworks. His foresight helped turn an already strong position into a formidable redoubt. Greene was also an able field commander. Once Johnson's assault on the upper hill began, Greene ordered his best shooters to the front while others reloaded and passed weapons forward. In this way, the rate of fire and the effectiveness of the New Yorkers were greatly enhanced. Johnson attacked with just three of his four brigades, roughly 4,700 men. Brig. Gen. John

M. Jones' brigade attacked the center of Greene's works, got the worst of it, and was quickly repulsed. The Louisiana brigade under Col. Jesse M. Williams suffered a similar fate. Only the regiments of Brig. Gen. George H. ("Maryland") Steuart fared better on the far Union right. His men drove ahead and climbed into the trenches and along positions recently abandoned by Colgrove and McDougall. The Rebels were now precariously close to the Baltimore Pike, the vital supply artery for the Army of the Potomac.

Once Johnson's attack began, however, Greene called for help. Within the next hour or two a few regiments from Brig. Gen. James S.

BRIGADIER GENERAL JOHN M. JONES

Wadsworth's I Corps division, stationed on Cemetery Hill, and Gibbon's II Corps on Cemetery Ridge, came to his aid. The Confederates maintained their occupation of the trenches and breastworks on the lower end of Culp's Hill, but were never able to break through Greene's defenses. The direct attacks did not end until well after nightfall, though gunfire would continue through much of the night. Both sides held these positions through the night of the 2nd and into the morning of the 3rd, awaiting whatever fate had in store for them the next day.

COLONEL ARCHIBALD L. McDOUGALL

Many historians and experts on the battle regard Pap Greene's masterful defense of Culp's Hill comparable to (or even more important than) the heroic stand of the 20th Maine on Little Round Top. Culp's Hill is a more remote corner of

BRIGADIER GENERAL GEORGE H. STEUART

MAJOR GENERAL EDWARD JOHNSON

the battlefield, and is less visited despite its overall importance to the outcome of the battle. Don't forget, it does have one of Gettysburg's three remaining observation towers. While it may seem to take you out of your way, the importance of Culp's Hill to the battle and to truly understanding Gettysburg make it mandatory to visit.

The Brinkerhoff's Ridge Diversion

There is one other facet of the fighting on July 2 that adds an interesting twist to the Ewell-Johnson attack on Culp's Hill: Johnson's missing fourth brigade. For most of the day, Union and Confederate forces had been contesting an area just west of the intersection of the Hanover Road and the Low Dutch Road east of Gettysburg. This elevated piece of land is known as Brinkerhoff's Ridge. As 3,000 Union cavalry under Brig. Gen. David M. Gregg

BRIGADIER
GENERAL
DAVID McMURTRIE
GREGG

approached from the south, Allegheny Johnson, recognizing the danger the Federals posed to the Confederate flank, ordered the famed Stonewall Brigade under Brig. Gen. James A. Walker to take up a position on the ridge.

Between 6:00 and 10:00 p.m. the fight for this crucial piece of high ground seesawed back and forth as additional units were fed in by both sides. The outcome was essentially a stalemate, with a slight advantage to the Confederates. The Union, however, maintained a strong enough presence near the Hanover Road that it was decided the Stonewall Brigade could not be spared to assist in the

attack on Culp's Hill. Had the 1,400 seasoned veterans of this brigade been available to Johnson for his assault on the hill, the outcome that warm July evening might well have been very different. Extend these Virginians beyond Maryland Steuart's flank and they would not have met much if any resistance. As it was, the Union position on Culp's Hill held, securing the north end of the Fishhook and keeping the Baltimore Pike open.

Before we move on to the nighttime fight for East Cemetery Hill and the end of Day Two, I want to visit Brinkerhoff's Ridge where the

BRIGADIER
GENERAL
JAMES A.
WALKER

Stonewall Brigade helped hold off Union forces and protect the Rebel left flank.

As I learned during an earlier visit to the battlefield, Brinkerhoff's Ridge, aside from the fraction you can see from the Hanover Road, is on private land and inaccessible. I complained about that fact to Ranger John Nicholas over at the Visitor Center. He explained to me in cautious tones that just past the equestrian statue was a small country road that headed north, and that if I turned there I would find access to a facility of a private utility company from whose driveway I *might* be able to take a picture of the back of Brinkerhoff's Ridge with a telephoto lens.

Telephoto lens? Well, refusing to be daunted by a little challenge, I headed over to Route 116, sans telephoto lens, found Hoffman Road, took the left (as I've come from town), and quickly found the entrance to the utility company, which, of course, has a formidable gate blocking its driveway. Brinkerhoff's Ridge was nowhere to be seen, blotted out, as it were, by the utility company's own buildings. Knowing that I was in the vicinity of the ridge, however, I continued north on Hoffman Road (accessible from the north from Cavalry Field Road off the York Road). Not too far along, I took note of a farmhouse set back from the road and a gentleman working on a pick-up truck with a rather nice sedan parked next to it.

"What the hell?" I muttered under my breath. "The worst that can happen is he tells me I'm on private land and to leave." Well, as Professor Minerva McGonagall might say, "by sheer dumb luck" I met David Craine, a software engineer who had been based in Washington, D.C. but wanted a quieter life so he moved to Gettysburg. The farm, it turns out, was one of three that had stood on Brinkerhoff's Ridge during the battle. David couldn't be nicer as we talked about the battle and, in his case, his newly found interest in the Civil War. When I asked if I could take a few pictures, David graciously offered me free rein to walk the property and take all the pictures I want—more serendipity. And speaking of "sheer dumb luck," it is from David's property that GNMP rangers begin their annual tours of Brinkerhoff's Ridge. I thanked David profusely and headed off to explore. (Make sure and do not trespass on his land without permission. Don't trespass on anyone's land without permission.)

The Fight for Culp's Hill—the Stuff of Legend

If you choose to visit Culp's Hill by car, as I have done on several occasions, you will need to leave the Visitor Center and make a right turn onto the Baltimore Pike. Just a quarter of a mile down the pike is a turn-off to the left named Colgrove Avenue. (Watch carefully, it's a little hard to spot.) Once committed to this little paved road, just follow its winding path.

You will arrive at Spangler's Spring. Park your car and take a moment to read the information tablets. Proceed to the second turn to the right (the first is East Confederate Avenue—another story entirely), and follow the little road as it increases in elevation until you reach the top. Be careful to follow the numerous one-way signs. You can't miss it because this is where you will find the last of the three extant observation towers.

I like this tower—buried in the woods it somehow feels kind of welcoming. It is also a lot shorter than the monster over on Warfield Ridge overlooking Longstreet's attack. In fact, the Culp's Hill Tower is a mere 60 feet tall and has a paltry 96 or so steps. The view from the top is good but would be better if the tower was higher than the trees. Still, it is still worth the climb. Once back on terra firma, however, there's a lovely statue of ole "Pap" Greene. He's pointing into the woods from whence came, or attempted to come, the Confederate assaults.

Once you've given it the once over, follow the one-way paved road taking you back down to the area of the southeastern part of Cemetery Hill, where you can reconnect with the Baltimore Pike. Having cursorily examined Culp's Hill a few times via the automobile route, it was my inclination to try a more extensive exploration of it on foot. In fact, I did it twice. The first time turned out to be quite an adventure.

I began by leaving my downtown hotel and proceeding on foot down the Baltimore Pike. It was a beautiful morning in early May. One block past High Street is Wall Alley, where I turned left. Go just one block and turn right onto Schoolhouse Alley, a quiet "lane" amidst a nice neighborhood on the periphery of the downtown area, which will give you a taste of another part of the community that is Gettysburg. On the right are private homes; on the left you will note the Lincoln Elementary School in the same complex that houses the Adams County Literacy Council and, a little farther down the road, the rather large complex that is the Gettysburg Area Middle School.

Schoolhouse Alley flows directly into Wainwright Avenue, a park road that extends into town. You are now approaching Cemetery Hill. Note the two blue water towers off to your right. Former Mayor Troxell told me they were located there due to the high ground, and were most convenient to the town. In a word: ugh!

After a short distance I reentered the GNMP. Wainwright Avenue runs along the base of the higher portion of Cemetery Hill and becomes Slocum

Avenue. Here auto traffic is one-way so if you are driving, keep a wary eye. A noisy NSP tractor was clearing some dead wood off to one side.

The ascent from the intersection of Slocum and Wainwright avenues to the top of Culp's Hill is about three-eighths of a mile. It is not terribly steep, although not for the faint of heart, and passes through the beautiful wooded lower portion of the hill. I arrived at the top, bound and determined to make my solo adventure something special. I decided to descend the hill by way of the Johnny Reb Trail, developed in cooperation between the Boy Scouts of America and the NPS (the other being the Billy Yank Trail).

As I begin to descend the hill, moving deeper into the more heavily wooded area, I come to what appears to be a "Y" intersection. The trail to the right looks as though it will just take me back to the road, while the trail to the left seems to be more challenging. So I turn to the left. Before long I am in ever-denser brush as I descend what is in fact not a trail at all. Oops! Well, to make a long, painful story shorter, I am now completely turned around—putting a pejorative spin on it, one might even say "lost." So far, I have no ticks on me that I can see, have not been bitten by any snakes or eaten by a bear, and despite not knowing where the hell I am, am still enjoying the nice morning. But, I would rather not be lost.

I pause for a brief respite on a fallen tree, take a drink from my water bottle and a few deep breaths when I hear the sound of a tractor off to my left: remember the tractor I mentioned above? Well, so did I! I could not move to the sound of guns, but I could trot to the sound of a tractor. Within a few minutes I reached a paved road.

I ended up on East Confederate Avenue at the base of Culp's Hill and have, once again, stumbled onto a little more serendipity. For it is here that elements of Ewell's Corps assembled in preparation for their assault on the hill. I speculate that at least some small number of Confederates must have attempted to climb the steep, rocky, wooded slope I had just descended. It also gave me a sense of the kind of obstacles the Confederates encountered when they attacked from positions farther east. And, despite the difficulties of my chosen path, there were some rewarding moments. In addition to those I've already mentioned, the fact that many regimental markers are in the most unlikely places on the battlefield was brought home to me as I encountered one to the 66th Ohio Vol. Inf. buried in the woods near the top of the hill.

Erring on the side of discretion, however, I head north on East Confederate Avenue and once again approach Gettysburg, emerging two blocks east of Lincoln Square on York Avenue. Civilization! So much for my first solo adventure to Culp's Hill.

COLONEL
ANDREW
L. HARRIS

Enis and I, however, returned to Culp's Hill on yet another beautiful day in May. This time I was determined to make a proper exploration of the hill, and trust Enis' skill with his Nikon to capture it all on micro-chip (had I said "film," I would really have shown my age). We retraced my journey on foot up to Culp's Hill. Everything is pretty much the same on the way up. The weather is stunningly beautiful. Having arrived at the top of the hill, we once more head down the Johnny Reb Trail. Having learned my lesson, this time we take the right fork. The trail itself is rudimentary, but clearly a trail. And, as I thought, the trail in the woods is very short and emerges onto the one-way road up (which, of course, wasn't here in 1863) to the summit. After carefully checking our maps, we conclude this is the position occupied by Union troops in defense of the hill, indeed, the very area where Pap Greene had the breastworks constructed and trenches dug. A century and five decades have taken their toll on the remains of the breastworks, and they are essentially gone.

In addition to its historical importance, for the modern visitor Culp's Hill and the area surrounding it are some of the most interesting parts of the battlefield. A series of short, undulating hills, surrounded by and intermingled with heavily forested areas eventually give way to what is the third highest point on the battlefield. Many tourist bus excursions visit here, but if you are on your own, don't neglect it. The one-way road to the summit is beautiful, historic, and filled with monuments and informative information tablets that will give you a complete understanding of this key Union position, and why the Confederate forces fought so hard to capture it. It is also very easy to lose your perspective, so bring an arm full of maps when you visit.

The End of the Day: The Confederates
Finally Attack Cemetery Hill from the East

Before we get to the final clash of Day Two I want to single out one of the most famous Confederate brigades—the famed "Louisiana Tigers" of Jubal Early's division, Ewell's Second Corps. The Tigers were comparable to the Army of the Potomac's Iron Brigade. One of only two Louisiana brigades in Lee's army, this collection of ne'er-do-wells earned a reputation as some of Lee's best fighters. Under the command of Brig. Gen. Harry T. Hays (whom we met briefly at the end of Day One), they were forced to lay low for most of the day due because of their position just east of town under the guns of Union artillery on Cemetery Hill.

The attack against Culp's Hill during the middle-evening of Day Two was well underway when Ewell sent two brigades of Early's division (the Tigers under Hays and another under Col. Isaac E. Avery) against East Cemetery Hill, slightly north and west of Culp's Hill. The Tigers are finally unleashed! Robert Rodes' division, also part of Ewell's command, was to assault Cemetery Hill from the northwestern side. Unfortunately for the Confed- erates, despite

COLONEL
ISAAC E.
AVERY

having had the whole day to plan this assault, there was no coordination or single guiding hand. Rodes (who may have been sick with a fever) did not have his division formed in time, and when his brigades finally crept forward to join the attack (Rodes was not with them), Early's men had already attacked, captured the hill, and been repulsed!

Howard's Union troops of the XI Corps, who had taken a beating the day before north of town, occupied Cemetery Hill with substantial artillery support. Early's twilight assault fell against Colonels Andrew L. Harris and Leopold Von Gilsa. Brig. Gen. Adelbert Ames also sent the 17th Connecticut to reinforce their position. Somehow, however, a gap developed

East Cemetery Hill looking toward Evergreen Cemetery.

in Harris' position. Confederates poured toward this weak point. The Rebs broke through at the base of Cemetery Hill, routing the defenders there and fighting up the slope in the darkness. Some of the attackers reached Capt. Michael Wiedrich's New York artillery battery and another manned by the Pennsylvanians of Capt. R. Bruce Ricketts. The Union gunners fought them with ramrods, spikes, fists, and pistols.

Early's men carried East Cemetery Hill, and for a few minutes the battle fell off into a fitful silence. Where were the promised reinforcements? Reinforcements in fact did arrive, but the Rebels held their fire, unsure whether they were Rodes' men or Union troops. In fact, they were from both Howard's XI Corps and Hancock's II Corps. Early's men tumbled back off the hill. The second day of Gettysburg now belonged to history.

Once the day's fighting ended, two XII Corps divisions unneeded elsewhere were returned to Culp's Hill to forestall any more incursions by the Confederates. Ewell reinforced the lower portion of Culp's Hill. Both sides busy were busy setting the stage for the following morning.

This is yet another area of the battlefield that is strikingly beautiful, with its steep slope that carried the attack against East Cemetery Hill on the evening of July 2. We entered it from the site of Spangler's Spring. The road winds northerly around the base of Culp's Hill, an area that was heavily occupied by Ewell's Corps during the night of the 1st and throughout the day on the 2nd and into the 3rd. For just about a half of a mile, the road passes through the wooded area surrounding the base of the hill. The woods soon give way to some of the prettiest open ground on the battlefield. To our right is farmland with some houses in the distance. This land, now owned by the NPS, is leased to local farmers for grazing. On the left is a series of rolling hills that terminate at the top of East Cemetery Hill. Once the sightlines open to the north (that is, directly in front of us), the edges of modern Gettysburg and many streets that can lead you back into town become visible.

Meade's Council and Lee's Authority

Late in the evening of the second day, after the fighting had ended, Meade convened a war council of his corps commanders at the Leister Farm. According to Stephen Sears in *Gettysburg*, his comprehensive history of the battle, the meeting began informally before the group of generals settled down to the business at hand. Daniel Butterfield, Meade's chief of staff inherited from Hooker just three days before the battle began, posed three questions to the assembled officers: "1. Under existing circumstances is it advisable for this army to remain in its present position or retire to another nearer its base of supplies? 2. It being determined to remain in present position, should the army attack or wait the attack of the enemy? 3. If we await attack, how long?" The answers of the nine generals in attendance determined the outcome.

To the first question, John Gibbon voted to "correct position of the army but would not retreat"; Birney, Sykes, Howard, Sedgwick, and [Seth] Williams simply said, "Stay"; Slocum was stronger with "Stay and fight it out"; Hancock wanted to "rectify" the position, but only "without moving to give up the field"; [John] Newton used the same phrasing as Gibbon. The army would stay put.

To the second question, the vote to await attack was unanimous, with Hancock offering the only qualification with: "No attack unless our communications are cut."

Question three brought a wider variety of responses, ranging from one day to "until Lee moved." Ultimately, this decision, too, was unanimous.

Gibbon, taking note of the unusual and decisive conclave, wrote, "I recollect there was great good feeling amongst the Corps Commanders at their agreeing so unanimously, and Gen. Meade announced, in a decided manner, 'Such then is the decision'."

On the other side of the battlefield, General Lee decided to reinstate his original plan to continue attacking without consulting a single one of his ranking lieutenants. "The general plan was unchanged," he later wrote.

Longstreet and Ewell were to renew their attacks on either end of the Union line in the morning. The newly arrived Jeb Stuart would operate on Ewell's left and rear, and the fresh troops comprising Pickett's division, who had yet to fire a shot at Gettysburg, would be part of a renewed assault against the Union center. Edward Porter Alexander, on his way to becoming the Army of Northern Virginia's favorite artillerist, reported that when he visited Longstreet's headquarters the night of the 2nd, "to ask the news from other quarters and orders for the morning . . . I was told that we would renew the attack early in the morning. That Pickett's division would arrive and assault the enemy's line. My impression is the exact point for it was not designated, but I was told it would be to our left of the Peach Orchard."

Conversation with an Expert: LBG Deb Novotny

Deb Novotny has been a Licensed Battlefield Guide for 38 years. "Only Antietam in Maryland, and Shiloh in Tennessee come close to Gettysburg for me," she explains. Deb is one of the most highly regarded LBGs, and regularly participates in bus tours to other historic sites organized by the other LBGs. Her "hobby" is going to cemeteries: "It's the way I visit my friends from the past—visiting the gravesites of Civil War-related men and women. I started doing this in 1978, and have probably visited about 1,000 of them. I've always been interested in the human side of the war. I love to do the research, but hate writing about it."

Deb notes that, for a time, she was the only woman out of 156 guides at Gettysburg (at the time of this interview, there were 15). When she got her license, she was the fourth woman to have done so (the first was in 1968). Currently, she is the 7th longest-serving guide. Less than 600 people have held the license since 1915, when the LBG Service began. Deb has recently served on the committee to revise the written test, and delights in the fact that they now have a mentoring program to get people ready for the oral exam.

Getting down to some specifics, she tells me, "I admire the common soldier. These men and women were volunteers; they left their homes, brave people. Courage, bravery, and sacrifice are my themes. You should know some think over 500 women fought disguised as men during the Civil War—one of them died in Pickett's Charge. There is more to the women's side of the story than just nursing, although they were the ones who did most of it. Elizabeth Thorn (of Gettysburg), six months pregnant, dug the graves for some 105 soldiers during July and August 1863. Her sickly baby died before she was 15.

And let's not forget the importance of the Sisters of Charity from Emmitsburg who came up here after the battle." Deb was on the committee to establish the Gettysburg National Civil War Women's Memorial.

Serving as a kind of memorial of their own are the "Rock carvings we have here, sometimes done within a year of the battle. For example, the carving about Strong Vincent's mortal wounding on Little Round Top."

I asked what aspects of the battle she found the most fascinating. "I love the story of Annie Etheridge," explains Deb. "A volunteer nurse from 1861, she traveled with the 3rd Michigan during the Gettysburg Campaign. This regiment was charged with filling in the gap between the Peach Orchard and the Stony Hill. She had a horse and had the wounded

DEB NOVOTNY

loaded on it, carrying them back to the Trostle Farm. Called "Gentle Annie" by the men, they lined up to observe when she was awarded the Kearney Cross given for bravery. Annie was one of the only two women to receive this honor. Her married name was Hooks and she is buried with her Union veteran husband in Arlington National Cemetery."

Deb continues: "The Battle of Gettysburg is chock full of the 'human stories' that I find so interesting: Union Maj. Gen. John Fulton Reynolds, killed in the first hours of the battle; Confederate Brig. Gen. Lewis A. Armistead mortally wounded at the end of Pickett's Charge on the Confederate side, who had been a close personal friend of Winfield Scott Hancock; Armistead's uncle had been in charge of Fort McHenry during the War of 1812. Sgt. Ben Crippen of the 143rd Pennsylvania, who stood there shaking his fist at the Confederates and winning praise from a Confederate general, only later to be killed by the enemy. And Confederate Sgt. Richard Kirkland, who had gained fame as the 'Angel of Marye's Heights' at the Battle of Fredericksburg, offering water to both Confederate and Union wounded after the fighting had stopped, and who served with the 2nd South Carolina near the Wheatfield. He would later die at Chickamauga. And, don't forget," she adds, "the Confederate soldier did not feel defeated after Gettysburg." That goes a long way to explaining why this horrible war dragged on for almost another two years.

Deb excitedly recounts, "My most memorable tour was in September 2012, escorting astronaut Jim Lovell, the Apollo 13 commander, around the battlefield. At the end of the tour, I asked him if NASA had ever offered him another trip? He replied: 'My wife Marilyn nixed the possibility.'"

"Over the years, my interests have changed: I've moved from Pickett's Charge to Little Round Top and the Wheatfield, and now it's the First Day. But the Second Day of the battle has so many examples of bravery and courage that I always enjoy reading about it. Even about Daniel E. Sickles, who changed the course of the entire battle by making a controversial move forward to the Peach Orchard Ridge with his III Corps. Though badly wounded near the Trostle barn, he survived to become a U. S. Congressman after the war, and then introduced and pushed the bill that created the Gettysburg National Military Park in 1895. Without him we might not have such a well-preserved battlefield to study." So, perhaps Sickles was good for something.

Aftermath

It is generally believed that while communication between Union officers and units was excellent, there was a marked lack of effective communication in Lee's army. To be sure, assembling an attack over such a wide expanse would be difficult under any circumstances. But command and coordination among senior officers in the Army of Northern Virginia was, at best, spotty, and at worst, woefully negligent. Personalities? The difficulty of coordinating an attack over such a large expanse? Terrain? Lack of accurate intelligence? All of these factors led Robert E. Lee to make what may have been his greatest mistake of the war.

Historians are in general agreement that his decisions about how to proceed on July 3 were based on a false impression of the outcome of the battle so far. While he had inflicted heavy damage on the Federal left, and had secured the lower parts of Culp's Hill, he had not gained much if any real tactical advantage, and Meade had successfully restored his defensive Fishhook. Just as important, he had large numbers of soldiers in reserve, including the entire VI Corps.

The cost of the fighting of Day Two was horrific. More than 10,000 Union troops fell killed, wounded, or captured. Sickles' III Corps was completely shattered, losing nearly one-third of its men. The II Corps and V Corps had also lost heavily. The Confederates fared little better, losing nearly 7,000 men, the greatest losses falling to Longstreet's Corps and the division of Richard Anderson. The casualty rate in the attacking Rebel brigades ranged between 30 and 40%.

Who came out on top on Day Two is open for speculation. Day Three would be a different matter.

Chapter 6

The Climax of the Clash, Day Three — Lee's Plan and Disaster, and My Final Personal Encounter with History

July 3—the climactic third day of Gettysburg—saw multiple actions occurring simultaneously across the battlefield. This necessitates some jumping around both chronologically and geographically, but with a little help from Tim's maps it should all make sense. The focal point of this day is naturally the Pickett-Pettigrew-Trimble Charge, with the cavalry action on East Cavalry Field about the same time playing a secondary role. We will conclude with South Cavalry Field and one of the hidden gems few people get the opportunity to discover.

If we compare our first map of the main battlefield with this one, we can see the Union position has tightened. The Fishhook is compressed and a bit shorter and thus more compact and in a word, stronger. Ewell's Second Corps and Slocum's XII Corps renew their contest for Culp's Hill, while Longstreet reluctantly prepares for the famous charge. In addition to the main Stuart-Gregg fight, there are two additional cavalry actions: one eight miles away near the Fairfield Road, and the second at the end of the day on the southern end of the Gettysburg field. We've already covered some of the Day Three battlefield while exploring the events of Day Two, so we're familiar with parts of this ground.

Any account of Day Three must begin with an examination of Lee's plan of attack. The results thus far convinced him to venture another major assault. He had beaten back the Army of the Potomac on July 1, routing two of its corps, and only failed to win a complete victory because the high ground remained in Union hands. The next day, Lee nearly cracked open Meade's line on the enemy left, lodged men for a time in the center on Cemetery Ridge, and carried part of Culp's Hill on the enemy right. Meade was about to break, his line stretched thin. Lee knew he had reinforced his left and likely had drawn from his center to do so. One more major thrust—this time against the extended center-right just below Cemetery Hill—would do it. Or so Lee seems to have believed.

His plan, generally speaking, called for renewed attacks by Ewell and Longstreet on either end of the line early on the morning of the 3rd to tie up Meade's forces. This would be followed by a massive artillery barrage against the Union center to silence enemy guns and soften the position, followed by a decisive infantry blow with a fresh division of Virginians under Pickett and other brigades drawn from A. P. Hill's Third Corps to break through on upper Cemetery Ridge and drive the Union army from the field. The orders Lee had sent both Ewell and Longstreet during the night of the 2nd were somewhat vague, and did not give either commander specific instructions when to attack. Once again there would be a lack of coordination, and Longstreet's continued reluctance to any major attack. Scott Bowden and Bill Ward in their award-winning *Last Chance for Victory* (required reading at the U.S. Army Command and General Staff College) argue that, despite the questionable nature of Lee's orders for the day, it was the failure of his subordinates to execute them as he envisioned that brought the Confederate defeat. It seems to me the Union army likely had a hand in the defeat as much as any Southern miscues.

The balance of the Union army had finally arrived at Gettysburg. The VI Corps under the command of Maj. Gen. John Sedgwick, the largest in the Army of the Potomac, was now on the battlefield. Its batteries and brigades were immediately dispersed to reinforce key positions on Culp's Hill, farther south on Cemetery Ridge, and on Little Round Top. In addition, Sykes' V Corps and Slocum's XII Corps are also now in position at full strength. It was becoming more apparent that the larger resources of the Union army (manpower and artillery) would play a decisive role in what lay ahead—especially since Meade held a compact interior line and could easily reinforce his front anywhere, while Lee held a much longer exterior line, and could not reinforce it rapidly at any point.

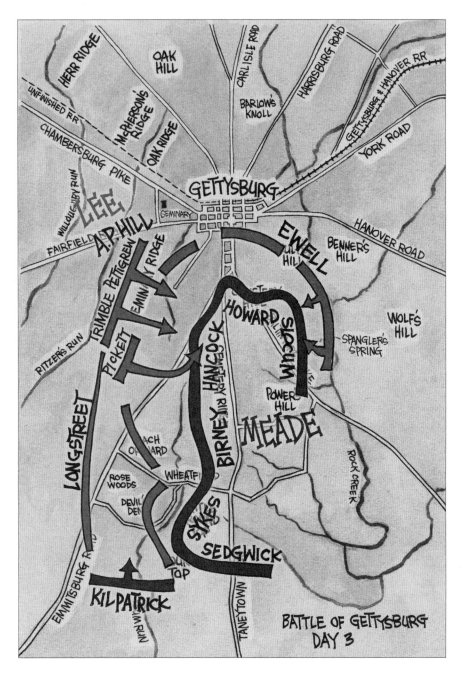

Was Lee wrong to attack on Day Three? Should he have been more specific in his orders to his corps commanders? Should he have finally listened to Longstreet (who wanted to move southeast and place the Army of Northern Virginia between Washington, DC. and Meade's army)? Should Lee have better recognized the strength of the Union position, holding as it did interior lines and the most desirable high ground from Culp's Hill all the way to Little Round Top? Would the proper execution of his orders really have made the difference between victory and defeat? I certainly don't have the expertise to know the answers, and since these things did not occur we can never know. In truth, even the experts don't agree. As you become more familiar with these events, walk the ground, and read the historical accounts, you'll form your own opinion or come to trust the interpretation of a favored historian. Or, to quote the English playwright and poet Christopher Fry, you may "rest content in the mystery" that Lee's actions imposed upon history. The result, though, is indisputable: The Confederate attack was a complete disaster and it heralded Meade's complete strategic and tactical victory at Gettysburg.

The Day Begins

In the previous chapter, we tread the very ground where the action would kick off the day's influential events. They began before the sun rose—not with the attacks Lee had hoped for (neither Longstreet nor Ewell were ready), but with a Union artillery attack. Union Brig. Gen. Alpheus S. Williams ordered 26 artillery pieces to open fire on Maryland Steuart's forward Rebel position, disrupting the advances made the night before. It was about 4:00 a.m. and still pitch dark.

During the night, Allegheny Johnson's Rebel troops, reinforced by other brigades, had taken up positions about where they were the day before on the eastern and northeast sides of Culp's Hill in preparation for renewing the attack the next morning. During the night, however, the two XII Corps divisions that had been pulled off the hill to assist Hancock had returned, determined to evict the Rebels who had taken advantage of their absence. Maj. Gen. John Geary was back with his men, as were Brig. Gen. Thomas Ruger's brigades. The cannonade was effective in some places, noisy everywhere, and triggered the action long before the Confederates intended to renew it. Heavy infantry fire followed. This was in essence a classic "spoiling attack," and indeed, it spoiled the Rebel plans. It also kicked off what would be at least six and probably closer to seven hours of unrelenting combat—the longest sustained fighting of the entire battle. And it settled once and for all who would control the wooded rocky heights.

When the fighting erupted off to the northeast on Ewell's front, Lee sought out Longstreet about his pending renewed attack against the Union left. What he discovered did not please Lee, who assumed all along that Hood's and McLaws' divisions would be ready to attack at first light. Longstreet, on the other hand, had a better sense of how heavily these divisions had suffered on the 2nd (surely Lee did as well?) and had spent time exploring a flanking movement around the Round Tops. Lee had had no interest in that option the previous day and today was no different. However, he did accept Longstreet's protests that his two divisions were in no condition for heavy fighting. Lee eventually pointed to Cemetery Ridge and replied, "The enemy is there, and I am going to strike him." Maj. Gen. George E. Pickett's newly arrived division was on the field, but not yet deployed for an attack.

BRIGADIER GENERAL JOHN W. GEARY

There was now little hope for a coordinated attack on either end, but Lee was unwilling to give up the idea of one last offensive action. It was time to reconsider the master plan for the day.

Lee sent for A. P. Hill to join him and Longstreet for a conference. After some discussion it was decided that a strong direct attack against Meade's right-center would take place after a massive artillery barrage helped clear the way. Henry Heth's division under J. Johnston Pettigrew (Heth had been wounded on July 1), plus two brigades form Dorsey Pender's division under Isaac Trimble because of Pender's severe leg wound on July 2, would join Pickett's division in the effort. Two additional brigades under Wilcox and Lang (both from Anderson's division of Hill's Corps) were apparently slated to support the attack on Pickett's right. The troops seem to have been chosen based upon where they were in line, rather than whether they were capable for the task about to be thrust upon them. Longstreet was dismayed by these decisions.

There remained the little matter of the Bliss Farm—a thorn in the side of both armies. Throughout July 2 and into the morning of the 3rd, possession of the farm changed hands some ten times. On the third morning of the battle,

BRIGADIER
GENERAL
ALPHEUS S.
WILLIAMS

Union Brig. Gen. Alexander Hays ordered 60 men of the 14th Connecticut to retake the farm. An interesting sidelight to what will become the last attempt by either side to control the farm was that these troops carried new breech-loading Sharps rifles, giving them firepower far beyond their numbers. When the Confederates vigorously contested the occupation by the 14th Connecticut, the aggressive Hays upped the ante. Using the discretionary orders given to him by Hancock the day before, Hays ordered the Bliss buildings burned to the ground to deny their use by the enemy. Within a short time the structures were aflame and the opposing troops pulled back toward their respective ridges.

Meanwhile, to the north and east, Jeb Stuart made a decision of his own. After watching the fight at Brinkerhoff's Ridge the previous day between Gregg's Federal cavalry and Walker's Stonewall Brigade, Stuart decided to draw Gregg out into the open and destroy him. Stuart gathered four mounted brigades along the York Pike and sought out a good place to confront the Federal cavalry. Two and a half miles from the town he reached Cress Ridge just south of the pike and gazed across the open fields of the Rummel Farm, which at this point seemed devoid of Union defenders. That would soon change.

My take on Stuart's action is consistent with most modern thinking about the fight at the East Cavalry Field, which was the largest mounted clash since Brandy Station at the start of the campaign in early June. For a long while many writers argued Stuart had been instructed by Lee to break through the rear of the Union line in conjunction with "Pickett's Charge." In other words, the cavalry action was part of the same attack, just separated by space. Eric Wittenberg, an award-winning cavalry author, has "led the charge" so to speak, in debunking this idea by using reason and facts in his fascinating book *Protecting the Flanks: The Battles for Brinkerhoff's Ridge and East Cavalry Field, July 2-3, 1863.* Eric will join us shortly for an interview.

Back at Culp's Hill, meanwhile, the fight was not going well for the Confederates. With Maryland Steuart's brigade completely stalled on the slopes of Culp's lower Hill under heavy artillery fire, the Confederates concentrated their efforts on taking Culp's upper hill. Col. Jesse M. Williams' Louisiana troops, supported by James Walker's Stonewall brigade, attacked the same ground bled over the evening before, with the same results. The meager Union force under General Pap Greene has been heavily reinforced, not just by units from the XII Corps but from the V and VI corps as well. The inability to capture the Union high ground had been apparent to most of the Confederates for hours. It was not until about 10:00 a.m.,

COLONEL
ARIO PARDEE JR.

however, that a change of tactics took place and Steuart's brigade shifted left to attack across a cleared patch of ground northwest of Spangler's Spring. This also failed when Union muskets blasted back the exhausted Rebels. Later in the morning, a counter-charge by a Union brigade under Col. Charles Candy reinforced the Union success, as did a sustained volume of infantry fire by Lt. Col. Ario Pardee, Jr.'s 147th Pennsylvania (which is why the meadow over which his lead flew was rechristened Pardee Field).

Near the end of the morning, presumably in an attempt to exploit the lack of progress on the Confederate side, two Union regiments attacked across Spangler's Meadow farther south near the spring. The unfortunate men ran into fresh Confederate reinforcements under Brig. Gen. William "Extra Billy" Smith and were shot down by the score, the 2nd Massachusetts losing half its number.

Why the Confederates insisted upon attacking Culp's Hill for as long as they did is something of a mystery to me. The position when even modestly manned so favored the tactical defense that assaulting it seemed madness. When you walk the ground—or even look at photographs—the strength of the position nearly shouts at you. Ewell had refused to attack Cemetery Hill at the end of Day One with the beaten Union troops streaming up the long mostly

BRIGADIER GENERAL WILLIAM "EXTRA BILLY" SMITH

open slope, but spent two days fighting for inches on ground once defended, he could never have taken. Or at least that is how it seems to me. Why didn't he tell Lee it was a bad idea and ask that his corps be used in a different capacity? Perhaps Union general Alpheus Williams said it best when he wrote, "The wonder is that the rebels persisted so long in an attempt that the first half hour must have told them was useless." The final result was that Meade maintained the northern end of the Fishhook and significantly strengthened it. The Confederates, on the other hand, expended resources they could not spare: nearly 2,800 men killed, wounded, or missing, compared to perhaps 1,100 Federals.

The single story from Culp's Hill that always tugs at my heart strings involves the Culp family, who owned the hill at the time of the battle. Henry Culp had a pair of nephews named John Wesley Culp and William Culp. The brothers joined opposing sides, with Wesley enlisting in the 2nd Virginia Infantry (the Stonewall Brigade) and William in the 87th Pennsylvania Infantry. In a magnificent twist of irony, the short bearded Private Wesley tramped back into Pennsylvania. Soon, he was fighting for Culp's Hill. He was killed there on his family property during the last hours of fighting. His body was never recovered, so where his remains were interred is unknown.

Preparations

As Ewell's bloody fight was winding down and Longstreet was reluctantly organizing his forces for the grand attack against the right-center of the Union line, the Federals were preparing to receive it. Meade was now wholly comfortable holding his ground and fighting a defensive action, and the strength of the Fishhook was no longer in doubt. His right was secure, and the Confederates did not appear to be making any renewed effort against his left.

He and Hancock rode the lines, moving units into position here and there to shore up potential weak spots. Meade predicted earlier that day that Lee would attack his center if he attacked again, but he hadn't done much to strengthen Hancock's position.

Meade probably found out Stuart was in the vicinity after the Hunterstown clash, and had the foresight to position Union cavalry under Brig. Gen. David Gregg along the Hanover Road behind the Union right flank. Gregg had with him the brigades of Brig. Gen. George Armstrong Custer and Col. John B. McIntosh. If the Rebels made a move against his right-rear, the Union cavalry would be ready. (The left flank was too

BRIGADIER GENERAL ALEXANDER HAYS

rocky and wooded for large-scale mounted actions.) Custer's men were positioned near the Hanover Road and the Low Dutch Road, less than two miles south of Cress Ridge where Stuart was contemplating waging a battle.

Like the preceding two days, July 3 was also shaping up to be a hot one. Fortunately for historians, the Reverend Doctor Michael Jacobs of Pennsylvania College, a professor of mathematics and science, recorded the weather three times a day, including temperature and cloud conditions. Because of that we know the temperature on July 3 hit the high 80s by mid-afternoon. The sky was clear, but the humidity high because of an approaching rainstorm.

Despite the fact that two of the three divisions slated for the main attack (plus Anderson's pair of brigades under Wilcox and Lang) belonged to A. P. Hill's Corps, Lee put Longstreet in overall charge. Longstreet called upon E. P. Alexander very early that morning to organize and position his artillery for the "sizable" barrage Lee requested before the attack. Alexander, you will recall, was put in command of Longstreet's artillery the previous day, and on July 3 given an even larger role. Lee's nominal chief of artillery, Brig. Gen. William N. Pendleton, was more of a figurehead than tactical leader, and relegated to

BRIGADIER
GENERAL
WILLIAM N.
PENDLETON

organizing the artillery from Ewell's and Hill's corps that would follow up the infantry and offer fire support.

Throughout the morning, the energetic Alexander placed artillery pieces and their limbers along a line stretching from the captured Sherfy Peach Orchard on the right (which the Confederates believed was a much stronger artillery platform than it proved to be) angling northwest across the open fields and then northward along Seminary Ridge. Including pieces from Ewell's Corps that would also participate, the Confederates amassed about 160 guns (sources conflict on this). It was the largest artillery concentration in North America to that time. I get a sense of the size of the effort each time I pass the woods next to the McMillan House on West Confederate Avenue and move southward down the ridge; one gun after another are pointed at Cemetery Ridge. The Federals had somewhat fewer cannon directly opposite on Cemetery Ridge, but there were others on Little Round Top and Cemetery Hill within range. The latter point would play an especially deadly role in the upcoming exchange.

The Confederates had to deal with a serious problem the Union army did not: Lee's guns populated a long exterior line, with few outstanding artillery platforms from which to concentrate them for an effective cross-fire. The same was not true for Meade, whose guns had been magnificently placed by General Hunt, an aggressive gunner who relished the thought of unleashing his cannon against any attacking Rebel infantry.

Out of sight of the Union forces behind the tree line west of Seminary Ridge is where the infantry under Pickett, Pettigrew, and Trimble assembled for the upcoming assault. Pickett's division aligned itself in the eastern reaches of Spangler's Woods, while the brigades of Trimble and Pettigrew assembled farther north well left of Pickett. The number of infantry involved in the attack varies widely. Original estimates were rounded to 15,000, but more modern studies generally agree the number was closer to 12,000–12,500.

The arsenal on Seminary Ridge.

The 38-year-old George Pickett was something of a dandy—a romantic in love with a 19-year-old named LaSale "Sallie" Corbell, whom he would marry later that year. One of Longstreet's favorites, the Virginian obtained a brigadier general's commission fairly early (January 1862) without having seen any combat. It was there his good luck took a turn. His solid performance at the head of his brigade on the Peninsula in the spring came with the price of a severe shoulder wound that kept him off the field during much of the army's high tide through Sharpsburg. He was promoted to major general and given a division of two brigades (his own going to Richard Garnett) soon expanded to five, but was barely engaged at the great defensive victory at Fredericksburg, and missed the stunning offensive victory at Chancellorsville altogether because of his detachment around Suffolk to forage. Pickett's late arrival at Gettysburg was not of his doing, but his was the only fresh division left in the army, and Lee intended to throw it directly at the enemy over a mile of open ground. Somehow, Pickett was happy with this turn of events.

The commanders of Pickett's three fresh Virginia brigades at Gettysburg—Richard G. Garnett, Lewis A. Armistead, and James L. Kemper—were all brigadier generals of long-standing and familiar to their men. Because the men had missed so much action as well as the first two days of

MAJOR GENERAL GEORGE E. PICKETT

Gettysburg, they were anxious to get at the enemy and prove their worth. Pickett would tell E. P. Alexander as much right before the attack began.

The other two divisions had been heavily battered on July 1, and many of their officers killed or wounded. With Heth absent wounded, the inexperienced Pettigrew was now in charge of the four-brigade division. Two of the brigade's four leaders (Davis and Brockenbrough) were unsuited to brigade command. Pettigrew's own brigade would go in under its senior colonel, James Marshall, as would James Archer's small battered command under Col. Birkett Fry. A small demi-division of two brigades (James Lane's and Alfred Scales') was given to Isaac Trimble, who had accompanied the army north but had no formal command and was unfamiliar to the men. Lane was with his men, but Scales' North Carolinians were put into the attacking line under Col. William Lowrance.

Conversation with an Expert: Chuck Teague — Observations on Day Three:

GNMP Seasonal Ranger Chuck Teague lives in the Gettysburg Historical District, where he and his wife built their retirement home. In addition to serving as a Borough Councilman, he has been a substitute teacher at the high school, a volunteer police and hospital chaplain, and a facilitator for troubled families. Not only was he a full-time career officer in the military [Chuck retired as an Air Force Lt. Colonel], but he has also served his country in the Army National Guard and the Army Reserve. After attending Gettysburg College and later law school, he practiced law for 10 years and served as a pastor for 23 years. As he puts it, "I retired from all my careers in 2003, became a Park Ranger, and, having had three heavy meals, entered the *dessert* phase of my life."

"What intrigues you most about the battle?" I ask.

CHUCK TEAGUE

"That the story is not settled!" he replies. "There are a number of pieces to this battle that are not clearly understood, or are mysteries. We're dependent on soldiers' accounts, and they didn't agree about what went on here." Chuck then quotes General Abner Doubleday: "You can only understand what went on in your immediate front."

"You can see," he continues, "how that would leave a great many gaps in the record. There were about 300 major battles in the Civil War. I want to get a handle on those related to Gettysburg. But truthfully, you'll never even get to the bottom of what went on here."

The topic turned to the third day. "Lee had a sensible, clear plan—he was confident. He now had ample artillery, infantry, and cavalry at his disposal, positioned where they could make a difference, and he planned a bold assault he believed would dislodge the Yankees from Cemetery Hill. It is revealing that one of the key men here, Confederate Brig. Gen. James Kemper, observed that what had been written 23 years after the battle [by way of analysis] was fantasy and mostly based on Federal perspectives—assumptions that have become part of the folklore of the battle: Lee was desperate, and after having been thwarted in attacking the enemy's flanks he sought to strike their center; Pickett's division waited in the woods; it was intended to be a frontal assault; the objective was the Copse [of Trees]; the tactics were to split the Union line on Cemetery Ridge."

Chuck next addresses the issue of Confederate over-shots during the cannonade: "The Yankee guns were likewise firing long. People who watch movies and reenactments don't realize that there was a 9–12-foot recoil when a cannon was fired, with the trail of the gun repeatedly pressing the ground behind. Even a half-inch difference would cause the muzzle to be elevated enough to make a difference in range, but the artillerists under fire never made the adjustment." The tragedy for the Rebels, he notes, "is that their infantry was waiting on the slope behind their artillery line," and for them "the cry of mortal agony could be heard every minute."

Chuck thinks Jeb Stuart's mission that day is often misperceived. "Lee expected him to swing around and get into the rear of the Union army, but that wasn't the back slope of Cemetery Ridge," he explains. "The rear of the army is its vital line of operations, which reaches to its supporting assets and, if the position collapses, becomes the route of retreat." For the Yankees, their rear was along the Baltimore Pike extending to Westminster. "Had the Rebel artillery and infantry succeeded in dislodging the Federals, Lee's expectation was that the panicked Union forces would be streaming down the pike right into the arms of Confederate cavalry." Lee said he wanted to "ruin," to "destroy" the enemy army. If that was to be the case, he could not let it get away. Chuck identifies Brig. Gen. David Gregg as deserving of as much honor as Custer in thwarting Stuart. [The cavalry fight on East Cavalry Field is discussed below.]

Where Did Lee Intend to Attack?

The massive Confederate infantry assault can be viewed as a demonstration of raw courage, sheer stupidity, or both. The fact that it was not a brilliant offensive plan is, for the most part, universally accepted. General Lee had determined after the course of two days of heavy fighting that a final coordinated attack against the right-center of the Union line would break apart Meade's army and drive it from the high ground. As we know, not all of his subordinates agreed with him. But was it a general attack, or an attack against a specific location?

It appears that Lee decided to strike the vicinity south of Cemetery Hill

from Ziegler's Grove (the right-center of Meade's line) down Cemetery Ridge. Several hundred yards south of the grove, accompanied by a tight group of trees that look like one tree, is "The Angle" [where a low stone wall running parallel to the ridge making a 90-degree turn west, and then turns back south once more]. Just slightly farther on, past The Angle is the famous Copse of Trees—which historian John Bachelder declared to be the focal point of Lee's attack. He also coined the area as the Confederate High-Water-Mark.

Bachelder was an accomplished painter and photographer who had accompanied the Union army on some of its campaigns. His primary life's work, at least what he is most known for, was his superb dedication to

BRIGADIER GENERAL JAMES L. KEMPER

documenting the battle of Gettysburg, and especially where the individual units fought on that sprawling and often confusing field. His untiring efforts played a large role in preserving and memorializing it for future generations.

After the war, a Virginia veteran from Pickett's division pointed out to Bachelder where they had attacked on July 3, and mentioned they had marched toward a small patch of scrub oak (where the Copse of Trees are today). It was Bachelder who came up with "Copse of Trees" tag line, helping to create the mystique that still surrounds that little umbrella-shaped group of trees (the most visited area on the entire battlefield). At the time of the battle, however, the trees were much smaller and General Lee probably never noticed anything special about them. None of the trees there today are "witness" trees; the originals were cut down by the local landowner after the battle. The ones you see today were planted in their place. If Lee had a single objective it may have been Ziegler's Grove which was there during the battle, but is mostly gone today. It was something of a joint in the long Union line. Anyway, the idea the Confederates would try to cross a mile of open ground and then under heavy fire funnel everyone toward a small spot always seemed rather nonsensical to me.

With the men now in position, the fighting at Culp's Hill winding down, and the Union forces on Cemetery Ridge waiting anxiously for whatever was coming next, the scene was set for the most famous charge in American history.

The Cannonade

At approximately 1:00 p.m., the Confederate artillery opened fire. Longstreet's order: "Let the batteries open, order great care and precision in firing." The Union batteries eventually responded with some 80 guns, the terrain hampering placement of more front-line pieces. Meade's army, however, had at least that number again in reserve, along with plentiful

BRIGADIER GENERAL J. JOHNSTON PETTIGREW

ammunition. Artillery chief Hunt makes sure the Union batteries return fire slowly and carefully to save ammunition and make every shot count. Noise and smoke did not interest Hunt; only results mattered.

This exchange is widely considered

BRIGADIER GENERAL LEWIS A. ARMISTEAD

MAJOR GENERAL ISAAC R. TRIMBLE

the largest pure artillery battle of the Civil War. The sound produced by close to 250 cannon was overwhelming and reportedly heard as far away as Philadelphia and Baltimore. The concussion damaged the ears of many of the men firing the guns. Within minutes the powder smoke on this still and hot July day nearly obscured the visibility on the field. The Rebels especially had trouble seeing through the smoke to determine where their shots were landing, and the natural tendency was to shoot high. They did the best they could, but their window of success was very small. Any undershot hit the front of the ridge, and any overshot of even a few feet sailed far into the rear and mostly exploded harmlessly there. (General Meade fled his headquarters at the Leister Farm for Power's Hill when shells dropped around his house and grounds.) Although unnerving at first, the Union men hugging Cemetery Ridge quickly got used to the noise and realized it was much worse than the bite. When Union troops overshot, the rounds fell among the Confederate troops

The storied "Copse of Trees."

behind their blazing artillery line massing for the attack. The iron rained on them mixed with deadly wood splinters.

It is important to note here that Union artillery ammunition was much better and more reliable than Confederate ammunition. Southern gunpowder was extraordinarily good, but Southern fuses were often defective. When and where they would explode—or if they would explode at all—was an expensive gamble and anyone's guess.

In a stroke of genius, as the Confederate guns pounded away, General Hunt gave the order for his artillery to gradually cease firing. He wanted to save ammunition for the coming infantry attack, and give the enemy the impression the Union guns were being destroyed or running out of ammunition and leaving the field. Winfield Scott Hancock, whose II Corps men hunkered down to wait out the barrage, and would have to repel the coming attack, was furious with the decision and contradicted Hunt. Hancock wanted to keep the guns firing to keep up the morale of his own men. The conflict led to a lifelong war of words between the two generals. (Once the Confederate assault began, some of Hancock's batteries were already out of long-range ammunition and had only shorter-range canister to throw at the gray infantry. The batteries that followed Hunt's directive to conserve plenty of ammunition had plenty on hand once Pickett's, Pettigrew's, and Trimble's men stepped out of the woods.)

The view from Cemetery Ridge looking across the valley to Seminary Ridge.
The Virginia Monument is the white speck to the left center.

Throughout the bombardment, Meade spent his time adjusting the placement of both infantry and artillery units so that when all was said and done, about 13,000 men—or roughly the same number that would be thrown at his position—would bear the brunt of the attack. Hancock was doing much the same, riding his line, giving orders, adjusting guns and men, and offering words of encouragement.

How Long?

Just how long the great cannonade lasted is anyone's guess. Watches back then were not synchronized—some were not even on the same hour!—and no one agrees. The troops had been on campaign for weeks, so how well a watch kept time also mattered. Most agree the bombardment opened at 1:07 p.m. Alexander later explained that he intended Pickett should advance within just 15 or 20 minutes of the opening of his guns, and that he wrote his first note to Pickett about 1:30 p.m.: "If you are coming at all you must come immediately or I cannot give you proper support; but the enemy's fire has not slackened materially, and at least 18 guns are still firing from the Cemetery itself." (Longstreet had put the burden on Alexander to notify Pickett once the guns achieved the expected results, so the infantry could then advance. Why he did this, and whether it was justified, could warrant an entirely different book!)

Like Hunt, Porter Alexander knew if his guns continued to fire at their current rate, they would soon run out of ammunition. Unlike their Union counterparts, the Rebel gunners were far from their logistical base and running low on fixed (artillery) ammunition. When Alexander noticed the fire from Cemetery Hill diminishing, he sent Pickett his second and final message about 10 or 15 minutes after the first one: "For God's sake come quick; the 18 guns have gone. Come quick or my ammunition will not let me support you properly." Several Union batteries had ceased firing, and some even appearing to be withdrawing. What none of the Confederates knew was that Hunt had ordered the firing stopped, and that fresh Union batteries and ammunition were on the way to the front.

When the first message arrived Pickett rode over to a sullen Longstreet, showed him the message, and asked, "General, shall I advance?" Longstreet was more convinced than ever that the attack was sure to be a bloody failure, and reluctant to give his reply. Instead, he turned away. Exactly what he said, or how or whether he conveyed permission, remains vague. Pickett replied, "I am going to move forward, sir," and rode off. He did not receive Alexander's second note until he returned to his division. Its receipt confirmed to Pickett that now was the time to go.

All of this suggests the bombardment last perhaps 45 minutes, if that. Some witnesses, however, thought it lasted for as long as two hours. We will never know for sure. Regardless, once the Southern fire slackened the Confederate infantry stepped out and begin its infamous march into history.

Conversation with an Expert: Matt Atkinson— Observations on the Third Day

If ever you are ever seeking a ranger with personality, Matt Atkinson fits the bill. Possessed of a slightly wicked sense of humor, the classic twinkle in his eye and a vast knowledge of Gettysburg and all things related to the Civil War, Matt is the epitome of a gregarious and charismatic Park Ranger Interpreter. Born and raised in Houston, Mississippi, Matt went on to college at "Ole Miss" and completed both a B.B.A. in General Business and a B.A. in History. He decided that teaching was not for him and landed instead a part-time job at the Petersburg National Battlefield. It was there, he explains with a vestige of his southern accent, that he discovered "My boss was getting paid to shoot a cannon—that's the life. The Civil War has always been my hobby—and now I get paid for it, too!"

One of the first things I ask Matt is how he got hooked on Gettysburg. Being from Mississippi, I would have thought he'd be more attracted to one of South's famous battlefields. Matt's answer is simple and catches me by surprise. He smiles broadly and offers two words: "We lost!"

MATT ATKINSON

One of Matt's ancestors served with the 11th Mississippi (part of Joe Davis' brigade). He missed the first day guarding wagons, but sallied out across the fields between Seminary and Cemetery ridges on July 3 and was killed in Pickett's Charge. "The words freedom and independence are interchangeable for both sides," he comments. "Men willing to die for their country whether it be the USA or the CSA." Matt began his tenure at Gettysburg in 1999, and is a full-time ranger. His wife Angie, who grew up in York County, PA, is a Supervisory Park Ranger. I can only imagine their conversations over the dinner table—perhaps a touch of Carville and Matalin? As far as Matt is concerned, "Gettysburg is the Super Bowl . . . the Taj Mahal. Don't go to other Civil War battlefields and tell them you've been to Gettysburg—you'll just make them feel bad."

"Day Three is notable for the sheer drama of it all," opines Matt, "like a play being acted out with an impending crescendo that hasn't happened yet." Clearly, for Matt, the larger scope of each day's actions draws his focus. "Faulkner was right," he says. "Every Southern boy imagines what might have been. Most visitors don't realize the scope and complexity of Pickett's Charge," he continues. "Lee and Longstreet only had the morning to plan the assault. Think about the details that would go into that plan for a moment, and in such a short amount of time. The generals want to send eleven brigades across an open field that measures a mile in length and a mile in width to have them all arrive at approximately the same place on Cemetery Ridge. Not to mention the preparation that went into the artillery bombardment. Of course, the original assault plan did not survive the first shot. First, the artillery bombardment, on which so much depended, proved ineffective. Second, the small details about the advance escaped Longstreet. For instance, he forgot to designate a 'Brigade of Direction'—in other words, the unit on which the brigades to the right and left of it would align upon. Birkett Fry's unit was chosen just as the brigades started forward in the attack. To compound the problem, Pickett's Division, which had the shortest distance to go, started forward first—leaving Pettigrew and Trimble's divisions in the position of having to make up the distance. Third, Pettigrew's (Heth's) division, had suffered extensive casualties on July 1 and was grievously undermanned, and should not have been included in the attack. The list goes on and on. Despite all the obstacles, it is a real tribute to the officers and valor of the Confederate soldiers that the attack even had, in the end, a slim chance of success."

Knowing of Matt's wonderful sense of humor, the question almost begs itself: Any favorite questions from the many tours you've conducted? "Certainly," comes his prompt reply. On the silly side was the question, 'Was the Battle of Gettysburg fought here?' On the not-so-silly side, 'If General Lee was so smart how come he lost?'" Matt has also spent a great deal of time studying Dan Sickles; perhaps he'll write a book someday.

The Charge Goes Forward, but the Union Line Holds

As the bombardment reached its fitful ending, Meade moved from his rearmost headquarters on Power's Hill closer to the position being held by Hancock's II Corps; he knew the infantry assault was about to begin.

As he was doing so, Rebel foot soldiers in three divisions (nine brigades total) from Spangler's Woods in the south to the McMillan House in the north—about 12,000 troops—emerged into the hot afternoon sun forming a line of battle stretching about one mile in length! (Two brigades under Wilcox and Lang would make a late appearance on Pickett's right, stepping out of Pitzer's Woods once it was clear the attack had failed. If considered part of the main attack, the charge consisted of 11 brigades). From the Macmillan Woods stepped the battered divisions under Generals Pettigrew (in front) and Issac Trimble (behind). Pickett's Virginians moved out from the area of Spangler's Woods. From the Union lines, it must have been a frightening sight to behold.

Given their general objective on northern Cemetery Ridge, Pettigrew and Trimble could traverse the open fields between the respective ridges pretty much dead-on. Pickett's division, however, was well to the south and a large gap of several hundred yards existed between these two columns. In order to combine the attacks into one punch, Pickett's men would have to execute a swing to their left to reach the objective. This was a tall order under fire, and also risked exposing their right flank to artillery fire from lower Cemetery Ridge and Little Round Top, as well as infantry fire when the Rebels approached close enough for that to matter. (I have often wondered why such a large gap existed at all, but have never had it satisfactorily explained.)

Whether the focal point was the Copse of Trees, Ziegler's Grove, or somewhere else on the ridge, there was no doubt Hancock's II Corps would bear the brunt of the attack. Along with attached artillery, the II Corps had the

COLONEL JAMES MARSHAL

divisions of Generals Hays and Gibbon straight in front of the charge, with Caldwell's division and Doubleday's division of the I Corps close by farther south. Other Federal units from the III, V and VI corps were also within reinforcement range. It is important to keep in mind that, except for Ewell's Second Corps off to the north and Stuart's cavalry engaging Gregg beyond the Confederate left flank, most of the Southern army is arrayed in a long rather thin line just behind the three attacking divisions. Most of those men are worn out and suffered grievously during the first two days of battle. With his interior lines, Meade's entire army is much closer to the center of Cemetery Ridge than most of Lee's, and many of his units are fresher.

When the Confederate infantry stepped out, two Confederate brigades in Pettigrew's division lagged behind: Col. Brockenbrough's small Virginia brigade on the extreme left and Joe Davis' next to it on its right. Many of their men had to run to catch up. Some of the infantry succumbed early to the stifling heat and humidity. Meade's artillery commenced firing once more. The shot and shell tore large gaps in the lines, which other soldiers quickly filled as they continued on. The horrific canister rounds would come later when the Confederates infantry stepped within that killing range.

As the Confederate advance continued, Pickett's division came under intense fire from the guns on Little Round Top and others on lower Cemetery Ridge. Garnett and Kemper (front line), and Armistead (in the rear) suffered as a result. On the northern end of the line, Brockenbrough's command bore the brunt of holding the extreme left of the line, its flank open to a shower of lead and iron. Before long it fell apart under the withering fire of the 8th Ohio, which had moved forward to enfilade the Rebel formation. The Virginians tumbled to the rear. One brigade was already out of the fight. Pickett's brigades spent a couple minutes reforming in a swale and then stepped out and angled left (to the northeast) in an effort to strike farther north along the ridge and close the distance with Pettigrew and Trimble.

Most accounts agree the majority of the Confederate infantry reached the vicinity of the Emmitsburg Road. No one, however, had been sent ahead to knock down the heavy fencing lining both sides of the route. As a result, the Rebels took significant casualties climbing the high barrier or standing there trying to tear it down. Either way the men had to reform, and they were within killing distance of thousands of rifled-muskets by this time. It was at this point that many of the soldiers simply refused to go farther. Some returned fire from around the road, and others began the long trek back to Seminary Ridge. Many hundreds more continued up the slope.

COLONEL BIRKITT D. FRY

On the left Confederate front, parts of Davis' brigade and soldiers from the brigades of Pettigrew (James Marshall) and Archer (Birkett Fry) reorganize and press ahead up the slope toward the crest. It was about this time the dreaded canister fire, together with a more concentrated musket fire, strikes them.

On the Confederate right, Pickett's brigades also cross the Emmitsburg Road (though how many will never be known), but the crisp alignment they arrived with is now mostly gone. Like their comrades to the left, the men now bunch more closely together, their parade-like lines merging into masses of bayonets and bodies struggling ahead against a storm of lead and iron.

It was about this time that Brig. Gen. George Stannard's large Vermont brigade swung out a giant hinge and fired into the exposed right flanks of Kemper's and Garnett's brigades. Back near Seminary Ridge, Confederate gunner Porter Alexander saw the threat to Pickett's right and tried to interdict it with fire. As Union Lt. Col. Edmund Rice recounted, "A Confederate battery, near the Peach Orchard, commenced firing, probably at the sight of Harrow's men leaving their line and closing to the right upon Pickett's column. A cannon-shot tore a horrible passage through the dense crowd of men in blue,

BRIGADIER GENERAL GEORGE J. STANNARD

who were gathering outside the trees; instantly another shot followed, and fairly cut a road through the mass."

It was also about this time that Hancock fell with a severe wound in his upper thigh-groin area that required he be removed from the field.

The pieces were in place for the unfolding of one of the most frequently cited acts of Union bravery. Federal battery commander Alonzo Cushing and his guns were firing from "The Angle" just north of the Copse of Trees. The 22-year-old veteran had already been wounded during the bombardment and his battery knocked to a shambles. Rather than evacuate, Cushing rolled a pair of guns forward closer to the low stone wall. It was there, in the very face of Armistead's massed Virginians flooding up to the barrier that he fired canister into the enemy and suffered his cruel fate.

Although cited for gallantry after the battle, it was not until 2014 that Cushing was posthumously awarded the Medal of Honor. Part of his official citation reads as follows: "As the Confederate Forces closed in, First Lieutenant Cushing was struck in the mouth by an enemy bullet and fell dead beside his gun. His gallant stand and fearless leadership inflicted severe casualties upon Confederate Forces and opened wide gaps in their lines, directly impacting the Union Forces' ability to repel Pickett's Charge. First Lieutenant Cushing's extraordinary heroism and selflessness above and beyond the call of duty, at the cost of his own life, are in keeping with the highest traditions of military service and reflect great credit upon himself, Battery A, 4th U.S. Artillery, Army of the Potomac, and the United States Army."

The men that killed Cushing probably belonged to Armistead's command, although by this time Garnett's men were heavily mixed in with them. A small number of Virginians surged over the stone wall, and with the gallant Armistead near the front, stormed ahead. Armistead had impaled his hat on a sword so his men could see it. Waving it above his head he urged his men on. The Rebel

The Angle near The Copse of Trees

general had been a close friend of Hancock's before the war, which makes their duel fates within yards of one another especially ironic. Armistead led his men on foot inside "The Angle" and with some of his men overran Cushing's abandoned guns. Armistead has just placed a hand on one of them when he was wounded twice. Although the injuries were not considered serious, he died two days later. The fighting Irishmen of the 69th Pennsylvania held their ground here with other Union men, some engaging the enemy in hand-to-hand combat.

Elements of other Union brigades on the right of Pickett's attacking Confederates—Stannard's Vermonters, as well as the 71st, 72nd, and 106th Pennsylvania—continued pouring a devastating musket fire into the crowded Virginians. All the while, additional Union units were moving up to help defend the embattled ridge. Despite their bravery, the Virginians were too few to make a difference. Most who made it over the wall surrendered or were shot down. Hundreds of others were scampering back toward the Emmitsburg Road and beyond, challenging fate a second time by trying to get back safely.

The most famous charge in American history had reached its grisly end.

*   *   *

It is like a magnet in the way it draws your attention. You can see it from so many places on the sprawling battlefield. From the Lee monument area the fields that carried the shoes, boots, and hooves of "Pickett's Charge" from west to east looks pretty much level until you get to the Emmitsburg Road, where it lightly slopes up to the Union position atop Cemetery Ridge. Looks are deceiving, and you have to walk it to figure out that the geography is lying to you. And you absolutely should cross here. Many thousands of visitors do each year.

I don't want to interrupt that narrative too much, but I think it is worth commenting on a couple things. The first thing that strikes me every time I walk across is how vulnerable the infantry was in 1863—it is painfully obvious as you tread across. There is no cover of any kind. Second, what looks flat—isn't level at all. There are swales out there that gobble you up, and from which you can no longer see the Union position or Seminary Ridge. (There was an ongoing feud between Virginians and North Carolinians after the war. The former argued that Pettigrew's men never crossed the road, or if they did they never much approached the stone wall. An expert on one of the walks pointed out to me that there are places on the walk not far from the Emmitsburg Road that Pickett's men could have looked north—off to their left—and not seen much of anything. This might have made them think their comrades had already fled, when if fact most of them had not.)

The Confederate "High-Water Mark" Memorial. *Library of Congress*

The George Gordon Meade Equestrian Statue on Cemetery Ridge.

The next thing that strikes me is the disruptiveness of the fencing along Emmitsburg Road, and how steep the final couple hundred yards are on the way to the Angle. It is a hike! By that time the Rebs must have been thoroughly exhausted and more than a bit worried about the attack's potential. Once you reach the stone wall and the Angle north of the Copse of Trees, turn around and look back; the strength of the Union position is overwhelming. If you don't want to walk the field, you can get out of your car on Cemetery Ridge and walk a short distance to the Angle.

Each time I visit the Angle, I place my hand on one of Cushing's guns, think about Armistead, sword up, hat likely down near the sword guard, and I walk to his memorial. I then move to my left (south) along the stone wall that slowly bends a bit back toward the Copse of Trees. Near the base of the trees is the High-Water Mark Memorial. Look west across the mile of open fields toward the Lee Monument and ponder what happened here. The bodies are long gone (though it is not unlikely some still remain buried out there), and the carnage that took place is—let's face it—unimaginable to modern sensibilities. How could anyone stand and receive that attack, let along make such a charge to begin with? And then I hear echoing in my head the words of the greatest poet who ever lived: "Cry Havoc! And let slip the dogs of war!" Never have I witnessed a place that brings home to me the true meaning of that phrase.

"It was All My Fault"

The retreating Rebel survivors fell back under a hail of continuing fire. How many fell just trying to make it back to Seminary Ridge will never be known, but surely it was significant. Union Gen. Alexander Hays, in responding to a burst of gunfire from part of his line, helped end the killing when he trotted

MAJOR SAMUEL H. STARR

over dragging a captured Confederate flag behind his horse. "Stop firing, you [——] fools; don't you know enough to stop firing!" he yelled. "It's all over—stop! stop! stop!"

The cost of this attack was almost unimaginable: approximately 5,600 Confederates had been killed, wounded, or captured, matched against some 1,500 Federals.

In the wake of the disaster, General Lee rode amongst his defeated men telling them "The fault is mine, but it will be right in the end," and they should rally and prepare to repulse the enemy. In one of the saddest exchanges of the war, Lee came across General Pickett and asked about the state of his division. Pickett replied, "General Lee, I have no division." (Pickett's report of the attack was rejected by Lee, who asked him to rewrite it. Apparently, he never did, and the original has never turned up.)

The Battle of Fairfield

The cavalry fight at Fairfield just eight miles to the west on Day Three is not considered part of the Battle of Gettysburg, but of course is part of the campaign. How some historians reach this conclusion is beyond me because it had some very important consequences for Lee. It began just before the opening of the Confederate cannonade.

On the morning of the 3rd, a farmer reported to Wesley Merritt, a newly appointed Union cavalry brigadier, he had seen a large unguarded Confederate supply train over near Fairfield. Merritt, in an ill-advised move, orders just one regiment, the 6th US Cavalry (some 400 men), to find the train and hold the town, with an eye to preventing the Fairfield Road from becoming a line of retreat for the Confederates. The relatively inexperienced regiment is led by an elderly martinet named Maj. Samuel H. Starr, and the unnecessarily harsh Capt. George Cram. On the Confederate side, elements of the 7th Virginia, and later the 6th and 11th Virginia Cavalry, are led by Brig. Gen. William E. "Grumble" Jones.

The action started about 12:30 p.m. The small group of Yankees sent ahead to find the wagons enjoyed some success in their initial advance against Confederate pickets, but were hampered in their charge by a series of fences and stone walls. Soon, additional elements of the 7th Virginia Cavalry appeared on the scene. The Yankees realized they were completely outnumbered and headed back south. Starr, however, eager for a self-glorifying cavalry action, led most of his men into position south of the James A. Marshall farmhouse and deployed mounted and dismounted

BRIGADIER GENERAL WILLIAM E. "GRUMBLE" JONES

troopers on either side of the road along a high ridge. (Cram had been sent with a few dozen men along a railroad grade to Starr's left to watch that flank, and would not join the battle until the end.)

The troopers of the 7th Virginia, eager for a fight themselves, charged the position but ran into the same difficulties with the fences and walls, as well as the .52 caliber breech-loading Sharps carbines of the Union troopers. The effort was thrown back. With the arrival of the 6th Virginia, Jones ordered an artillery battery into a nearby field, which opened fire to good effect. Starr, on the other hand, has no artillery with

BRIGADIER GENERAL WESLEY MERRITT

BRIGADIER
GENERAL
JUDSON
"KILL-CAVALRY"
KILPATRICK

him. The battle continued, with each side briefly gaining the upper hand. Grumble Jones was reported to have said, "Shall one damned regiment of Yankees whip my entire brigade?" The answer to his exhortation was a resounding "no."

The remnants of the 7th Virginia rallied, the 6th Virginia and some additional troopers from the 11th were added into the mix, and a series of well-coordinated attacks turned the tide in the Confederates' favor. Lacking any artillery in support of their mounted unit, and outnumbered almost three to one, the bluecoats fell victim to the repeated Confederate assaults and suffered a resounding

defeat. Of the 424 Union troopers engaged, six are killed, 26 wounded, and 208 missing and presumed captured. Confederate casualties number a total of 34, with eight killed, 21 wounded, and five missing.

The cavalry battles that swirled around the main event where the ten roads came together in southern Pennsylvania were a mixed bag. Hunterstown was something of a draw, but Fairfield was a clear-cut Confederate victory that secured the Hagerstown Road that Lee would use to help evacuate his army. East Cavalry Field—one of the largest mounted battles of the war—was a

COLONEL
JOHN B.
McINTOSH

decisive Union victory. Probably. Maybe. It depends on how you look at it. History can be confusing.

Before we jump to that part of the discussion, let me introduce Brig. Gen. Judson "Kill-Cavalry" Kilpatrick, yet another of the interesting and, without a doubt, controversial Union generals. According to Stephen Sears, Kilpatrick was "all flamboyance and burning ambition. He was mindlessly reckless with the lives of his men, and their nickname for him—'Kill-Cavalry'— was not intended as a compliment." He is one of three cavalry division commanders under the overall command of Maj. Gen. Alfred

COLONEL
JOHN R.
CHAMBLISS

BRIGADIER
GENERAL
ELON J.
FARNSWORTH

Pleasonton, the other two being John Buford, with whom we are already familiar, and David Gregg. Custer commands the 2nd Brigade in Kilpatrick's division and Col. John B. McIntosh leads the 1st Brigade in Gregg's division.

This coterie of Union equestrians was balanced by the large and often flamboyant personalities of their Confederate counterparts. We've met the man in charge, Jeb Stuart, as well as Southern grandee Wade Hampton. The South lacked many things, but it never lacked for capable cavalrymen. Joining Stuart and Hampton at Gettysburg were Brig. Gen. Fitzhugh

BRIGADIER GENERAL FITZHUGH LEE

Lee and Col. John R. Chambliss, both commanding brigades, as did Wade Hampton.

Wait. Another Lee? If you are wondering whether Fitzhugh Lee was related to Robert E., the answer is yes. Fitzhugh was the army commander's nephew. One of General Lee's own sons—Maj. Gen. William Henry Fitzhugh ("Rooney") Lee—was also a general of cavalry, but had been severely wounded at Brandy Station and captured. Of Lee's two other sons, Maj. Gen. George Washington Custis Lee served as aide-de-camp to President Jefferson Davis, and Capt. Robert Edward Lee, Jr. served in the Rockbridge Artillery.

Kilpatrick led Pleasonton's 3rd Division, which included the brigades of Brig. Gens. Elon J. Farnsworth, Wesley Merritt, and George Custer. Horse artillery was divided among the various cavalry brigades. A series of decisions ended up with Kilpatrick moving into the area south of the main battlefield with Farnsworth's brigade, and Custer's brigade remaining farther north in Meade's right-rear near the intersection of the Hanover and Low Dutch roads with Gregg's men.

Custer was there for the big cavalry battle because Gregg had spotted Jeb Stuart's own shift on that front and asked Custer to remain with him—which was the same as asking Custer to violate his orders to follow Kilpatrick. With the Confederate approach promising one of the great cavalry clashes of the war, Gregg told Custer he would welcome his assistance. Not one to miss a fight, Custer replied, "If you will give me an order to remain, I will only be too happy to do it.'" So with Gregg, Custer, McIntosh, and a larger artillery force than the Confederates could muster, Union forces totaled somewhere between 3,250 and 5,000 troopers (estimates among credible sources vary considerably).

Stuart had four brigades with him on Cress Ridge. In addition to his own reliable officers Hampton, Lee, and Chambliss, he had Brig. Gen. Albert G. Jenkins' brigade, now under the command of Col. Milton J. Ferguson (Jenkins

BRIGADIER GENERAL ALBERT G. JENKINS

had been wounded; his brigade was attached to Ewell's Corps during the first phase of the campaign). Including this brigade, Stuart had at hand between 5,000 and 6,500 men. It is a fairly wide swing, but different historians have come up with different numbers—just like with them damn Yankees.

The battle at East Cavalry Field, which deserves more popular acclaim than it has heretofore received, is about to begin. And like the main battle itself, it has a curious beginning.

Despite Stuart's cautious approach to avoid drawing attention to his movement, once he arrives Stuart orders an artillery piece to fire

four rounds in various directions. Historians have come up with two possible motivations for this strange behavior. First, he was letting General Lee know he had arrived in position behind Meade's right flank. That makes no sense at all, however. How on earth would Lee be able to distinguish four discharges from a lone gun firing miles away when hundreds of cannons were conducting the largest barrage in American military history up to that time, all around him? The second possibility is that Stuart was looking for the enemy, a tactic known as "reconnaissance by fire." This makes much more sense. And if that was

COLONEL MILTON J. FERGUSON

Stuart's intent it worked well because Gregg promptly responded. (After the war, one of Stuart's staff officers explained that Stuart fired the cannon as he did simply to get a response from Gregg.)

Conversation with an Expert: Author and Historian Eric Wittenberg—The Cavalry

A full-time lawyer, Eric is a prolific writer and historian on all matters concerning the Union cavalry in the Eastern Theater. He also maintains a blog at "Rantings of a Civil War Historian" at www.civilwarcavalry.com. His first book, *Gettysburg's Forgotten Cavalry Actions*, which I am pleased to say is available once again in an expanded revised Sesquicentennial edition, won the coveted Bachelder-Coddington Literary Award. Since then he has written many more books, and more award-winners.

I had heard several variations surrounding the meeting between Jeb Stuart and Robert E. Lee when Stuart finally arrived in Gettysburg on July 2. Neither man wrote about the meeting, so what they said to one another will remain speculation. What does Eric think?

"We don't know what happened," Eric tells me. "Only four people were present when the meeting occurred: Lee, Stuart, and two officers on Lee's staff, Major Charles Venable and Colonel Charles Marshall. Neither staff officer reported any hostility on Lee's part after the meeting, and not even Stuart—who was notorious for communicating his feelings openly in letters to his wife—discussed anything like that. The one man upon whom some historians base the notion that this meeting was a nasty confrontation, Colonel Thomas Munford, was fifteen miles away at the time. All we have is hearsay." The truth may lie somewhere between the extremes of these various interpretations, explains Eric, and "may be found in a brief comment by Stuart's Adjutant, Major Henry B. McClellan, that 'Lee was short with Stuart.'" Clearly, an understandable reaction on Lee's part, but this is well short of a severe reprimand.

I ask Eric if he agrees with the generally held opinion that Stuart had been ordered by Lee to attack the Federals from the rear on the afternoon of July 3 in coordination with Pickett's attack? Eric scoffs at the idea.

"Let's look at the record," he insists. "Stuart had been ordered by Lee to 'protect the flank.' By Day Three the Union cavalry had four full brigades operating east and south of Ewell's position. An attack by them could have been disastrous for Lee's plan to concentrate on the center and break the Union line with a direct assault there. Now that Lee had Stuart's cavalry force at his disposal once again, he wanted to prevent such an attack. So he had Stuart lead his three and a half brigades of seasoned troopers east and south to confront the Federal cavalry at what has become known as East Cavalry Field.

ERIC
WITTENBERG

Furthermore," adds Eric, "does it make any sense that Stuart would have ordered the retreat of his cavalrymen after just one charge if his orders required him to break into the rear of the main Union position? I think not."

While he was on the subject, Eric observes: "Young General Custer's heroics have been a little exaggerated over the years. No doubt brave—or just foolhardy—he did lead several charges against Stuart's troopers. But to give credit where credit was due, it was General Gregg who ordered those charges, sometimes even going around Custer and speaking directly with the regiment-commanding colonels."

This reminds me of a comment J. D. Petruzzi made, which directly supports Eric's observation about "the notoriously competent David Gregg, who defied orders and stayed in place at the intersection of the Hanover and Low Dutch roads, leading to the massive July 3 cavalry battle at East Cavalry Field." Thanks to cavalry experts Eric and J. D., we may have discovered another of Gettysburg's "unsung heroes."

When Jeb Stuart sallied out east and south of Ewell's flank at the head of his cavalry, Gregg had only McIntosh's brigade of his division at hand, plus Custer's brigade on loan from Kilpatrick. Custer was determined to play a major role here, and he did. He had certainly dressed for the occasion. Quoting once more from Stephen W. Sears in his superb work *Gettysburg*:

> Twenty-three-year old George Custer, West Point '61, youngest brigadier in the Potomac army, was dressed for battle in a sailor's blouse with silver stars on its wide collar points, red cravat, black velveteen hussar's jacket spangled with gold braid, olive corduroy pants, gleaming jackboots, and wide-brimmed felt hat. It was said he looked 'like a circus rider gone mad.' Yet for all the gaudy trappings, George Custer always led his Michigan troopers by example and always from the front.

As cavalry-on-cavalry actions go, this one had it all: ferocious noisy charges, bloody hand-to-hand fighting with pistols, sabers, and fists, and daring single encounters where individual lives hung by a thread (or an ill-aimed saber stroke). The men pushed themselves and their mounts to the point of complete exhaustion.

Stuart's force, deployed in various dispositions around the Rummel Farm, assaulted south toward the Hanover Road intent on brushing aside the Union brigades under Gregg. If he succeeded, a possible route into the rear of the Union lines would be open (see the map here). He might also have been in position to cut off the Baltimore Pike as the Union army's supply or escape route. But the interestingly attired Custer had other ideas. "Come on you Wolverines!" screamed Custer and he set his spurs, waved his saber, and charged headlong into Hampton's front along with several hundred fellow Michiganders. The charge, frankly, shocked the hell out of the Southern riders who were still not used to the recently discovered Union competence. A series of charges and counter-charges followed, blunting Stuart's intentions—whatever they are.

And then the mounted affair got more complex. Dismounted skirmishers and artillery from both sides began their battle in earnest for dominance of the field as Stuart prepared a stronger thrust. During another series of charges by Custer against yet another larger Confederate force, McIntosh, leading cavalry regiments from Pennsylvania and New Jersey, emerged from a line of trees and slammed into Stuart's main body. Yet another series of bloody charges and countercharges ensued. By this time Stuart determined that one of his brigades was running low on ammunition and decided to withdraw north. Maybe he also determined he had accomplished his mission of protecting Lee's flank and retiring from the field was prudent?

Whatever his motivation, Stuart's decision brought the battle of East Cavalry Field to an end. The fighting lasted less than an hour. Despite its intensity and close nature, casualties were not as heavy as one might expect. Union casualties numbered 254—the vast majority of them Custer's men—while Confederate losses were at least 181. (Jenkins' brigade failed to report its losses.) Tactically the battle was a draw—inconclusive at best. If Stuart's goal had been to get his troopers behind Meade's army, the battle was a strategic loss for the Confederates. If his goal was to protect Lee's flank from any potential Union incursion, Stuart was successful (though he likely did not have to fight at all since Gregg was not trying to dig into Lee's flank and rear). See what I mean? History can be so confusing.

I love visiting East Cavalry Field and you will too. It is easily accessible from both Route 30 in the north, from whence came Jeb Stuart and the Confederate

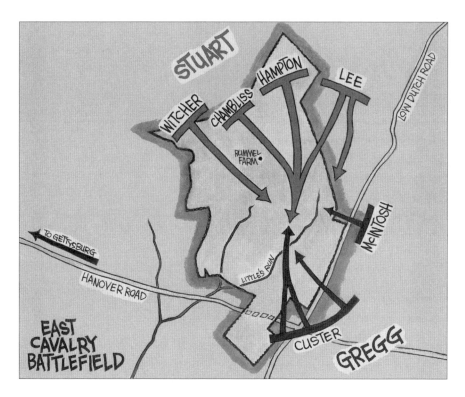

cavalry, or from Route 116 in the south, the position of the Union troopers under Gregg and Custer. It is a lovely undulating open area, through which the NPS has built several access roads. I usually park my car by the roadside along the places I want to see and, with maps in hand walk out to the different monuments placed back from the road denoting the position of the various units that fought the action. Many monuments are close to the roads and so easily viewable from your car. Right in the middle of it all sits the Rummel Farm. It is private property, so don't get too close.

I recommend driving Route 30. It is just a little over half a mile past the intersection with Route 15. Just watch for Cavalry Field Road off to the right. If you approach from the north off 30, you will initially pass through a suburban area. As the road narrows you will see the sign announcing the entrance to the GNMP at the north end of Cavalry Field—pretty much the place where Stuart approached to get the lay of the land and what he might be up against.

If you decide to enter from PA 116 south of East Cavalry Field, the area held by the Union cavalry, be very careful as you will be making a left turn off the little road. The sign is not easy to find, so you will naturally slow down as you watch for it—and, like us on our first visit, you'll undoubtedly have

Stuart's view of the
East Cavalry Battlefield.

someone in an oversized pick-up truck not paying much attention trying to get past you. It can be a terrifying experience, and one in our case compounded by the fact that we were in my little Mini!

This part of the battlefield is interesting for a lot of reasons, but one of them is its absolutely serenity. When entering from the south, off the Hanover Road, you come in on East Cavalry Avenue and cut across the southeast corner to exit back onto the Low Dutch Road; this is in the area occupied by Gregg and Custer. After a very short distance you find the entrance to Gregg Avenue on the left, which takes you back onto the battlefield. Gregg Avenue essentially defines the separation between Stuart's troopers and those of the Union.

After a small jog, the road runs straight west until it turns north and becomes Confederate Cavalry Avenue—same road, different label. There are about 25 monuments and information tablets here. A visit to ECF takes no more than a couple of hours, tops, and this includes several excursions on foot. If you want to stay in your car, browse your maps, and drive slowly along you can cover it easily in less than an hour.

An Overlooked Corner: "Lost Avenue"

Every so often, we find ourselves presented with an opportunity that is just too good to pass up. Have you ever heard of "Lost Avenue?" I hadn't either until Ranger Matt Atkinson mentioned it.

The official name for Lost Avenue—which has an air of mystery about it—is Neill Avenue, named after Union Brig. Gen. Thomas H. Neill. It runs along a secluded hillside on the southern slope of Wolf's Hill. Because it is surrounded by private land it is also almost inaccessible, but there are a convoluted series of small trails leading to it that avoid trespassing on anyone's property. I had no idea where these trails were, and most of my mountain goat-like capabilities faded when I entered my 50s. Matt explained that the best way to see Neill Avenue was to contact Dean Shultz, the owner of the land surrounding this little piece of overlooked history—and hope for permission to see it.

Always on the hunt for more knowledge of the battle and its grounds, I did just that. Mr. Shultz, who could not have been nicer, not only agreed to meet with me, but asked if I'd like to "go up to Lost Avenue?" My luck gaining access to this unusual place was holding—I should have played the lottery that day.

Dean Schultz is an amazingly

DEAN SHULTZ

energetic man in his mid-seventies. Enis and I met him at his office just across the Baltimore Pike from his farm and shared the pleasure of meeting his wife Judy, who helps run his surveying business. Dean enjoys puffing on any one of several corncob pipes—the shorter variety—he has planted around his office.

BRIGADIER GENERAL THOMAS H. NEILL

He puts them down and picks them up as the need arises. Gracious to a fault, he speaks with me while puffing away on one of those ubiquitous corncob pipes. It was then I noticed two small bent metal rods stuffed into a back pocket—a project he had been working on around the farm and had forgotten to remove before he met us, I tell myself. We walk to the farmhouse to make a brief stop for Mr. Shultz to change into boots. The refurbished interior is just as charming as the exterior. Dean points out several bloodstains on the wooden floor beneath one of his rugs. This farm was behind Union lines, and like nearly all of the buildings at Gettysburg, served as a hospital. Dean really does have

The Peter Barker Farm now owned by Dean and Judy Shultz.

these corncob pipes all over the place because he grabbed yet another one from inside the house as we headed out.

My friend Enis and I learn that Dean's property was once part of an original tract of land called "The Manor of Maske"—43,000 acres the William Penn family acquired in 1765 for their own use and future sale. Dean has a plaque on the side of the house saying as much. We leave the house and head up toward the barn, where we are greeted with tolerant interest by a pair of the largest Hereford cows I have ever seen. They don't appear to be fenced in, and as they turn away from us and amble back toward a small trough, Dean informs them he will feed them later and they need not follow us. Dean and Judy keep the cows as pets and living lawnmowers, and have buried three of their predecessors on the farm. They also leave evidence of their presence in the form of "Confederate landmines," as Dean calls them, telling us to "watch where you step."

Judy names these gargantuan pets and calls them after individuals associated with Gettysburg. In this case, we are happy to have met "Lydia Leister" (since deceased) and "Solome 'Sally' Meyers." "We once had a bull named "Jeb Stuart," joked Dean, "because he was always behind!"

Moving up the hill, just above the barn, Dean pauses and points out that more than 7,000 Union and Confederate soldiers were originally buried on the battlefield, including a number who died from their wounds and were buried on the very ground where we now stand. (I should note at this point that Dean is considered by everyone in the Civil War community as one of the *foremost* experts on Gettysburg.) Dean reached into his back pocket and withdrew the two curiously bent pieces of metal and informs us they are "dowsing rods," most commonly used to look for water. Apparently his are capable of much more. Dean demonstrates this by locating the area of an old buried pipe that once carried water between a well and an old cistern. He stands on ground that he knows to be on one side of the pipe and, holding the rods loosely, walks across the area of the pipe. Without any manipulation on his part, the ends of the rods move together! He adds that the rods also react to human remains, or even to where human remains once were. Enis and I are, in a word, skeptical—until Dean demonstrates it by finding a grave of a soldier who had died at the farm and was buried there. He lets both of us give it a try—guess what? They work for us, too.

Dean informs us that in the hands of a skilled "dowser" they are even capable of defining the shape of the human remains buried under the ground, mentioning an instance where a friend of his pointed out that the particular skeleton he was passing over had lost a leg. You are skeptical, right? I would not have believed it either had I not experienced it myself. I only know that not only did I observe this phenomenon, but I succeeded in doing it myself. Apparently, Shakespeare's maxim, "there are more things in heaven and earth, Horatio, than are dreamt of in your philosophy" is quite true.

Slightly shaken by the experience, we proceed up the hill. The field to the right is beautiful in the full glory of spring. Dean is charging ahead with surprising alacrity, and that "youngster" Enis has no trouble keeping up with him. I admittedly lag behind trying to figure out the mystery of the dowsing rods. (I kept waiting for Dean to call me "Jeb Stuart.") The large and slightly wooded lot to the right (as one ascends the hill) was where, on the afternoon of July 3, an initial reconnaissance was launched by a Union brigade under Brig. Gen. Thomas H. Neill. It was Neill's task to move out and make sure no Confederates were trying to slip around the extreme right of the Union position and seize, or at least harass, the traffic moving along the Baltimore Pike. It was probably a good thing for the Union that they checked.

Confederate infantry of the 2nd Virginia had taken up positions behind a stone wall at the top end of the field we are now ascending—probably less than 300 yards from the pike. As Neill's men approached, they were taken under fire by the Confederates. Neill ordered Col. Seldon Connor of the 7th Maine to

Lost Avenue, looking east.

bring up his regiment, as well as the 43rd New York, while he rode back to Slocum's headquarters on Powell's Hill for reinforcements. Adding elements of the 49th New York and the 61st Pennsylvania, his force grew to about 1,450 men. The Confederates, only about 160 strong, were easily driven from their positions and retreated about 200 yards north of the stone wall that still marks the forward-most point of their advance. Casualties were few, probably fewer than 15 Union troops killed, wounded, or captured. There were no known Confederate casualties. One Union officer among the fallen was Capt. William Gilfillian of the 43rd New York.

As we approach Neil Avenue Dean points out that "roads" throughout the park were here at the time of the battle, and that "avenues" were designated memorial stretches of ground filled with monuments mostly provided by the men who fought there. He reminds us that Neill Avenue is the only avenue in the entire park still unpaved. Given its location, and the care Dean takes of it, my guess is that it will remain that way. The meeting was small in comparison to everything else that had taken place at Gettysburg, and main the battle was over by the time these few triggers were pulled.

Neill Avenue runs almost parallel to and northeast of the Baltimore Pike just above where it crosses Rock Creek. Approaching it is like stepping back in time unencumbered by the intrusion of the modern world. Dean tells us we can photograph whatever we want. His enjoyment at being able to bring yet another visitor into the special world of this remote spot is palpable. Acknowledging the fact that he has taken time out of his busy day to do so, I am especially grateful. Gettysburg never ceases to amaze, and the discovery of another of its "special places" is one of the things that keeps drawing me back to the power and beauty of its domain.

As soon as you step onto this secluded lane, history envelops you. Looking east, the lane extends about 275 yards. West, the open ground quickly gives way to a wooded area about 25 yards distant; the trees descend toward meandering Rock Creek near the site of the McAllister Mill, which before the war was an important stop on the Underground Railway. This far from roads and traffic makes it easier to sense "the way it was." Aside from the few monuments here, this part of the battlefield appears as it did in 1863. The wall on the left as you face east is the actual wall behind which Confederate sharpshooters fired until driven back by Neill's Yankees, who moved to occupy this spot. The wall on the right was added later.

Monuments along Neill Avenue include those to the 43rd and 49th New York, the 61st Pennsylvania, and the 7th Maine. As we head up the lane (east) Dean provides numerous details of what went on here, demonstrating his encyclopedic knowledge of not only this action, but of the entire battle. Committed to preservation, Dean was one of the founders of the Land Conservancy of Adams County. Finally, ascending a small hill, we proceed to the eastern end of the lane and arrive at what was the extreme right end of the Union lines after 10:00 a.m. on July 3, 1863.

After giving Enis and I the full tour of Lost Avenue, Dean asks if we would like to head over to Spangler's Spring, which I'd not seen before from this side. When I ask if it's okay if we do that, Dean replies, "Why not? It's my land." Jumping at the opportunity, we walk along a track that had once been the boundary of the Manor of Maske.

After descending a modest grade on an old farm road, we come upon the ruins of the Zephaniah Taney farm. Hidden in the abundant overgrowth are the vestiges of its foundation. The farm was here at the time of the battle, just yards above Rock Creek. The farm is now owned by the NPS, but due to its inaccessibility across private land, is rarely visited. Thanks to Dean, however, we have found it.

Its owner, Zephaniah, enlisted in the Union army but was wounded and captured during the Seven Days' Battles in June 1862. He was discharged that year, but did not take part in the action at Gettysburg. During the battle his

COLONEL
NATHANIEL
P. RICHMOND

farmhouse was occupied by Confederate sharpshooters firing at the Union troops of Silas Colgroves' brigade, part of the Union right flank near Spangler's Spring. After examining the Taney Farm, we head down toward Rock Creek.

If we were to wade across, we would be very near Spangler's Spring below the southeastern slopes of the tallest part of Culp's Hill, where Confederate brigades once assembled for their assault. Within this part of the Gettysburg battlefield, ownership of the land shifts between private ownership and the GNMP. As we head toward the spring, Dean points out land "we" own (meaning park property), versus land "he" owns.

LIEUTENANT
COLONEL
WILLIAM P.
BRINTON

Farther down the creek we find ourselves standing directly across from what had been the McAllister Farm, and just to its left, the McAllister Mill. Sadly, just above the ruins of the mill is the Gettysburg town dump. Thankfully, it's not for garbage but brush and trees, and soil from various excavation projects. Trucks and other equipment are parked out of sight just over the hill. Dean and other preservationists are doing their best to get Gettysburg to find another location for this facility, which is not located on the battlefield itself.

Heading up a small hill we find ourselves back at Dean's farm. We offer him our profound and heartfelt thanks and bid Dean a fond farewell, hoping our paths will cross again.

The South Cavalry Field and the Futile Death of General Farnsworth

There is, unfortunately, one more action that took place at the end of Day Three. The battle was for all practical purposes over, but General Judson Kilpatrick, operating with part of his cavalry division south of the main battlefield, spotted an opportunity for glory. He ordered the young Elon Farnsworth to take his brigade and attack Confederate infantry behind a rock fence running from the Emmitsburg Road to the base of Big

MAJOR WILLIAM WELLS

Round Top on the Slyder Farm. The Confederates belonged to Jerome B. Robertson's brigade and included the 1st Texas Infantry. The initial attack came when Kilpatrick ordered Col. Nathaniel P. Richmond's regiment of West Virginians to move out against the Texans. These Union troopers overcame the obstacle of a rail fence and then charged into the waiting Confederates, taking fire from three sides before being driven back.

Next up was the green 18th Pennsylvania Cavalry under the command of Lt. Col. William P. Brinton. Despite being joined by elements of the 5th New York Cavalry, and fighting dismounted to try and overcome the Confederate position, no progress was made. Refusing to listen to his subordinates as they argued against another cavalry charge, Kilpatrick insisted on another charge, challenging Elon Farnsworth to lead it. Farnsworth, along with three battalions of the 1st Vermont Cavalry, proceeded to attack. One of the North's rising cavalry stars, Maj. William Wells (who would be awarded the Medal of Honor for his actions here, and later rise to the rank of brigadier general), chooses to ride with Farnsworth. Another battalion would dismount and fight on foot opposite the mounted attack of Farnsworth and Wells in a failed attempt to envelop the enemy in a pincer movement.

The result was one of the most ill-conceived actions of the battle—a waste of good men on the part of General "Kill-Cavalry." The most notable loss was Elon Farnsworth himself, who had been promoted to brigadier general less than a week before. The site of "Farnsworth's Charge" is clearly visible from South Confederate Avenue opposite the base of Big Round Top.

The term South Cavalry Field is usually thought to describe only the area of the ill-fated charge by Farnsworth, but in reality covers a lot more ground. Farther south along the Taneytown Road is the place where Union cavalry forces collected before they moved north. The area is completely neglected compared to its more famous cousin farther north. Open fields on both sides of the Taneytown Road provided the Union a perfect point to concentrate their cavalry under Kilpatrick's command. I visited the open field east of the road that cuts through a small stand of trees *en route* to the spot where Farnsworth was killed. It has a kind of serenity today that must have been very different in 1863 with the gathering of Union cavalrymen and their excited steeds.

The Battle of Gettysburg is Over

The armies spent the remainder of July 3 in fitful exchanges of small arms fire as both sides scoured the field for wounded. Foraging parties picked over the battlefield to scoop up whatever materiel would prove useful. Nearly every structure from tents to hotels overflowed with wounded men of both armies. For those in both armies who suspected the fighting was over, they were right. The fight at Gettysburg now belonged to history.

Chapter 7

After the Battle and the
Gettysburg Address

Although many Southern officers, Lee among them, worried that Meade would aggressively follow up with a counter-attack, none came. Some historians maintain that Lee *hoped* the Union would counterattack. If so, he was disappointed. Meade's army had also been battered, his men needed rest, the units needed to be reordered, and Union ammunition was a concern. Meade was also not the sort who would impulsively throw a large force back across an open field to repeat Lee's mistake. He had witnessed Fredericksburg, and had just beaten back one of the largest attacks of the war. He had firmly defeated Lee by remaining on the defensive. And for Meade, that was enough.

Lee knew he had been beaten, and his first concern was for the safety of his army. Ewell's Second Corps was pulled back to Seminary Ridge to consolidate the line, which extended now from Oak Hill southward. Some of the men bolstered their new positions by throwing up light breastworks of dirt and fence rails. Around sundown on July 3, according to Rebel Maj. Jedediah Hotchkiss, "The Generals had a council at General A. P. Hill's headquarters on the Cashtown Road . . . and decided to fall back."

Lee's losses, which he had not yet tabulated with any specificity, were horrendous. All told, his casualties would exceed 28,000 men: 3,903 dead,

18,735 wounded, and 5,425 missing/captured. The Army of Northern Virginia was about 150 miles from its nearest railhead at Staunton in the Shenandoah Valley, and Lee knew his entire communications and ammunition supply was now exceedingly vulnerable. His wounded, packed into wagons that formed a train of misery many miles long, would begin rolling out the next day, July 4. Cavalry would escort them. The infantry would leave last.

Meade's army had also been roughly handled. The costly Union victory came in at more than 23,000 men: 3,155 killed, 14,529 wounded, and more than 5,000 captured or missing. Of those wounded on both sides, many hundreds more would die, and large numbers would never be able to serve again, making each the equivalent of a kill.

Gettysburg was a significant victory for the Union, and one that many historians view as some sort of turning point of the war. Although the Civil War would continue for nearly another two years—with 1864 being the bloodiest single year—most of that time the Confederacy fought on the defensive in an attempt to stave off defeat. At Gettysburg, which turned out to be Lee's last invasion of the North with his entire Army of Northern Virginia, the Southerners still had hopes of achieving outright victory.

I must confess feeling a sense of closure tinged with a little excitement and a bit of sadness. I have been lucky enough to cover a significant portion of this great battlefield on foot. I'm excited just knowing there are many areas I have not yet explored. Fortunately, my home in Pittsburgh is just four short hours from Gettysburg, so I have every intention of making the journey as often as I can with my wife Marilyn, friends Enis and Mimi, and others I hope to meet along the way.

I'll admit it: I indeed suffer from a severe case of GAS.

July 4, 1863

The Fourth of July was a miserable one for the survivors of both sides, who endured a heavy rain while wondering what more Fate had in store for them. For the large number of wounded still lying where they fell, the misery must have been nearly unbearable. They didn't know it yet, but the garrison at Vicksburg, Mississippi, was about to surrender. The loss of an entire army, together with the Mississippi River in Union hands, was a catastrophe for the South. The Confederacy was now split firmly in two and, in Lincoln's phrase, "The Father of Waters now flows un-vexed to the sea."

Meade was still in something of a wait-and-see attitude. He would finally discover that Lee's lines had contracted and his army retreating, and sent out Sedgwick's mostly un-bloodied VI Corps after it. The heavy rains also impeded Lee's retreat, affording Meade time to prepare his pursuit. Meade had sent Maj. Gen. Henry W. Halleck in Washington a cautious dispatch that made no claim to "victory," but described instead how the enemy had suffered severe losses after twice assailing Meade's center—leaving the *implication* that the Army of the Potomac had been victorious.

QUARTER MASTER MAJOR JOHN A. HARMAN

The Wagon Trains

Before Lee's wagons rolled, Lee sent Meade, under a flag of truce, a request for an exchange of prisoners. Meade knew the Confederate was planning a general retreat and denied the request. There was military advantage in leaving Lee to guard and transport large numbers of enemy troops during his flight south. The wagons Lee set in motion contained both wounded and some of the abundant food and other supplies his army had collected during its time in Pennsylvania.

The initial train of wagons and ambulances under Brig. Gen. John Imboden headed out the Chambersburg Pike and back through the Cashtown Gap to Greenwood, where they would turn south for the Potomac River at Williamsport some 42 miles distant. The wagons and Imboden's 2,100 cavalrymen and half a dozen artillery batteries were also protected by Hampton's and Fitz Lee's cavalry brigades, which watched the flanks. Once underway, the train stretched for some 17 miles.

A second train was organized by Ewell's Corps under the command of Quartermaster John A. Harman. Harman's train took a more direct route over South Mountain at the Fairfield Gap to reach Williamsport by way of Hagerstown, a concentration point for the Confederates. (Recall that this route had been kept open by the defeat of the Union cavalry at the small Battle of

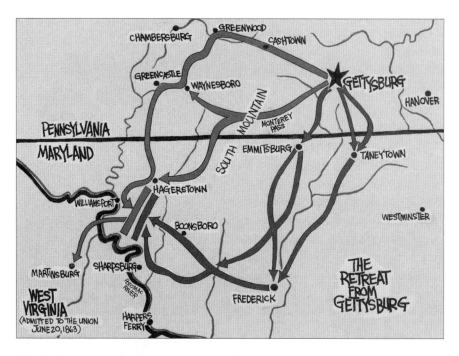

Fairfield on July 3.) Imboden's train had a longer march to reach the Potomac, but its route kept it farther from the reach of the Union army.

Lee's infantry took the same route as Harman through Fairfield to help punch back any Union pursuit. Hill's Third Corps led the way out on the Fairfield Road, followed by Longstreet's First Corps. Ewell's Second Corps brought up the rear. The infantry move southwest was toward and through Monterey Pass. After a few miles more the foot soldiers broke off on different routes to coalesce once more at Williamsport. The Army of Northern Virginia completed its withdrawal from Gettysburg on July 5.

The End of the Gettysburg Campaign

Retreat

Today, Fairfield is a pleasant little community and boasts the Historic Fairfield Inn, originally the Mansion House of Squire Miller, one of the town's founders. It was a stop on the Underground Railroad and later saw service as a Confederate Hospital. One of the five oldest continuously operating inns in America (1757), it offers its modern guests a choice of six suites and guestrooms as a B&B (all completely updated), fine dining in either the Mansion House Restaurant or Squire Miller's Tavern, along with dinner theater

The Fairfield Inn in downtown Fairfield.

entertainment. Historic guests have included Patrick Henry, Thaddeus Stevens, and Generals Lee and Stuart, with more recent guests including Baseball Hall-of-Famer Eddie Plank and Mamie Eisenhower. The establishment's 27th Innkeeper, John G. Kramb, will be delighted to welcome you to the landmark inn.

Lest we forget a visit to the "other side," the Historic Fairfield Inn is reputed to be haunted. (I wonder if the ghosts over at the Cashtown Inn ever pop over here for an evening, and, in the spirit of "turn-about is fair play," vice versa?)

Most of Stuart's cavalry followed a more easterly route to screen the army and its wagons, riding down the Emmitsburg Road into Maryland before heading west at Mechanicstown (now Thurmont) through the Catoctin Mountains to link up with Lee at Hagerstown. A large portion of Lee's army retreated across the Sachs Covered Bridge (we had visited that earlier).

Various Union cavalry units jumped in pursuit of the retreating Southerners. Judson Kilpatrick and George Custer caught up with Harman's wagons at Monterrey Pass, and in the ensuing fight in the dark and rain recovered some of the wagons of Union bounty and took some prisoners. Unfortunately, horror stories associated with their treatment of a few of the wagons full of wounded Confederate soldiers ring true. The Union troopers made no attempt to stick around long enough to confront Confederate infantry taking the same route.

Waynesboro, Pennsylvania is home to the new Monterey Battlefield Park and Museum. In a tribute to what is billed as only the second battle fought in Pennsylvania during the Civil War, this little museum of one room was built near the site of the battle. (Preservationists are working hard to add battlefield acreage.) The museum contains interesting artifacts, maps, and more and is the brainchild of John A. Miller and run by volunteers. On our visit we enjoyed the outstanding docent services of R. Lee Royer. Two of their treasures to look for are a genuine "carpet bag" and a rubberized "talma"—a kind of rain cape. Despite its diminutive size, this museum is a real pleasure, long overdue, and is working to develop programs of interest to the public. You can find them on the Internet.

Imboden's column was repeatedly harassed along its more northern route, but the strength of its supporting troops prevented serious damage. When Imboden finally arrived at Williamsport, he found to his dismay that the Potomac was swollen from heavy rains. Worse, the pontoon bridge left in place at Falling Waters six miles below had been destroyed by Union cavalry dispatched on July 4 by Maj. Gen. William H. French from the garrison at Harpers Ferry. Only a small ferry was in place to serve the escaping Confederates.

July 6 saw a flurry of sharp cavalry clashes as Stuart's and Kilpatrick's divisions fought for Hagerstown. In loyalty-divided Maryland, locals on both

The Monterey Pass Battlefield Park and Museum.

sides joined the fighting. Additional Union and Confederate troops were fed into the fight, but the arrival of Confederate infantry forced the blue-clad cavalry to break off the action.

Meantime, a more dangerous situation developed for the Rebels. Imboden and his wagon train of wounded were attacked at Williamsport when Buford's cavalry division caught up with them. Buford dismounted most of his 3,500 men to fight on foot, while Imboden rustled up every man he could find—including teamsters and the lightly wounded. His efforts allowed him to field some 2,500 effectives.

The cavalryman turned in the performance of his life, juggling his

BRIGADIER GENERAL JOHN D. IMBODEN

forces well while somehow holding off several assaults. In the nick of time, and with his ammunition running low, two wagons stuffed with just what he needed arrived on the ferry from across the Potomac. By this time, however, Kilpatrick was approaching to support Buford after the former's repulse at Hagerstown. The situation looked grim for Imboden until word arrived from Fitzhugh Lee: His brigade was on the way if Imboden could only hold out for another half-hour. New gunfire broke out behind Kilpatrick—Jeb Stuart was on the way, too. The Union cavalry withdrew. This was the closest the Federals would come to cutting off Lee's entire line of retreat. Imboden gave credit to the teamsters who assisted his defense and dubbed it the "Wagoners' Fight."

On July 7, the full Confederate army began taking up positions between Hagerstown and Williamsport. When Lee learned of the loss of the pontoon bridge at Falling Waters, he dispatched engineers and his young artillerist, Porter Alexander, to create a defensive line along Salisbury Ridge strong enough to hold off any Union assault. Quartermaster John Harman was assigned the task of replacing the lost pontoon bridge. Over the next several days and nights, the Confederates built a formidable line of defense amply supported by artillery. This position, eventually approved by Lee, set the scene

MAJOR PETER A. WEBER

for the final confrontation north of the Potomac River during the campaign. The remainder of Lee's forces concentrated at Williamsport.

Meanwhile, elements of Meade's Army of the Potomac arrived to find themselves facing this formidable Confederate defensive position. They had learned the hard way that attacking Lee's men at any time was dangerous, and when holding a strong fortified position essentially impossible. Meade telegraphed Halleck on July 12 that he intended to attack the following day, but a council of war that night voiced concern that Lee's lines had not been thoroughly examined. Meade and others spent the 13th scouting the front and ordered his corps commanders to launch a reconnaissance-in-force the next morning. Lee had remained in position hoping Meade would assault. By this time the river had fallen enough to ford, and a pontoon bridge erected. The Rebels began retreating that night, and by the time Meade's infantry went forward the enemy was gone.

The final act of the drama came about when the impetuous Union cavalry under Judson Kilpatrick confronted Henry Heth's rearguard during the last stage of the Confederate retreat. Ordered to pursue the Rebs, George Custer decided to err on the side of caution—which was unlike his usual recklessness. Rather than charge ahead, he had two companies of the 6th Michigan under Maj. Peter Weber dismount and reconnoiter the enemy's position.

The even more reckless Kilpatrick, however, countermanded Custer and ordered the men to mount up and charge. Heth was initially surprised by the arrival of what he thought was additional Confederate cavalry, and so did not immediately engage the approaching horsemen. The engagement that followed was short-lived but sharp. The Confederates rallied, Major Weber was killed, and about one-third of his men were shot from their horses. General Pettigrew, who had assumed command of Heth's division when that officer was wounded on July 1 and survived the final grand infantry charge on July 3 with but a slight hand wound, was mortally wounded and left behind.

Gettysburg, Thereafter

July 4 was a Saturday. Union Sgt. Henry Monath was at his post at the foot of Cemetery Hill that morning when he spotted a group of citizens moving along the Baltimore Pike "waving their handkerchiefs for us to come." Surprised and curious, Monath led the small group back down the pike all the way into town and Lincoln Square, where he discovered that, except for a few Confederate stragglers, the town had been evacuated.

With the battle over and the Rebels gone, the little community of Gettysburg was left with the aftermath of the terrible battle. The reality of what that meant must have been

GOVERNOR ANDREW CURTIN

astonishing. The citizens of this small Pennsylvania town faced with an unbelievably difficult task. The support of the Army of the Potomac and its resources helped ease some of the burden and suffering.

Every possible building was commandeered to serve as a hospital to treat wounded of both armies—almost 20,000 men! Sanitary conditions being what they were in 1863, many of these men would die before they could receive treatment, or perish because of the treatment they received and the infection that would set in. Across the sprawling battlefield awaited the torn bodies of some 7,000 dead men and untold thousands of wounded, at least 3,000 horses and mules, and an almost inconceivable amount of debris—from human and animal waste and canteens to muskets, uniforms, haversacks, and everything else an army carried with it. The stench was overwhelming and could be smelled miles away. Within hours millions of flies covered the fallen and filled their air with endless buzzing.

The Union dead received better and faster treatment simply because Meade's army still held the field. Wherever possible, Union soldiers were identified and sent back to their hometowns for burial. Others were assigned graves in Evergreen Cemetery or were given proper burial on the battlefield

JUDGE DAVID WILLS

itself. Those who had been interred in shallow makeshift graves, many of which had been exposed by the falling rain and pigs and dogs rooting through the soil, were reburied or moved to more suitable sites.

The Confederates, on the other hand, were for the most part thrown into shallow mass graves with little attempt made to identify the individual remains. Richard Garnett, for example, one of Pickett's generals who fell at the height of the Pickett-Pettigrew-Trimble Charge, was never identified. Wounded Confederates were generally afforded the same quality of treatment by the Union surgeons and their civilian helpers. Lee had also left behind some medical personnel to assist with the thousands of wounded he was forced to abandon because they would not have survived the long and arduous retreat to Virginia. Union soldiers and civilians scoured the battlefield for anything that might prove useful, and families who had learned of the fearful battle arrived in an effort to identify their fallen brothers, sons, and fathers. The dead animals were hauled into piles and burned.

Fortunately, the town's strained resources would soon receive help. While the country knew a great struggle had taken place at Gettysburg, just how large it was—the costliest battle of the war—was not yet fully understood. Within hours of the end of hostilities, civilian volunteers, the resources of the U.S. Sanitary Commission, and the Christian Commission and Sisters of Charity arrived in Gettysburg by the hundreds. They helped organize hospitals, relieve surgeons, nurses, and staff attending the wounded, and provided a much-needed boost in morale. In addition to the buildings pressed into use as hospitals, Camp Letterman—named for Dr. Jonathan Letterman, the visionary Medical Director of the Army of the Potomac—was established on the York Pike. It would serve thousands of wounded troops from that hot July all the way to November.

As alluded to earlier, the burning of thousands of dead horses and mules, coupled with decomposing human bodies and the infected wounds of the living, created an overpowering stench. Stories confirm this sickening odor lasted for months and could be smelled from miles away. Albertus McCreary, a young lad living in Gettysburg at the time, would later write the article "Gettysburg: A Boy's Experience of the Battle" for *McClure's Magazine* in 1909. According to him, "the stench from the battlefield after the fight was so bad that everyone went around with a bottle of pennyroyal or peppermint oil."

DAVID McCONAUGHY

The Birth of a National Cemetery and Its Dedication

Recognizing the importance of this battle and the magnitude of the task of burying the dead, David McConaughy, a prominent citizen of Gettysburg who had been the organizer of a ring of citizen-spies furnishing information to Gen. Meade, bought land throughout Gettysburg including some acreage adjacent to Evergreen Cemetery. As president of the Evergreen Cemetery Association, he contacted Pennsylvania Governor Andrew Curtin regarding a more formal internment for the Union dead—not only those from Pennsylvania but for the dead of all the Northern states that had fought there. Along with Theodore S. Dimon, who had been sent to Gettysburg from New York to help deal with the fallen from the Empire State, Judge David Wills, at the urging of Governor Curtin, took up the cause to create a national cemetery to re-inter the men and thus honor the dead.

McConaughy sold 17 acres (at cost) adjacent to the civilian Evergreen Cemetery to the Commonwealth of Pennsylvania, while David Wills spearheaded the effort to turn this hallowed ground into a national cemetery. Much of the land McConaughy purchased also became the foundation of the Gettysburg National Military Park as we know it today. Landscape architect

WILLIAM SAUNDERS

William Saunders was called upon to create a design for the new cemetery. The process of transferring the Union dead to this site was undertaken, and despite efforts to identify each soldier, some 1,600 of the 3,512 bodies are marked "unknown." Most of the Confederate dead, although not all, were eventually relocated to cemeteries in their native states, although some Confederates still lie in unmarked graves on the battlefield [and a handful are also in the National Cemetery buried along their Union counterparts among the "unknown."]

The final act honoring the dead came on November 19, 1863. David Wills invited Edward Everett, a former president of Harvard University and the man generally considered the greatest orator of his day, to dedicate the cemetery with a speech. Indeed, Everett's address was billed as the main event of the day. Wills also considered adding one of America's greatest poets to write a dedication, but none were available. As an afterthought, Wills invited President Abraham Lincoln to add a few remarks at the ceremony. Lincoln agreed to attend. Everett spoke first, and droned on for two hours. Once he finished, Lincoln stood and delivered his 272-word "Gettysburg Address" [versions vary from 270 to 275 words]. It took just two minutes. Everett later wrote Lincoln to express his wish that he had been able to be as

EDWARD EVERETT

Abraham Lincoln

eloquent. Ironically, Lincoln's address met with criticism at the time. Today, his words resonate as the most powerful and eloquent tribute to "these honored dead" history has ever recorded:

> Four score and seven years ago our fathers brought forth upon this continent, a new nation, conceived in liberty, and dedicated to the proposition that all men are created equal.

> Now we are engaged in a great civil war, testing whether that nation, or any nation so conceived and so dedicated, can long endure. We are met on a great battlefield of that war. We have come to dedicate a portion of that field, as a final resting place for those who here gave their lives that that nation might live. It is altogether fitting and proper that we should do this.

> But, in a larger sense, we can not dedicate—we can not consecrate—we can not hallow—this ground. The brave men, living and dead, who struggled here, have consecrated it, far above our poor power to add or detract. The world will little note, nor long remember what we say here; but it can never forget what they did here. It is for us the living, rather, to be dedicated here to the unfinished work which they who fought here have thus far so nobly advanced. It is rather for us to be here dedicated to the great task remaining before us—that from these honored dead we take increased devotion to that cause for which they gave the last full measure of devotion—that we here highly resolve that these dead shall not have died in vain—that this nation, under God, shall have a new birth of freedom—and that government of the people, by the people, for the people, shall not perish from the earth.

The Soldiers' National Cemetery Today

Sitting adjacent to the Evergreen Cemetery, the Soldiers' National Cemetery at Gettysburg was the first of its kind in the nation and is a powerful tribute to the men who fought and died here. There are three main entrances to the cemetery: one from Baltimore Street just below the entrance to the Evergreen Cemetery, another from Steinwehr Avenue, and the third from the Taneytown Road.

On my first visit there, I entered from the Taneytown Road side. A moderate-sized dais just ahead and slightly to the left immediately caught my eye. A natural assumption is to think this is the place Lincoln gave his famous address. Alas, it is not true. The dais was built in 1879 and is known as "The Rostrum." It is used for the annual tributes that have become a part of the

The Soldiers' National Monument (left).
The real site of the Gettysburg Address
(above).

legacy of Gettysburg. Off to the right is a memorial commemorating Lincoln's immortal words. The actual location of the speech (it is now believed), was slightly farther south and east just behind the iron fence that now separates the two cemeteries; the fence was not there in 1863. In other words, Lincoln was in the Evergreen Cemetery when he delivered the Gettysburg Address.

This cemetery has grown to include military personnel from other conflicts who are now buried around its perimeter. I walked along the asphalt path toward the site of the graves themselves, struck by the simplicity of the place. It doesn't take long to note the presence of Civil War cannon and flank markers denoting the lower slopes of the Union position on Cemetery Hill. Their presence does not disturb the peacefulness and gentle tranquility that somehow manages to shut out even the hustle and bustle of the tourist-laden areas that surround the cemetery on three sides.

The graves are arranged in a series of semicircles around the Soldiers' National Monument that marks the Union victory and the valor of the fallen soldiers. The original plan was to arrange the plots in essentially random order, but because of resistance from the states, the graves are grouped by state, with two additional sections for unknowns and for soldiers of the Regular Army.

Spaced around the central core of graves are four poetic tributes to the fallen engraved on steel tablets. In addition to the Soldiers' National Monument at the center of the concentric semi-circle of graves, there are four large monuments—one to Maj. Gen. John Reynolds, the New York State Monument, the Collis Monument, and the Masonic Monument—along with

The Evergreen Cemetery Gatehouse.

several smaller ones. All four are kept outside the perimeter of Civil War graves—reverence and simplicity being the intention.

If you exit the Soldiers' National Cemetery on the Baltimore Street Side, a short stroll to the right will take you to the Evergreen Cemetery. This is where Gettysburg's civilians rest, a holy place that had been there well before the battle in that hot July of 1863.

Chapter 8

The Gettysburg National Military Park Museum and Visitor Center, and the Eisenhower National Historic Site

"If you haven't been to the new Visitor Center, you haven't been to Gettysburg."
—Ed W. Clark, Superintendent, GNMP

*J*ust a mile from the town's Lincoln Square is the entrance to the new Gettysburg National Military Park Museum and Visitor Center. A little road twists and turns as it carries you to the one of the numerous parking lots surrounding the Visitor's Center (or, more commonly, VC). If you prefer, you can also reach the VC via its back entrance off the Taneytown Road. The landscaping looks a bit like scruffy weeds, but is a selection of native drought-resistant plants that require no irrigation.

The new Museum and Visitor Center is a remarkable facility. Completed in 2008 as a joint project of the National Park Service and the Gettysburg Foundation, it is both beautiful and spectacular. Inside, the grand lobby extends the full length of the building, the interior just as impressive as the outside.

Inside are ticket counters, two information desks (one manned by Rangers and GNMP volunteers, the other by Gettysburg Foundation volunteers), the museum itself, the entrance to two theaters, a great bookstore and souvenir shop, a snack counter, another small souvenir boutique which changes its

The Gettysburg National Military Park Museum and Visitors Center

offerings as the occasion warrants, access to Paul Philippoteaux's world-famous cyclorama painting of "Pickett's Charge," meeting and conference rooms, a large cafeteria, and of course, restrooms. Beyond the public access facilities are a library housing extensive research materials, curatorial rooms, storage for period artifacts, and a large office suite on the second floor.

On our first visit, we pay the fee for A New Birth of Freedom, the wonderful film narrated by Morgan Freeman that explains the battle and some of the important events surrounding it. In addition to Freeman, the powerhouse vocal talents of Marcia Gay Harden and Sam Waterston enrich the short film. Your fee provides access to the film, museum, and the famous cyclorama. To keep the wait to a minimum, two theaters offer the film every fifteen minutes, and are handicapped accessible. (If you join the Friends of Gettysburg—as Gettysburg Foundation members are known—there is no fee.) Interestingly, Abraham Lincoln was known to have had a rather thin, reedy voice, so Waterston—with his wonderful versatility—was an excellent choice to portray him. But being an actor myself, I disagree with his choice to continually stress the word "people" in the immortal phrase, "of the people, by the people, for the people," thus minimizing the nuances of the prepositions that carry the true meaning of the sentence; it's catchy, but it's just wrong.

After *A New Birth of Freedom*, we ascend to the dramatic space that houses the cyclorama itself. This building replaces an older structure and was created to hold the entire painting, which has been meticulously restored. A cyclorama is a large panoramic painting intended for viewing "in the round." As such, it requires a special facility built uniquely to house and show it. This painting has enjoyed three different housings during its time at Gettysburg, including the state-of-the-art building we are in now. Fortunately, under the care of professional preservationists, the Gettysburg Cyclorama by French artist Paul Philippoteaux has been restored to its full glory.

To get a full sense of its size, it is important to understand that this grand oil on canvas is 42 feet tall and 377 feet long! It also includes a life-size diorama running along its entire base (remember, the painting wraps 360 degrees around the viewing platforms) depicting in surprising detail the panoramic sweep of "Pickett's Charge." The effect of this astounding presentation is palpable. When the painting was first displayed, veterans of the battle often cried when viewing it. Its current environment, with its affecting narration, dramatic sound effects, and stunning light show, highlights perfectly this amazing work of art. If you want to learn more about this magnificent artwork, an oversize full-color book dedicated solely to this giant painting and all the mysteries and intricacies embedded within it, was recently published. *The Gettysburg Cyclorama: The Turning Point of the Civil War on Canvas*, by Chris Brenneman, Sue Boardman, and Bill Dowling offers the insider's view of the cyclorama. All three authors are Licensed Battlefield Guides, and two of them work with the painting itself. I highly recommend it.

The Museum at the Visitor Center features one of the best collections of Civil War material found anywhere in the country on all aspects of the war, not just Gettysburg.

The exhibits are beautifully presented in modern climate-controlled rooms and include everything from the causes of the war and slavery in the territories, to secession, the opening shots, military objectives, lives of the soldiers, and much more. Additional exhibits meticulously document the battle itself, along with its horrible aftermath and the many weapons and accouterments of war. Still other exhibits on the Soldiers' National Cemetery, the election of 1864, Lee's surrender at Appomattox, Lincoln's assassination, and the cost of the war will also be found here. And don't miss the additional displays throughout the

A portion of Pickett's Charge as painted by Paul Philippoteaux.
Photo courtesy of the Gettysburg Foundation.

lobby. (The rear lobby accommodates additional restrooms, a unique relief map, and the Ford Education Center.)

The bookstore is right in keeping with the standards set by the rest of the VC—and it's huge. Many of the books focus just on Gettysburg, and include biographies of major participants, many specific actions, unit histories, and particular battlefield locations. Thankfully, since people interested in the Civil War tend to be interested in a lot more than one battle, the bookstore also carries dozens of books on other Civil War battles and topics.

There's a lot more here than just books. During my frequent visits to the bookstore over the years I've added to my growing collection of battlefield maps, souvenirs, and hats (and have even picked up a rain jacket, CDs of Civil War songs, and some commemorative coins). This is also the place where I pick up "guilt gifts" for my wife Marilyn, which have included pottery, tea towels, and even delicious jam. My lovely wife is a cosmopolitan woman who would much prefer jewelry, but recognizing my limited resources on some of my solo trips, has graciously accepted these "tokens" of my guilt for being away—although, I always end up eating the jam (a tough job but someone has to do it).

For your first visit, I recommend you purchase the "Official Guidebook" entitled *Gettysburg National Military Park—Museum and Visitor Center*. It provides an excellent overview, and your purchases made here help support the VC.

The "Refreshment Saloon" was clearly built to accommodate a lot of people, and while we adults over 30 might wish for an additional "fine dining" opportunity, there likely isn't enough of a demand for it in the VC. There are many fine restaurants in and around Gettysburg, but do take advantage of the convenience of this facility—especially at lunchtime—and enjoy some of their tasty offerings. While you are at it, don't miss all the wonderful Civil War photographs, many having to do with commissaries serving the soldiers in 1863. The extra 15 minutes will be time well spent. If the weather is nice don't stay inside; take your tray outside and enjoy dining al fresco on the large patio.

If you are in a hurry, the "Grab and Go" section just to the left of the entrance offers prepared fast foods and snacks. There is also a small snack and coffee concession at the far end of the main lobby, just adjacent to the little boutique.

The Eisenhower National Historic Site

Dwight and Mamie Eisenhower purchased the farm in 1950 and at the instigation of a friend, began breeding and raising Black Angus cattle. After an extensive renovation during Eisenhower's presidency, he used it as a second home whenever he was away from Washington and made it a focal point for informal diplomacy, inviting foreign leaders and dignitaries to stay in the little guesthouse on the property. In 1955, after Ike's heart attack, the farm became a temporary White House the Eisenhowers used during his recuperation. They moved here permanently in 1961, when the general's presidency ended (affording Rick Beamer those opportunities to occasionally see them in church.)

The farm and the home were donated to the National Park Service in 1967, two years before Ike's death. Reverend Macaskill, their Gettysburg pastor, presided over the president's funeral. By prior arrangement with the National Park Service, Mamie continued to live on the farm until her death in 1979. One year later, the NPS opened the facility to the public.

The farm is accessible only by shuttle buses to and from the VC (you cannot drive there!), and tickets must be purchased in advance on a first-come, first-served, basis. The fees are very reasonable. The bus schedules vary from season to season, so it's best to check ahead.

The farm is open year round (except Thanksgiving, Christmas Day, and New Year's Day), and is an unexpected treat. The farm also hosts special seasonal events. The home is filled with gifts given to the Eisenhowers. Don't miss the Secret Service office, the golf pitch built especially for Ike, and the working part of the farm—the so-called Farm 2—a short distance from the main house. You can avail yourself of guided tours or just wander the property on your own as we did. For a complete listing of what's there, grab one of the NPS brochures marked "Eisenhower" at the VC. It's not surprising that the Eisenhowers, who were briefly posted to Gettysburg early in Ike's career, were so drawn to the place they decided to buy this large farm. (Even generals and presidents can get GAS!) The location is close to Washington and was very convenient once Ike became president. It's also an idyllic spot and quite beautiful. For a unique look at the Eisenhower years, and the feeling that you are stepping back into that "golden age" of America in the 1950s, it's well worth a visit.

Good Children Need Good Parents: The National Park Service

The Museum and Visitor Center and the extraordinary preservation and maintenance of the battlefield, along with the Eisenhower National Historic Site, make the Gettysburg National Military Park the "jewel in the crown" of the cultural parks of the National Park Service system. J. Robert "Bob" Kirby became its superintendent in March 2010 until he retired in 2014. Back in 2012,

BOB KIRBY

Bob and one of his park historians, Ranger John Heiser, generously shared some of their time with me to talk about the Park.

Bob, a veteran administrator, was a perceptive and articulate spokesman for the park and the NPS. He likened his job to that of a "steersman" on a racing skull, and talked about managing the "many moving parts" that are his job—all those "oarsmen." Making policy decisions and formulating new projects, keeping track of more than 85 full-time employees, maintaining the unique relationship with the Gettysburg

Foundation and their numerous staffers, overseeing the 150 or more Licensed Battlefield Guides, and helping host events for the 25,000 or so Friends of Gettysburg—affectionately referred to by Bob as "grippin' and grinnin'"—kept him fully engaged. When I asked him how important the relationship is between the town itself and the GNMP, he refused to mince any words in reply. "The Park is the town, and the town is the Park," he shot back without hesitation. "We work very hard here at being good neighbors."

JOHN HEISER

While the not-too-distant recession has affected Federal budgets across a broad spectrum of services, the Gettysburg National Military Park and its sister site, the Eisenhower National Historic Site, have been somewhat spared to date (relatively, speaking—more on this later). "Of course, we can always use more, but our budget is pretty good. We receive $1,100,000 for the Eisenhower Farm, and $7,000,000 for the Park." This may sound like a lot of money, but it's not. For example, not long ago, a two-year long project was completed to resurface the roads in the park. This alone cost $12,000,000 (in 2012 dollars)!

Frankly, the ace in the hole for both sites is the Gettysburg Foundation. Bob uses one carefully selected word to describe their relationship: "crucial." Successful projects during and shortly after Bob's tenure included: the acquisition of the Lincoln Train Station and a tract of land in the Plum Run area; the demolition of the former home of the Philippoteaux painting, and the restoration of the land around it to its 1863 appearance; and the sale of the famous "electric map," which now resides in Hanover, PA—once one of the highlights (pun intended) of visiting the park. It's a shame that it had to be sold, but its technology was hopelessly out of date; maybe someday there will be a spot for it at the Smithsonian.

As a guardian of a significant part of America's heritage, I'm curious about Bob's take on the "reenactor/living historian" phenomenon: the surprisingly large number of men and women, young and old, who enjoy capturing what to them is the essence of the Civil War experience by dressing in period garb, accoutering themselves with period equipment, and participating in the recreation of period life. Since battles are a particular fascination they seem especially numerous here in Gettysburg. Sensitive ground here, but Bob tactfully replies, "I believe it's important to allow people to follow their passion in their own way." The man is a genius.

John Heiser, a ranger and historian, is a font of useful information. He identifies his Civil War specialties as "soldier life, supply and uniforms, and army operations." He confesses that he leans toward the "history of military campaigns and commanders, rather than social and political history." In addition to the actions over the three days of the battle, he studies "the command strategy for those days, and the development and history of the battlefield park itself, along with the Great Reunion of 1913."

*   *   *

The 1913 Anniversary and Great Reunion witnessed the return of hundreds of survivors from both sides. It was a significant event in the history of the battlefield and the largest mutual gathering of Union and Confederate veterans in the US during the 50th anniversary observances of the war. Many regimental monuments, brigade and battery markers, several of the state monuments, and most of the equestrian officer statues were placed on the battlefield between 1879 and 1910. Following these tributes, the Great Reunion marked the time when former adversaries reached across half a century to recognize the sacrifices of their compatriots as well as their former enemies.

John was first drawn to Gettysburg on a childhood visit. He became fascinated by "the perspective of the battle's veterans who returned to this field for many years after and placed monuments and markers so that future generations could understand not only the service and sacrifice of the armies at this battle, but the individual stories told by each and every monument and cannon that stand in the park today."

Curious about the Eisenhower Farm being so nearby, John points out that it was, indeed, part of the 1863 battlefield. The buildings there at the time housed Longstreet's headquarters and a Confederate hospital. John also mentions the importance of another site: "Camp Letterman was a general hospital that qualifies as the first modern military field hospital. Established in tents on a farm east of the town on the York Road (Route 30 East), it served 14,000 Union and 6,800 Confederate troops." Today, commerce is closing in on it. Because it falls outside the 6,000-acre tract of land that is the GNMP, it may not survive encroaching business interests. Time will tell. It always does.

John explained that an 1895 law originally established the Gettysburg National Military Park "in order to serve as a memorial for the two armies that fought here." (Our friend Old Dan Sickles played a large role in getting the legislation passed and the placements of early monuments!) Between 1895 and 1933, the park was administered by the Department of War. In 1933, this passed to the National Park Service, which had been established in 1916 by President Woodrow Wilson. Yellowstone National Park was the first, designated as early as March of 1872 "as a public park or pleasuring-ground for the benefit and enjoyment of the people."

I asked John about events of the battle other than the two most famous (Pickett's Charge and Little Round Top) that were of interest to him that people should not miss. "My interest would focus you more on the horrific fight between the 24th Michigan and 26th North Carolina—both regiments were nearly annihilated," he explains. He adds that he certainly would not want you to miss the actions on the McPherson Farm, or the Herbst and Harman farms. And don't forget "the heroics of Captain Irsch of the 45th New York, the famed efforts of Captain Hubert Dilger's Ohio Battery, and the fight for Culp's Hill on the night of the 2nd."

Knowing that Bob and John have had more than their share of questions over the years, I am as always compelled to ask my favorite question. Bob, who also spent time as a ranger at Alcatraz in San Francisco Bay, recalls that a visitor once asked him, "How much does the island weigh?" John returns to Gettysburg with another variation on a subject that keeps coming up regarding the monuments and the fighting: "It's wonderful that they (the two armies) didn't destroy the monuments." (Dang, those Yankee and Confederate gunners were really good.) John ends our pleasant discussion by adding another question that took him aback: "How did they know to fight the battle here?" (In a variation on this theme, I know one historian who replied, "That's where all the cannon were!")

The Gettysburg Foundation and the Friends of Gettysburg

The subject of the Gettysburg Foundation is a popular one, and if you are like me, you have the same question: What is it? Simply put, it is a remarkable non-profit organization that provides an unprecedented level of financial,

JOANNE
HANLEY

material, and personnel resources in support of the Gettysburg National Military Park.

For example, the extraordinary facility that is the VC was the first privately owned and operated visitor center in the entire National Park Service. It was built with a combination of private, state, and federal funding, but now operates solely on its private revenue streams without government funds. That in and of itself is remarkable. Drawing on support from its large membership (the "Friends of Gettysburg"), the Foundation is at the heart of this thriving piece of history.

As a partner to Gettysburg National Military Park, the Foundation reaches countless individuals through its membership drives, public outreach campaigns, and fundraising initiatives. It fosters lasting partnerships with academic institutions and private organizations through educational and leadership programs, facilitates extensive monument and land preservation projects, and funds acreage and property acquisitions pivotal to the historical interpretation of Gettysburg. All of this and more has been accomplished so that this national treasure will be sustained for years to come—ensuring the soldiers who fought here "shall not have died in vain." The Foundation and members are proud to be a partner of the National Park Service.

Joanne M. Hanley was appointed as the Foundation's president in February of 2011. She is now retired, but through the good offices of Interim President Barbara Sardella, a new president, Dr. Matthew Moen, has been installed. As we began our chat, Joanne immediately acknowledged the immeasurable contribution of some of her compatriots: Bob Kinsley, who was the heart and soul of the partnership concept; Barbara J. Finfrock, a key player who began her relationship with the Friends of the National Parks at Gettysburg as a volunteer in 1993, and was instrumental in the creation of the present organization; and finally, her predecessor, Robert C. Wilburn.

"The Gettysburg Foundation's mission, in partnership with the National Park Service, is to enhance preservation and understanding of the heritage and lasting significance of Gettysburg." She adds, "We do several things here: we make sure the Museum and Visitor Center operates at the highest quality possible; we strive to keep the experience fresh, raising friends and funds to help sustain the Park, and we contribute to its ongoing rehabilitation, preservation, and education efforts. We see ourselves as being here to serve both the visitors and the National Park Service." She observes, "Every single one of those monuments out there has a story behind it." [Keep in mind that Gettysburg leads all the National Battlefield Parks with almost 1,400 of them.] "People who come here will be surprised—moved and inspired beyond expectation."

What's the managerial relationship like? She speaks to the fact that "trust, candor, and mutual respect make for a successful partnership. The key to the success of such relationships is in the mix of the right individuals who share the same goals and are willing to share credit." She emphasized the excellent relationship she enjoyed with former Park Superintendent Bob Kirby. "Both organizations initiate projects. The intersection between the NPS's needs and the capabilities and resources for funding of the Gettysburg Foundation, is the sweet-spot." She sums it up in one sentence: "Our job is to support Gettysburg."

Employing 40 full-time personnel, 40 part-timers, and another 20 or so seasonal employees, the Gettysburg Foundation provides a full menu of involvement for its members. You can simply contribute and enjoy the many benefits of membership. (Even at the most basic level of contribution, you will not pay for admission to either the museum or the film and cyclorama, and are entitled to a 10% discount at the Bookstore and the Quartermaster Store at the Rupp House, as well as many other businesses in and around Gettysburg.) It's a good deal, and your membership helps support the park. You can also participate in their many hands-on efforts in support of the GNMP; they have an incredibly full schedule of opportunities.

Joanne loves the stories of Father Corby and the famed Irish Brigade, notes their appellation "Fightin' Irish," and concludes our talk observing how the words of Lincoln's Gettysburg address resonate with meaning for her: "We can never forget what they did here. It is for us the living, rather, to be dedicated here to the unfinished work. . . ." She takes these words as a personal challenge, and is delighted to have found in her present position such an important venue to discharge what she sees as a tangible responsibility to history and our country.

One additional organization that should not be overlooked and is crucial to the preservation of Civil War sites nationally is the Civil War Trust. It has recently started a campaign to preserve important Revolutionary War sites (and recently acquired and restored General Lee's headquarters out on the Chambersburg Pike). If you are interested in preserving these memorials to history, please become a part of the ever-growing number of concerned individuals and consider joining both the Friends of Gettysburg and the Civil War Trust. They both maintain excellent websites.

Chapter 9

The Greatest Little Town in America

A Confluence

Why? The answer must include the unique confluence of offerings
presented by Gettysburg.

*T*he town's Civil War history is without question what defines the
place. The Civil War battle fought here, for better or worse,
defines the community itself. The town proper drips charm with its ability to
mix history with modernity through its wonderful array of shops, galleries,
antique stores, specialty shops, architecture, and everything else that makes this
place so special. Given that this small town is home to a mere 8,000 or so
people, its educational resources, anchored by Gettysburg College, remain
abundant.

The 75th Anniversary of the battle and the dedication of the Peace
Memorial by President Franklin Delano Roosevelt in 1938 makes a good
starting point for the transition from a sleepy bit of history to modern town.
Gettysburg had marked the occasion of other anniversaries previously (the 25th
Anniversary, for example, in 1888 saw the construction of the Prince of Peace
Church on Baltimore Street, and the 50th Anniversary the building of the rather
grand Post Office on Baltimore Street close to Lincoln Square, now the
Gettysburg Library.)

By 1940, all the main roads into Gettysburg had been paved, while many of
the secondary roads running through the surrounding townships and leading to
the farms were still dirt following the same routes since colonial times. While
the paving of even these smaller roads continued, many still follow their original

tracks and thus provide a scenic tour of the remaining rural areas—and a small taste of what the Gettysburg area looked like in 1863.

There was little development of the farm properties in the area until the 1950s, when out-of-town people started buying them up and turning them into residential developments. After the Eisenhowers bought their farm in 1950, it was not surprising that other military personnel started buying property in the area. The 1950s also saw the start of more intense development of tourist attractions: souvenir shops, motels, restaurants, etc., proliferated. In the last 25 years, however, there has been an extensive effort by the GNMP and its partners to push back on some of that commerce to restore the area to its appearance at the time of the battle.

Following a trend in the 1940s and 1950s to put modern facades on the historic buildings in the Borough, the 1960s saw a movement to promote the restoration of the buildings in Gettysburg to their original appearance, and was successful in getting many property owners to do so. The Borough now has a "Historical District," and regulates the appearance of buildings and signs within it. Indeed, older buildings whose foundations had become weakened by the constant traffic and vibration of those behemoths of the highways became a real concern.

The Borough of Gettysburg, of course, was only part of the battlefield, with most of the combat having been fought on the farms and fields beyond its boundaries: in Cumberland and Straban Townships, along with a small area in Mount Joy Township. The battlefield area where the armies fought, camped, and traveled covers many square miles, but the GNMP boundary includes a little less then 6,000 acres. The GNMP boundary does not cover the entire battlefield, but it does include many of the areas that witnessed the most intense fighting. While it is unrealistic to expect the whole battlefield can be recovered—there are simply too many homes and too many businesses and too much private land—there are always efforts underway to recover more battlefield acreage.

The 1960s also saw changes in the town's commercial center. Downtown self-owned buildings, with the merchants frequently living on the upper floors, gave way to absentee landlords. During the 1980s, when a Walmart and other large chain stores, hotels, and businesses moved in on Route 30 east of town, most of the downtown businesses left, leaving in their wake a host of empty store fronts. Like in most towns there are still a few around, but businesses catering to the tourist trade are always popular and usually fill up fairly fast. As tourism grew, so did the commerce to support it (the "tour bus" trade, for example).

The 1990s began the final phase of the transition to the modern town. Today, Gettysburg enjoys the best appearance it has had in the last century. Moreover, in the past two decades it has seen the development of excellent hospital and medical facilities in support of the burgeoning community and its vast numbers of annual visitors. The partnership that exists between the Borough of Gettysburg, the Gettysburg National Military Park and its partner, the Gettysburg Foundation, along with Gettysburg College, has worked extraordinarily well. Together they have made Gettysburg into one of the most attractive historical centers in America.

Clever Gettysburg

One of the special aspects of Gettysburg is the way it has managed to retain its small-town charm and historical flavor as it has grown into the exciting tourist attraction it is today. Downtown Gettysburg is like a finely wrought chain, with one jewel-like link leading to another. I have now been to Gettysburg dozens of times. Am I a member of that community? No. Has that community become part of me? Yes.

But the town is the history: the James Gettys Hotel, the Gettysburg Hotel, the Farnsworth House, and the Dobbin House—key historic points we discussed in Chapter 3. Take note of the historical markers around Lincoln Square and take a close look around the Square itself. Poke your nose into some of those curio shops or ask to see a restaurant menu if one isn't posted outside. Notice a few antique shops? Throughout the town you will find dozens, some of a general nature and some specializing in Civil War memorabilia. Many look like innocuous storefronts, so watch for them carefully. Right there on the Square, in nice weather between mid-April and October, you can enjoy a variety of wares at the Farmer's Market—open-air tents set up for various merchants and farmers.

Head north along Carlisle Street and you'll discover "Racehorse Alley" on your left. You guessed it: Back in the day, when the Chambersburg Pike was otherwise engaged, they held horse races over a five-block stretch here in the alley. Farther north, diagonally across the street and the railroad tracks from the Lincoln Diner, is the Gettysburg Transit Center, a very important place for getting around town or out to the battlefield. This is the home of Freedom Transit, which operates trolley buses year-round, either free or inexpensively.

Right there is the Lincoln Railway Station. Remember, this is the station where Lincoln arrived the night before he delivered the Gettysburg Address (he spent the night with Mr. Wills). As you proceed back toward the Square you pass the Majestic Theater on your left. Now owned by Gettysburg College, this historic theater shows films and hosts a variety of other activities of interest to the community as well as the College itself. (It's especially fun to go see movies about the Civil War in there.)

Take a short side trip down Racehorse Alley to your left—careful though, there's a lot of car traffic and no sidewalk. This part of the alley leads to the largest municipal parking lot in Gettysburg, with the fancy name Racehorse Alley Parking Plaza—it's on the left, as is the large boulder and plaque marking the site of the Samuel Gettys' Tavern. Looking to your right you'll see the back entrance to the Gettysburg Hotel. Enter the lobby and on the left is "One Lincoln," the hotel's moderately priced restaurant serving a nice selection of offerings for breakfast, lunch, and dinner; they have a nice bar, too.

Strolling down York Street you'll enjoy many nice shops along the block. The Union Drummer Boy, for example, sells authentic Civil War artifacts. And speaking of "authentic" memorabilia, check out The Horse Soldier back over on Steinwehr Avenue and the Gettysburg Museum of History on Baltimore Street. It gained national attention when it was featured on the History Channel's *American Pickers*. You'll also find the excellent military bookstore called For the Historian, managed by Larry Weindorf. Indeed, the entire area around Lincoln square is "Tourist Central"—take your time and enjoy all it has to offer.

This entire area offers a wide variety of wonderful eateries catering to your every taste. From the Gettysburg landmark: Ernie's Texas Lunch, to Thai Classic Four (are there three others elsewhere?), to The Parrot, arguably one of the best restaurants in Gettysburg (it also has a very capable upscale bar). Then there's Mama Ventura's—wonderful Italian food—and they'll even deliver a pizza to your room, Ping's for some good Chinese food and sushi, and, finally, if you want to eat "fancy" (and pricey), hop in your car and head out to the historic Herr Tavern. There are so many more, including the Lincoln Diner!

As we now head back down Baltimore Street, you'll find Dirty Billy's Hats—one of the most distinctive stores in town. Indeed, Dirty Billy's was one of the first places that caught my attention. Owner Bill Wickham has become something of a legend in the Civil War reenactor community. He produces beautifully made historically accurate replicas of Civil War hats (be sure you check out his website) and one of the foremost experts on Civil War headgear.

FRAN & BILL WICKHAM

Bill's wife and business partner is Fran Wickham—always cordial and pleasant, they complement each other beautifully. Located at 20 Baltimore Street, Dirty Billy's Hats: Military and Civilian Caps and Accessories—Exact Reproductions is filled with glass cases containing all sorts of attractive hats whose quality is unequalled. The shop offers a combination of reproductions, modern hats, and authentic antique Civil War headgear.

Bill first started collecting Civil War materials during the Centennial Celebration of the Civil War in the early '60s. He remembers Jack Kennedy once saying, "Remember the greatness that made this country," and was inspired by it. A veteran reenactor himself, he believes strongly the people who reenact are the true historians trying to recreate, and not just study, historical events. By 1964, Bill was making his first attempts at reproducing hats. He recalls the many people who helped him learn his trade, not the least of whom was his grandmother. Business-wise, Bill handles the reenactors and the history buffs while Fran focuses on the modern hats.

Bill also has an extensive historical collection of authentic hats ranging from the French and Indian War up to the Spanish American War. Having learned the trick from his grandmother, he stores many of these rare finds in emptied lard cans, packed with moth balls and old newspapers to protect their special contents. One such treasure trove he showed me contained four Confederate Civil War hats: a sailor's cap, a marine's hat in their odd greenish-gray color, a kepi, and a blood-stained forage cap with the owner's name written into the crown! Talk about a moment with history. Of course, I let Bill do all the handling; I would have been a nervous wreck for fear something I touched fell apart. As it turned out, they were all quite sturdy.

Bill adds that the owner of the bloodied hat had been taken to the main hospital in Frederick, Maryland, which had been set up at the former Hessian Barracks there. Mainly a hospital, it also served as a hospice housing men with head wounds or severe wounds to the torso, which could not often be successfully treated. While made as comfortable as possible with the use of morphine and other pain-killers, given the limited medical resources of the day

BARBARA FINFROCK

they usually died from their wounds. Terry Reimer, Director of Research at the National Museum of Civil War Medicine in Frederick, found one hospital in the town that had a particularly high mortality rate and speculates the "hopeless" cases had been sent there.

Bill enjoyed talking about the many different people he encounters: the visitors, always curious, inquiring, and sometimes "just silly"; the business people and their concerns of making a living here; other townspeople and how they find themselves constantly surrounded by history as they live their lives; and the Park Service, which he finds a little over-protective of the historical legacy of Gettysburg. "History doesn't belong to the government," he opines, "it belongs to the people." I am the proud owner of one of Bill's reproductions: a slightly modified Winfield Scott Hancock-styled "Slouch Hat." Unlike Bill and tens of thousands of others, I'll admit reenacting is just not for me. As an actor since the early '60s I have worn just about all the hot costumes I ever want to wear. Today, I shudder at the idea of wearing authentic reproductions of cotton and wool uniforms in temperatures anywhere above 70° with high humidity.

Gettysburg is full of interesting secrets. As one might suspect, numerous buildings are full of bullet holes and the occasional unexploded artillery shell (which you can often discover by simply by looking up). (Don't forget the Cannonball Ole Tyme Malt Shop.) These relics are often found in the walls or window frames of the upper stories of buildings. In fact, when you visit Dirty Billy's, look at the third-floor wall of the building on the right side of the alley (East Zerfing's Alley) just across the street. There is a Union Parrott Rifle shell stuck in the wall near the roof. Ironically, it had been moved there from the second floor when the building was expanded as a B&B for returning veterans in the late 1890s—the owners just didn't want to lose their little bit of history. And as we discovered earlier, Gettysburg lies on something paleontologists refer to as Dinosaur Ridge. Remember the dinosaur tracks built into the little bridge across Plum Run? Who knew?

On a more somber note, Bill wonders about the way some of the real history of the battle may be getting lost as the little town continues expanding. Fortunately, national organizations like The Civil War Trust, and the locally operated Gettysburg Foundation, and the NPS/GNMP are doing everything they can to preserve it.

The "boy" next door, John Fidler, owns and runs Martin's Shoe Store, Barbara Finfrock's favorite—remember, she was a key player in the development of the Museum and Visitor Center and is still a community stalwart when it comes to all things concerning the GNMP. It's a typical shoe store that you would find in most medium-sized towns in America. Sharing the neighborhood with Dirty Billy's, it's been around a long time.

John is an amiable man in his middle years born in 1961 in nearby York. The last of six kids, he remarks, "I was born on a kitchen table above the store." His father rode with Jim Tate in the famous winter-time ride from Gettysburg to the Indiantown Gap—and on February 21, 1941, Gettysburg added to its fame when Troop C of the 104th Cavalry rode their horses from Gettysburg to Indiantown Gap in a snowstorm, where they were federalized into the US Army. His father bought the store from George Martin in 1972, moving the family to Gettysburg when John was twelve. He remembers his first job washing dishes at the Avenue Restaurant on Steinwehr Avenue (which is no longer there). His classmate in Gettysburg was Rick Beamer, manager of the Dobbin House.

John sheds some new light on the old days. "We'd ride our bikes all over town: over to Hanover; over to the National Tower (from 1974 to 2000, the privately owned, and always controversial, viewing tower near the battlefield). As kids, we'd play fox and hounds in Devil's Den using certain tunnels that we thought no one knew about. It was a lot of fun to go out to the battlefield and watch the deer." John adds, "Back then the Majestic Theater was a great place to go. The town was so much busier. There was even a five and dime store across the street."

But, John notes, there have been a lot of changes in the town from about 1975. "There's less and less retail; the five and dime is gone, we used to have a dress shop, and there were three shoe stores in town. You used to be able to buy everything you needed in town." But, as in many towns large and small across America, those stores have moved to the suburbs. "We used to ride horses out where the Walmart store is now," he muses. He clearly misses the era.

John's personal connection to Gettysburg history was late in coming. "I read a lot of Civil War books; I just finished a book on Shiloh. As we live close to East Cavalry Battlefield, my son is named Jeb, and we own the Cavalry Field Mini-Storage located nearby." He still loves what he calls "the living history of Gettysburg. People walking around town in period garb—where else can you see that?!" Gettysburg is a special place for him: "The beauty of the battlefield; the way it's laid out; great restaurants and hotels. One very safe little town." And don't forget Gettysburg's best kept secret: "the fried chicken at the Hillside Restaurant on Route 15. They fry it in lard in black cast iron skillets. The place looks just like the pictures of restaurants I've seen from the '50s."

As we have discussed, the town is full of historic buildings. For example, if you're interested in historic churches in Gettysburg, get a historic town map and visit them on your own. There are a lot of them, including The Prince of Peace Episcopal Church, Saint Francis Xavier Roman Catholic Church, St. Paul's AME Zion Church, Christ Lutheran Church, Gettysburg Presbyterian Church, Trinity United Church of Christ, United Methodist Church, and St. James Lutheran Church.

On the civic side, be sure to take note of the Adams County Courthouse on the corner of Baltimore and Middle Streets, The Gettysburg Municipal Building (once the Adams County Prison), the Adams County Housing Authority (formerly the High-Street School), and in the same vicinity, the Gettysburg Area Middle School (a more recent addition), and the less-traveled entry to the GNMP, Wainwright Avenue. Take a moment to appreciate the wide variety of interesting period homes, many marked by historical tablets, from the affluent to the humble, not the least of which is the interesting Jack Hopkins House on South Washington Street.

Note the inscription on the Hopkins House plaque, which reads: "This house (#219) belonged to John Hopkins, an Afro-American citizen, from 1851 until his death at age 62 in 1868. His wife Julia continued to live here until she passed away in 1891. John Hopkins enjoyed a distinguished career as a janitor at the Gettysburg College beginning in 1847. Known as "Jack the Janitor" he was immensely popular with students and faculty alike as attested by the presence of the entire college staff and student body at his funeral service. Like most of Gettysburg's 200 Afro-American citizens the Hopkins family probably fled the town prior to the battle to avoid capture by the Confederates. The experience may have been a motivator for his son John Edward, who joined a US Colored Troops regiment shortly following the battle at Gettysburg and served to the war's end."

Sadly, Gettysburg, has some unpleasant memories in its dealings with its African-American community. As Jim Tate, our nonagenarian LBG, recalled: "In the 1920s the Klan held a rally here. It started on Seminary Ridge at Washington Street (to this day a neighborhood which is home to many African-American families), and went through town. Some of the Klansmen were carrying a huge flag, holding the edges—people would throw money onto it."

Back on Baltimore Street, you enter the fringes of the realm of the "other-worldly"—that is, the many businesses that cater to ghosts and all things that go bump in the night. Mark Nesbitt, the man generally credited with starting this industry back in the 1990s, owns the Ghosts of Gettysburg Tours. Entrepreneurial "spirit" that he is, he also owns and operates a similar business in Fredericksburg, the "heart" of four great Civil War battles: Fredericksburg, Chancellorsville, The Wilderness, and Spotsylvania Court House.

On a more serious note, when you cross Breckenridge Street you will notice the Tillie Pierce House on the right. This was the home of the fifteen-year-old girl whose family not only remained in the house during the battle, but successfully hid and tended five wounded Union soldiers including Colonel William Colvill of the 1st Minnesota, nursing him to a successful recovery.

Next to the Tillie Pierce House, it is my great pleasure to introduce you to the Shriver House Museum and its open, friendly, and extremely well-informed-of-all-things-Gettysburg owner Nancie Gudmestad. The Shriver House Museum is one of the real treats of the town of Gettysburg's historical scene. This well-preserved family home highlights the experience of Gettysburg's civilian population during the battle. In fact, the museum is so important to the town's history that is the only civilian facility that annually hosts reenactments of what occurred here in 1863.

The Shriver House Museum is located at 309 Baltimore Street. Hours and costs vary depending on the season and special events—the safest bet is to check their website. They do, however, always offer free admission to all active military members and their families.

The Shriver House Museum

Growing up in Philadelphia, Nancie and her husband Del, a Floridian, decided they wanted to find a venue for their "skillful salesmanship." After doing a fair amount of research on where to settle, they decided to open a B&B in Gettysburg, "not for the history, but because it fit our business plan." It was their goal to "treat people the way we wanted to be treated." They spent four years as innkeepers, but after becoming more familiar with Gettysburg decided to try something a little different. Looking around town, they discovered the derelict Shriver House.

Why the Shriver House? After countless conversations about Gettysburg, they concluded that, while there is so much said about the battle, "Somebody needs to tell the story of the people who lived here." They discovered the house had been built as the Civil War started, specifically for George and Hettie Shriver. The Shriver family had arrived in the area in 1721. Once purchased, Nancie and Del renovated the home and turned it into the fine museum it is today.

Nancie stresses the emphasis the Shriver House Museum places on the fate of the civilian population during that horrific three-day struggle. "We don't emphasize the military side of it—we tell history through the back door." It's an interesting point of view. "It's about people, not just about generals and dates.

NANCIE GUDMESTAD

Every single day I meet people who came here for a tour of Gettysburg—some had been here as kids and thought it was boring—and now I say, isn't it so much more exciting?" And having visited with Nancie, and having toured the Shriver House Museum twice, both my wife and I would add an emphatic, "YES!"

This is one of those "special" places that define Gettysburg. In addition to the house, the saloon, and the site of the Ten-Pin Alley, Shriver House Museum offers a small bookstore and gift shop. Your guide will take you through the Shriver home, now furnished with furniture and odds and ends from the period (although not the original pieces in the home—they were all destroyed). The tour really hit home for me as we entered the attic space that had become a Confederate "sniper's nest." It recreates the physical environment that had gone from a residence to a battlefield; a little taste of how the great Battle of Gettysburg foisted itself upon the community. As with just a few other places in Gettysburg, here the visitor experiences the truly personal side of this struggle, not just for the soldiers, but primarily for Hettie, and her daughters Sadie (7) and Mollie (5)—its innocent victims.

Time for a treat? Further down Baltimore Street is G's Old Fashioned Ice Cream—I can think of no better way to relax and take a break than with some ice cream. Of course, the ice cream hits the spot, but so too did Yankee *minie* balls on the south side of the building—take a close look around those windows. Those holes ain't from termites.

For the adults, right next door at 400 Baltimore Street is the new home of Reid's Winery Tasting Rooom and Cider House, formerly housed in the Jennie Wade Birthplace up the street. Maybe a nice Pinot Noir to go with your pistachio ice cream….

Back on the right side of the street and slightly south of the ice cream parlor is the historic Rupp House. This is not just important as an historic building, but also because it is the home of the Gettysburg Foundation. This is the headquarters of the Foundation and, houses a small museum and bookstore.

The Rupp House.

The Gettysburg Foundation also has administrative offices at the Museum and Visitor Center, and its volunteers man an information desk in the main lobby there. If you want to join up, you can do so here at the Rupp House or at the Visitor Center. Please don't hesitate: Do it now and enjoy all those benefits and help support the many projects undertaken by the Friends of Gettysburg!

The Steinwehr Avenue Corridor

Just before making the turn onto Steinwehr Avenue, you'll find the Gettysburg Emporium, and along with the Jeweler's Daughter just around the corner, these two specialty shops are a must if you're interested in authentic reproductions of period clothing. Each is filled with treasures that are either already made or can be custom made to fit your needs. As Baltimore Street turns onto Steinwehr Avenue, there's another fine Gettysburg bookstore called The American History Store—one of several stores owned by Deric Bardo. Don't overlook this fine place. It is quite extraordinary and offers a varied selection of titles and other offerings.

Speaking of books, Eric Lindblade (once the co-owner of Ten Roads Publishing), was born and raised in eastern North Carolina. He stayed there for the first 25 years of his life and attended East Carolina University. After college, he got involved in politics, becoming a town councilman in his hometown of Newport at the ripe old age of 22. At that time, he briefly held the distinction of being the youngest elected official in North Carolina.

ERIC LINDBLADE

"I remember hearing about the Civil War in kindergarten. Then, in 1989 (when I was six years old), my family took a trip to Maine to visit relatives. But as fortune would have it, we stopped at Gettysburg for lunch and spent a couple of hours there, and from that moment on I got hooked on the Civil War—history was always my passion." During his time in office he became "involved in trying to develop and promote the Civil War history in my hometown." His many visits to Gettysburg (at least twice a year after that first visit), means that "Gettysburg has been the one constant for me." Then, in 2008 he moved there! "One of the real reasons I moved to Pennsylvania," he jokes, "was to offset all those Pennsylvanians that moved to North Carolina! I've always been fascinated by the experiences of North Carolina soldiers, and the important role they played here in the battle, and the war itself. On an every-day basis, Gettysburg has one of the largest concentrations of Civil War historians and research sources in the United States—an unprecedented access to history, historians, and historical research."

He continues enthusiastically: "It's the only place in America where you can simply walk into a bar and hear in-depth discussions about the Civil War. Gettysburg as a Civil War site attracts people from all over the country and world—there's no other place like that. There is a collective captivation about this place—the battlefield itself, that's the 800-pound gorilla—and that's why I'm here, that's why everything is here."

There's much more to Eric than bartending at the famous Reliance Mine Saloon (more on that little treasure later). Eric is also a writer and historian, in addition to being involved in living history. "I have been doing that for 16 years now; my 'impression' is that of a typical enlisted soldier from North Carolina. I prefer the living history events to reenactments since I feel it is a much better way to educate the public about the lives of a soldier from that era." Eric's first book was on the Battle of Newport Barracks, which took place in his hometown. He is also working on a regimental history of the 26th North Carolina. At Gettysburg, the 26th North Carolina suffered the most casualties of any regiment in the Army of Northern Virginia.

Eric explains it this way:

> It was the largest regiment in Lee's army—starting out with about 900 men. After forty-five minutes of fighting against the 24th Michigan of the Iron Brigade, and then the 151st Pennsylvania, there were between 250 and 275 men left. On July 3, the regiment is involved in the Pickett-Pettigrew-Trimble Assault and advances all the way to the stone wall on Cemetery Ridge. When all was said and done after the battle, one account places the strength of the 26th at two officers, and sixty-eight enlisted men.

> Gettysburg is arguably the most chronicled battle in history," he suggests, and he remains struck by "how welcoming people are here today—it's a very welcoming place. The modern history of Gettysburg is as interesting as the 19th Century history in many ways.

Next up is the House of Gallon. Dale Gallon is one of the foremost Civil War artists in the world. Indeed, many of the historical tablets in and around Gettysburg contain his artwork. His work, both the original paintings and prints, can be purchased at his gallery. Be warned: this is outstanding art by a living painter who is extraordinarily popular, and it is not cheap. But if you can afford it, don't miss this wonderful opportunity to peruse his wares. Of course, Mr. Gallon is not the only noted living Civil War artist. Some of his better-known contemporaries include Don Troiani, Mort Künstler, and Keith Rocco. Gettysburg galleries are filled with their works; go on their websites for access to their paintings and prints.

As you stroll along this section of Steinwehr Avenue, you can't help but notice the concentration of businesses that cater (once again) to the "ghost tour industry." One, Gettysburg Ghost Tours, features the services of Johlene "Spooky" Riley—one of the "premier" storytellers and the Founder and Lead Investigator of the Gettysburg Paranormal Association. She is the author of *Ghostly Encounters of Gettysburg*, and seems to be one of the shining "candles" of communion with the netherworld. I took one of their tours in November 2013 as part of the research for this book and learned some fascinating things about Gettysburg that I hadn't known before. Unfortunately, "Spooky" was not available for my tour, but I was left in the very capable hands of Bob Withrow. For better or worse, ghost tours have become one of the main attractions of Gettysburg after dark. Given the interest in the paranormal throughout the country, this is not a phenomenon unique to Gettysburg.

Leaving the paranormal behind, we next turn to the Regimental Quartermaster for souvenirs more in keeping with the military side of Gettysburg history. I love going into this store and just looking around. (I've bought a few things here over the years, as well.) It's one of the better of the many stores that sell a vast array of "Gettysburgiana"—mostly reproductions, but also a few antiques. Along with the downtown area, this stretch of Steinwehr Avenue offers the greatest concentration of Gettysburg's Civil War-related businesses, restaurants, and lodgings.

Before we leave this area and move on to some other highlights of the town, I want to call your attention to a few more places. Restaurants abound here: the Dobbin House and, in the same block, Tommy's Pizza, one of the most popular pizza parlors in town. Across S. Washington Street is Gettysburg Eddie's. The place is always full, attesting to the good food and fun atmosphere. The restaurant is a tribute to Gettysburg's baseball Hall of Famer, Eddie Plank—give it a try.

And, just across the street, is one of the most famous places in town, at least among the writers, historians, and readers of Civil War history: The Reliance Mine Saloon. It can be hard to find unless you know where it is. Once you enter and pass through a "mine shaft" of sorts, you step into a darkened pub with tables, chairs and a small bar at the far end. But it isn't the atmosphere or a drink that draw people here as much as the special camaraderie that echoes within these walls. Of course average everyday folk like me might stop in for a brew, but the Mine (as it is popularly called) is known for certain "sorts" of people: Historians, authors, guides, and out-of-towners come here to swap stories, get books signed, and even sell their own books.

The Dean of this special group is William "Bill" Frassanito. Bill pioneered using modern landscapes to locate where Civil War-era photos were taken. His works include, among several others: *Gettysburg: A Journey in Time*, and *Antietam: The Photographic Legacy of America's Bloodiest Day*. Bill lives in Gettysburg and around 10:30 p.m. every Monday, Wednesday, and Friday slips quietly into the Mine. Everyone knows him, or wants to know him. And for good reason: He is a nice man with a rich history. Buy Bill a drink and he'll tell you about his career (and it is fascinating). Bring in a book and he will sign it. He might even have one there to sell to you.

As an aside, my publisher Ted Savas told me when he was visiting in 2009 with his son Demetri, Bill struck up a conversation with the 12-year old. While Ted, Jim Hessler, and a few other authors discussed publishing, Bill and "DT" slipped off to another table and talked for a full hour. The younger Savas—not yet hit by the Civil War bug—still recalls the occasion with fond memories. I bet if you can snag Bill for a while, you will too.

Farther down Steinwehr Avenue are other popular spots in town: the Gettysburg Heritage Center, the "Lincoln Train Museum," a gas station, several less expensive motels, a McDonald's, a KFC, General Pickett's Buffet, the Battle Theater and Gift Shop, the new home of the Appalachian Brewing Company, and lots more. Nestled among them, as mentioned at the beginning of this chapter, is The Horse Soldier. So many choices to define *your* Gettysburg!

The western edge of Gettysburg hosts a concentrated array of educational and historical institutions that combine to make a resource of great value, not only to the community of Gettysburg itself but to students, educators, historians, and even theologians from around the world.

Lying just north of the Chambersburg Pike is Gettysburg College (formerly, Pennsylvania College). It was founded in 1832 by anti-slavery

PETER CARMICHAEL

theologian Samuel Simon Schmucker, and five years later moved into Pennsylvania Hall on land provided by abolitionist Thaddeus Stevens. Pennsylvania Hall, the administrative heart of the College, is one of the three buildings that were here in 1863, the other being the Norris-Wachab Alumni House, originally the home of the President of the College. Today, Gettysburg College is one of the better liberal arts colleges in the United States and offers, as you might expect, substantial programs related to the Civil War: The Civil War Studies Program that is part of the regular curriculum, and the internationally known Civil War Institute, founded by Professor

Gabor Boritt and now run by Fluhrer Professor of History Dr. Peter Carmichael. The college's president, Dr. Janet Morgan Riggs, did her undergraduate work here before moving on to Princeton for her two graduate degrees.

In addition to being near the center of the fighting on Day One, the college's connection to all things military includes the former home of Dwight and Mamie Eisenhower, when they lived here during Eisenhower's command of Camp Colt, the training center for America's fledging tank corps beginning in 1918.

JANET MORGAN RIGGS

It now houses the Eisenhower Institute. (Gettysburg's rich educational culture also includes Harrisburg Area Community College, Gettysburg Campus, across town at 731 Old Harrisburg Road.)

BARBARA FRANCO

Heading farther west, and just south of the Chambersburg Pike, is the Lutheran Theological Seminary, also founded by Samuel Simon Schmucker. It is one of eight evangelical seminaries of the Lutheran Church in America whose mission is to train the leaders of the church in modern society. It is the oldest of the seminaries, and is central to the mission of the American Synod. Situated athwart the very Seminary Ridge that was held for so long by Union forces, and then after it fell by the Confederates for the duration of the fighting. Today, the seminary's 52-acre campus boasts more than two dozen buildings. As part of its commitment to modern Gettysburg, the seminary has "donated" two of

their buildings for important historical uses, as well as some land for Gettysburg's YWCA. The Reverend John R. Spangler, Executive Assistant to the President for Communication and Planning, was kind enough to provide me with many details about this key religious institution.

One of those donated buildings is Schmucker Hall with its famous cupola, which can now be toured as part of your admission to the new Seminary Ridge Museum there, which officially opened on July 1, 2013 to mark the beginning of the Sesquicentennial. Barbara Franco, its former executive director, led the transformation of this old building into the outstanding museum it is today. It has been refurbished into a wonderful historical resource that traces the events of the First Day, the care of the injured, and the general human suffering witnessed by Schmucker Hall; it also focuses on the larger issues of freedom and faith.

The seminary also provided the Adams County Historical Society with its new, albeit perhaps temporary, home in Wolf House, one of the older former residences on the campus that sits at the southern edge of the Seminary grounds. Its young and energetic executive director, Benjamin K. "Ben" Neely, identifies it not as a center of Civil War studies, per se, but as "the County's attic" because it houses thousands of letters, deeds of many of the farms and buildings in the area, and other papers and artifacts related to Gettysburg and Adams County. As the only full-time paid employee of the ACHS, Ben points out that the "funding for our organization comes from membership dues, private donations, and a small stipend provided by the county, some $12,000 annually." If you should be at all inclined, consider visiting and supporting this worthwhile operation.

Chapter 10

The Creators of Living History and the Phenomenon of Reenactors and Reenactments

*T*here is a phenomenon sweeping the Civil War world. It has been for many years: reenactors (or "living historians") and reenactments.

Before we meet some of the people involved, let's make a distinction between "living historians" and "historical reenactors." As it was explained to me, for the most part, reenactors are primarily concerned with the recreation of a particular battle (or part of that battle). Living historians, on the other hand, are individuals steeped in the history of a facet of life in the 1860s (or whatever period they study), not necessarily just the warfare. When these folks meet tourists, they often feel an obligation to pass on a sense of what life was like back then. Many people are both reenactors and engage in living history programs. Frankly, I am amazed at the degree to which these people steep themselves in the minutiae of the history of the war, of the period, and in some cases, of specific individuals who lived and died during that significant period in American history.

Reenactors come from all walks of life. They derive satisfaction and personal reward from assuming the guise of a Civil War persona. It often means participating in organized Civil War reenactments, traveling all over the United States to get to specific places where they occur, and outfitting themselves in the most authentic reproduction of wartime clothing and equipment their budgets will allow. Fortunately, the reenactments tend to avoid the battles fought in winter weather. I'm in awe of how they manage to do what they do in the summertime heat. If reenacting a soldier, they dress head-to-foot in heavy cotton, wool, leather, and a variety of accoutrements. In many cases they camp in mosquito-laden fields for several nights, with limited access to porta-pottis or showers.

Women portraying upper class ladies of the past find themselves ensconced in multiple layers of fabric over corsets and close-fitting underwear. If lower class, we're back to the heavier fabrics. Another factor, of course, is how committed each person is to the authentic clothing of the period. Since there are a plethora of sutlers available, along with online suppliers, it's not hard to find reproductions and, in some cases, original pieces available for sale. As the poet once said, if you can stand that heat, "You're a better man than I, Gunga Din."

By the way, if you've never read the magnificent *Confederates in the Attic*, by Pulitzer Prize-winning author Tony Horwitz, you owe yourself a very good read that will shed even more light on this phenomenon. It will also give you a new perspective on the generous acceptance by many Southerners of the Confederacy's defeat. But wait, as Sheldon Cooper of *The Big Bang Theory* might have asked, "Is that sarcasm?" Unfortunately, yes.

In many cases, reenactors associate themselves with specific units, like a regiment or brigade from a particular state. Often, this association involves regular meetings and drill, and even a commitment to help maintain the monuments to that unit on the many battlefields where they may have fought. Is it just a hobby? For some, surely it is. But for many is a much deeper commitment. Let's turn to some of the reenactors themselves to better understand all this.

Michael Kraus

Michael Kraus is the Curator/Historian of the Soldiers and Sailors Memorial Hall in Pittsburgh, and a captain in the National Regiment of the 116th Pennsylvania Volunteer Infantry, Company 1, Irish Brigade Reenactors.

Michael is also a self-employed sculptor with several Civil War statues to his credit, including a life-size figure of Colonel Strong Vincent for the Erie,

"CAPTAIN" MICHAEL L. KRAUS

Pennsylvania library. But for several days each week Michael can be found at Soldiers and Sailors Memorial Hall.

Michael came to reenacting through a series of fortuitous events: his discovery of an ancient Native American artifact that piqued his curiosity; a junior high-school teacher who formed a group called the Antiquities Club; a chance viewing of the Hollywood version of history *They Died With Their Boots On*; and a field trip to Fort Ligonier with a group of boys to "re-enact" a battle from the French and Indian War. "As Michael told me, Despite all this, "I found myself attracted to the aesthetics of the Civil War—its colors, materials, papers, and paintings." In 1971, a friend's father took him to Gettysburg, where he observed a lot of makeshift costumes common at the time. He was intrigued by a group called "Sherman's Bummers" who were far more authentic in their clothing and gear. Realizing he also wanted to go for the "authentic," he quickly joined this group of reenactors.

"Reenactment is a tool to understand the Civil War soldier," he explains. "And I wanted to do that from the inside out. I wanted to know how they did what they did, who they were, how they lived." Eventually Michael found his way into the 116th Pennsylvania. Knowing my background, he compared reenactment to theatre: "There is a degree of egotism involved, but that's secondary—for me, I can put those people on ego trips in their place. I actually admire the first-timer, their freshness in approaching history. Sure, there's a role-playing element—from the new inductees getting over their initial hesitance, to the seasoned veterans. Over the years I've played corporals and lieutenants, and done reenactments at Antietam, The Wilderness, Spotsylvania Court House, and Petersburg. Then in 1980, I was elected to be the overall Federal Commander of the reenactments at the 125th Anniversary of Gettysburg, which, by the way, I think was larger than the recent 150th. Serving as the Federal Commander was a lot of work."

"There are a lot of personal rewards for me," he continued. "First, I'm just very comfortable in 19th-century clothing. Everything I carry is 100% authentic; if it's not an original piece, it's a totally accurate reproduction. My tent, for example, is completely hand sewn. And it took me fifteen years to find an example of drawers to make a pattern. But there's a lot more: our regiment is like a fraternity, a fraternity of Civil War soldier brothers—seeing the same group of guys for twenty-five years. Camping out, we slow ourselves down. We consider it a hobby. Our unit does not allow women; there's no 'social component' to it. Our wives just have to stay home when we head out for our re-enactments."

Wow! But, I'm curious about the level of historical knowledge reenactors take to their events, so I ask.

"It depends on the level. Colonels and above have to know the history—you're ordering the men to reenact what actually occurred; for captains and below, not so much. The battles bring us the soldier's perspective, all you experience is just what's around you—what it's like in that noise, the confusion, the smoke."

Being nosey, I ask, "Isn't this frightfully expensive?"

"Sure, but people tend to start out in introductory gear or loaners," Michael replies. "Once committed, you start to buy the better stuff: my kit, for example, runs about $5,000—$2,500 for the uniform plus the buttons (apparently authentic), another $2,000 for my sword, and about $500 for the boots. Cavalry gear, and the equipment for artillerymen, is the most expensive though." Michael is totally committed to what he is doing. "I feel very strongly that my commitment to and extensive experiences with reenacting have contributed significantly to my expertise as both a curator and a historian."

Articulate and sensible, I understand the reenactment phenomenon a little better after talking with Michael.

Commander Michael S. Wassuta, who I contacted as the coordinator of reenactors for the Gettysburg Anniversary Committee reenactment of the 150th Battle of Gettysburg, is a retired law enforcement officer for New Jersey. He served in the United States Marine Corps, is the Commander of the Sons of the Union Veterans of the Civil War Camp #112 Gettysburg, Pennsylvania, and has been a reenactor since 1999.

Reenacting, says Michael, "is the spice that drives the soul." Michael is married to Cynthia Tutoli, having met through a cousin back in 1992. Cindy is also a reenactor, and they moved to Gettysburg shortly after Michael's retirement. In addition, Michael was recently elected vice-president of the

Adams County Fire–Police Associat- ion, "We deal, with traffic, security, and assistance to local and state police."

Michael was always fascinated by General Robert E. Lee, but being a good Yankee he joined the 2nd New Jersey Cavalry of the 2nd New Jersey Brigade. At the time, the brigade consisted of 153 members of which 19–23 were mounted. Initially they leased horses for weekend outings, but Michael now has his own horse (four, actually), and usually rides his #1: Kiwi, a Tennessee walker. "On occasion, I lend Kiwi to General Custer (Steve Alexander, see below), then I ride Nugget, also a Tennessee walker. Often, however, I play the mounted flag-bearer on the staff of Lieutenant General Ulysses S. Grant as played by Tony Daniels, another famous Civil War reenactor. But I've played a variety of characters: from private to general, from courier to flag-bearer, even a civilian scout."

Michael is a big man, and I ask him, "How do you stand the heat in wool uniforms?" "As long as I'm up on my horse, it can get as hot as it wants. If I had to do this on foot, I wouldn't be able to because of a back injury."

Cindy Tutoli is a warm and outgoing woman who worked for twenty-two years as an account manager for a large insurance firm. She moved to Gettysburg when Michael retired, and has now been reenacting for over a dozen years. Some of her best-known stops include Cedar Creek, Manassas,

New Market, Spotsylvania, and Culpeper, all in Virginia, as well as Little Bighorn in Montana, and of course, Gettysburg. It all began for Cindy when Michael took her on a trip to Amish country near Lancaster, Pennsylvania, and suggested they stop in Gettysburg. "It's on the way," he told her.

Cindy started her reenacting career to be with her husband, joining the 7th New Jersey Hospital Group: "I play a lot of nurses and civilian wives." Knowing of her role in setting up and breaking camp, I asked her if she finds that at all satisfying, or if she's still doing it to be with Michael? "I enjoy it as well," she explains. "It's a

"COMMANDER" MICHAEL WASSUTA

CINDY TUTOLI

lot of work: set-ups, maintenance, and breaking camp, but what I like most is the simplicity—getting back to the way things used to be. I enjoy the quiet of the encampments and the camaraderie I develop with the other reenactors."

"Other than Michael, are any other members of your family involved?" "No," she explains. "My mother was Belgian, and my dad a second-generation Italian—neither had any connection to the Civil War." She adds, "Not all reenactments are just about the battles; often they are original creations based on Civil War experiences. And as I watch the kids watching us, I enjoy the fact that we help motivate them to read and study history instead of being glued to their video games."

"Since I've learned to ride," Cindy continues, "I sometimes play a Union trooper. That's fun." She started horseback riding after she met Michael. "I started riding but then broke a hip. As soon as I could, I got back to it. We have four horses: Kiwi, Nugget, Brody, and Woody. Michael first got me interested in riding by hiring Kiwi, but the woman who owned him was planning to move—which worried me as I really liked that horse. Michael surprised me: he had already bought Kiwi." "Reenacting can be difficult sometimes," Cindy adds. "When we did Manassas last year it was really hot! They were selling ice for $6 a bag—somebody was making a lot of money! But mostly the experiences are very good."

"Then there was also New Market, Virginia," she laughs recalling another incident. "On that one I burned my hand tending the fire, had Nugget bite me, and Kiwi stood on my foot. Then, simply trying to get a lead line out of the back seat, I broke some ribs!" That sounds as though it might have been a good day to just stay home.

I asked Michael what his best and worst experiences have been: "My best was the 145th Anniversary of the fight at Bentonville, North Carolina," replies

Michael. "We were completely encircled by Confederates when a Federal unit came marching out of the woods—and we won the battle! Bentonville that year was special to me as I found out a month before I was going that I had a distant uncle who had served at Gettysburg with the 123rd New York Infantry, eventually going west and joining General Sherman's XX Corps on their march through Atlanta to the sea and up through Bentonville. He lived all the way up to the 20th century." This is an amazing discovery for someone as committed to Civil War history as Michael. "My worst experience," he adds, "was the First Manassas reenactment in 2012: the heat index reached 118 degrees—5,000 reenactors left that Saturday night after the first day." Many had passed out from the heat.

Michael also adds a word about unusual experiences. "At Little Bighorn a few years ago," Michael explains, "we glanced up and saw five or six Indian warriors on their horses in full regalia. We found out they were ghosts."

That sent my eyebrows up. "Do you believe in ghosts?" I ask.

"Oh yes, ghosts, spirits, and aliens, as well." Imagination is an integral part of role-playing, and in Michael's case, it extends into the supernatural. When I ask Cindy to relate her most unusual experience, she repeats Michael's account of seeing the ghosts of Indians at Little Big Horn. Cindy, too, is a believer.

On the humorous side, Michael tells me of how closely the horses can bond with the men: "One day I was giving Cindy a hug when my horse butted her out of the way, demanding my attention! They have their own personalities. I ride a lot now. We're busy from St. Patrick's Day all the way to Remembrance Day. Generally, the horses are not involved from November to March."

Steve Alexander

Steve Alexander is an unusual man, having found a level of commitment that is rare even within the more intense levels of the reenactor community. Steve impersonates General George Armstrong Custer—and only him.

Well known in the reenactor community, Steve has traveled all over the world bringing Custer to an untold number of spectators. His most frequent stops are Gettysburg, and of course the site of the Battle of the Little Bighorn, where Custer met his end. Steve has published two books on the subject: *G. A. Custer to the Little Big Horn*, and *Believe in the Bold: Custer and the Gettysburg Campaign*. He also maintains a rather elaborate and extensive website (www.georgecuster.com). Appearing in more than forty films as Custer, even suffering a severe injury in one of them when a horse fell on him, Steve is not in it for the money, as is true of most reenactors. Steve maintains that he has only been paid for a couple of the films he has done. He bears the full cost of his uniforms, all of which are authentic, his equipment, and travel to and from reenactments.

"I was born in Jackson, Michigan, at a time when westerns predominated on television," Steve related. "I grew up on a dairy farm, which meant that I milked cows twice a day, 365 days a year. The cows were not unionized in those days so they never got Christmas, New Years' Day, or Martin Luther King Day off (so neither did we!). My interest in the Civil War was spawned and nurtured by Disney's 'The Wonderful

STEVE ALEXANDER "BRIGADIER GENERAL GEORGE ARMSTRONG CUSTER"

World of Color' documentaries during the Civil War Centennial, a Marx's play-set of plastic toy soldiers, and *Old West* magazine. There were no cable stations, and the only 'reality shows' were those enacted by people willing to work, pay their debts, and accept their own responsibilities in life. The country was united in their beliefs in God, the flag, and their fellow man."

Steve spent thirty years working as a surveyor, but in the last recession in 2009 lost his job and had to find other employment. During his time as a surveyor crisscrossing Michigan, Steve found his path covering much of the same ground that Custer—who grew up in Monroe, Michigan—had traveled. "I found myself becoming ever more fascinated by Custer. Then, in 1986 I made a trip to the Little Big Horn, camped, ate beef jerky, and literally lived the soldier's life. Stopping at a museum in the area, I was asked to portray Custer for their upcoming Festival. I've been doing it ever since."

Steve's commitment to Custer led him to be named one of the "ten most fascinating people in the State of Michigan." He is the subject of dozens, and perhaps hundreds of newspaper and magazine articles chronicling his interest in Custer, and the many places and events at which he has been portraying him. After applying for some 250 jobs when he lost his position as a surveyor, Steve was "forced to humble myself in accepting unemployment for three months before landing an exciting career in Janitorial Service." And while his new full-time employment secures for him three meals a day and a roof over his head, Steve says that, "Throughout this humbling experience I have tried to maintain a dignified and historically accurate portrayal of an American figure who epitomized our western expansion. Through plays, films, books and reenactments I have continued to do my part to bring history to life and memorialize those values that had once made us a great nation." A self-admitted libertarian, Steve has a strong commitment to those essential values that once characterized the American spirit. He is also very religious.

"In the beginning of my 'Custering' I strived to learn everything there was to know about him. I did my research. Historical accuracy is very important to me. I recognize that my interest in Custer is beyond the norm; it's an obsession and I'm comfortable with it. Even as a teenager, while my classmates experimented with hallucinogenic drugs I spent my time traveling via books across prairies and the battlefields of the Civil War. Before I walked that hallowed ground I had made transcendent trips in my mind to the slopes of the Little Big Horn and the rolling fields of Rummel's Farm. There is a passion beyond the norm that drives me. I don't think that I'm reincarnated, but I have thought about 'why have I gone to so much trouble developing and playing Custer?' I believe when a person dies, the spirit—their energy—goes somewhere. Maybe when Custer died and his energy was dispersed, it reunited in an empathetic young boy growing up in Michigan." Steve now lives in Custer's Michigan home, or "living in Custer's womb" as he refers to it.

The spirituality represented in Steve's commitment to Custer is something new to me, and I find it quite amazing. I remember Bob Kirby's answer to my question to him about what he thought of the reenactment phenomenon: "I believe it's important to allow people to follow their passion in their own way." Certainly, Steve Alexander is unique among the reenactors I've encountered. There are times when he must believe that he is the 21st-century version of this great Civil War figure. That he devotes much of his life to it is, for him, the right thing to do. An internationally recognized authority on Custer, Steve has sought and derived great reward and satisfaction from his "obsession." It is for each of us to determine what holds value for us. In Steve's case, it is his becoming "The Foremost Custer Living Historian" in the country—as he was proclaimed to be by the United States Congress.

The events celebrated here in this little town confirm that Gettysburg is, above all, the focal point of that war that once tore our nation apart.

These shared experiences help me better understand what makes Gettysburg so special. If we grant that the Civil War was the most momentous, nation-changing event in our country's history, it becomes more understandable how it attracts the following it does.

Appendix

An Interview with the New Superintendent of the Gettysburg National Military Park

In January 2014 Robert J. "Bob" Kirby retired as Superintendent of the Gettysburg National Military Park after many years of distinguished service. I would like to extend a hearty welcome, and my very best wishes, to Ed W. Clark, the new Superintendent, for his own successful tenure.

According to an information release by the NPS/GNMP, Ed's background thoroughly prepared him for his new role:

> Previously he served as Superintendent of Manassas National Battlefield Park, where he provided Service-wide leadership for the Sesquicentennial of the Civil War and the broader Civil War to Civil Rights commemorative effort. He has also served as the acting Associate Regional Director for Operations for the National Capital Region of the National Park Service and the acting National Coordinator for National Heritage Areas for the Service. Prior to Manassas, Clark was Deputy Chief Ranger at Shenandoah National Park and Supervisory Park Ranger at the Blue Ridge Parkway among other posts.

He graduated from the Senior Executive Service's Candidate Development Program. The program is designed for the National Park Service's most promising senior leaders.

ED CLARK

Superintendent Clark is the beginning of a new era for the GNMP; he is clearly one of the most energetic, bright, and promising rising stars of the NPS.

Of all the people I have met in the preparation of this book, meeting and chatting with Ed, was one of the most memorable. Originally scheduled for an hour, we gabbled effortlessly for almost 90 minutes. An eleventh-generation Virginian, "raised in appreciation of my home state of Virginia," he experienced the emotional commitment to where he grew up, something he feels is getting lost in our modern, constantly mobile, America. Only in his mid-forties, Ed has spent a lot of time in his native state, but it is his new assignment that intrigues me.

"What are your impressions of Gettysburg?" I asked.

"Wow! This is just an amazing place," he began before elaborating. "It's such an evocative place—it stirs emotions in people—frankly, more so than any other place I've worked. There is such a sense of ownership here, how 'directly' you can feel it even now. Look what's here: of course, the battle itself, the Confederate High-Water mark: the storied Pickett's Charge—I had ancestors in that charge—the chill I got the first time I stood at the Virginia Monument and thought about which of my ancestors were in the line to my right, to my left, there were several here. That amazing Cycloramic painting of the Charge—all of it so emotional and moving, awe inspiring, and not just for me, but for so many of our visitors. Gettysburg was my Christmas gift—they called me on Christmas Eve, 2013." But Ed doesn't forget the men who have gone before him: "My predecessors have given me gifts, as well—their legacies provide the means to give the visitor here a better experience."

Clearly wanting to continue in that tradition, Ed has many things he would like to see accomplished. Hampered by the limited budgets provided to the NPS these days, he still sees ways of getting things done. Ed acknowledges the unique relationship of the GNMP and the Gettysburg Foundation: "It is at the core of our being; we're always striving to have the two entities function as one. At a recent NPS's 'Friends Alliance' nationwide meeting, we blew peoples' socks off—we always endeavor to bring our strengths to the table." He notes, "Always a struggle for even our combined resources is our fight with mother nature. The movement among the historical parks, for example, to try and restore them to their Civil War conditions. In our case that involves clearing 500 acres and planting over 3,000 orchard trees. Looking to the future, we want to finish restoring the area around Cemetery Hill, particularly, Ziegler's Grove, site of some of the most intense fighting on Day Two—we'll have to take out some of the parking lot that's there to do it."

Professionally, his resume speaks for itself, but I want to know more about the man. He jokes: "How many biologists do you know who carried a gun [when he became a law-enforcement ranger], and then became Superintendent of one of the Parks?" He still makes his home in Leesburg, Virginia, and commutes an hour each way to and from Gettysburg. His wife Heidi is a teacher, and his two sons are in school there.

"Are they interested in history?"

"History in general, absolutely," boasts Ed. "Years ago I gave them the choice of going to Disneyland or going to England, looking at a bunch of old castles, and the like—they jumped at going to England." His boys regularly volunteer at an old working gristmill in Leesburg. "My sons are qualified millers," he adds proudly, and then proceeds to show me one of his favorite photos of the two of them sitting on Hadrian's Wall in England. A man of many interests, Ed's hobbies range from fly-fishing to fiddle playing, but he adds quickly, "I'm the biggest museum geek who ever walked the face of the earth!"

A total Civil-War buff, Ed speaks of his role in the Civil War to Civil Rights commemorative effort: "I started looking at the broader context of the Civil War—how the Union 'victory' at Antietam led to Lincoln issuing the Emancipation Proclamation. I want to help folks make the connection that these events are not single occurrences, but part of a continuum of history."

And, that brings us to a passion of his: education. "It's important to place what went on here in the context of the modern era. Over 100,000 school kids visit Gettysburg every year; how do we bring more to the place?" He feels the answer lies in reaching out to organizations that could be a resource for future leaders: here at Gettysburg and the Eisenhower Farm, as well as in the NPS, generally. "And, not just the traditional organizations, but into new places to find those kids for whom history can become a passion—just look at the museum resources we have here! They can become the means to attract those young people: tell them the 'stories' behind the objects, acquire new ones, bring our history into context for them, get them excited about it."

Ed brings up Maslow's "Hierarchy of Needs." In their simplest form they constitute, from the most basic to the most advanced: biological and physiological, safety, love and belongingness, esteem (achievement, mastery, independence, status, dominance, prestige, self-respect, and respect from others), and self-actualization (realizing personal potential, self-fulfillment, seeking personal growth and peak experiences). It is in these last two categories, as difficult as they may be today, that the new leaders will be found. And Ed is not only clearly committed to finding them, but perhaps even more important, helping them get there.

Facing the practical realities of taking on the supervisory responsibilities of a place like the GNMP and the Eisenhower Historical Site, I ask him if he can share some insights into his budgetary concerns. "Sure: 2010 was the high-water mark for our budget; and it's only recently shown growth with a 9% increase for the National Park Service for our Centennial year in 2016. Currently, however, there is an estimated $11.5 billion backlog in Park maintenance nationally."

At this point my jaw drops.

"Here at Gettysburg, just to give you some idea of our needs, the cost of acquiring Lee's Headquarters out on Buford Avenue was significant, but paid for by private donations. It will cost an additional $1,000,000 from private funds to restore it to its 1863 appearance [since this interview, it has been accomplished]. Restoring the Phillipoteaux painting, for example, took $15,000,000 of federally appropriated money."

These numbers are staggering, but Ed is talking about our heritage, with Gettysburg being perhaps the most iconic site of the struggle that almost split our nation in two. It also reminds me of the vital role played by private organizations like the Gettysburg Foundation, where contributions are not only appreciated, but desperately needed. Nationwide, the Civil War Preservation Trust is continually deserving of funds and does tremendous work.

There is no doubt in my mind that Ed Clark is the right man for this monumental job. He is brilliant, amiable, and generous to a fault with both his time and energy. With someone as articulate as Ed to help, introducing you to the "greatest little town in America" and the reason it has become so becomes a lot easier.

And so, as we say in the theatre, "break a leg" Mr. Clark, and I sincerely hope we find an opportunity to chat again.

Afterword

When I undertook to write this book, I had no idea what I was getting into. It was much harder than I imagined, and it took much longer than I anticipated. And now I am done, and my adventure in "discovering" Gettysburg is behind me.

Perhaps it is silly to imply that I am leaving Gettysburg. Even when I do so physically, the resonance of my experiences here linger, always. They will stay with me for the rest of my life. And with each subsequent visit, with each new encounter with someone closely connected to this place, Gettysburg, the meaning of it all burrows its way deeper into the fibers of my being. It is now part of what defines me. If this sounds silly to you, it is only because you have never been there.

I was talking all this over with my wife recently about how completely taken I have become with Gettysburg. "Are you familiar with Ray Oldenburg's notion of a 'third place' in our lives?" she asked. I readily admitted I had never heard of it, so she filled me in.

The term "third place" (also known as "third space") revolves around the concept of community building—a reference to social surroundings separate and distinct from our home and our workplace. Ray Oldenburg wrote about this in his influential 1999 book *The Great Good Place: Cafes, Coffee Shops, Bookstores, Bars, Hair Salons, and Other Hangouts at the Heart of a Community*. These "third places," he argues, are important for civil society, democracy, civic engagement, and establishing feelings of a sense of place.

As one might imagine, if there is a "third place," there must be two preceding it. According to Oldenburg, "first place" is home and those we live with. "Second place" is the workplace—where many people spend most of their time. "Third places," then, offer the "anchors" of community life. They facilitate and foster broader and more creative interaction. All societies have informal meeting places; what is new in our modern time is that we intentionally seek them out as vital to current societal needs.

The hallmarks of a true "third place," argues Oldenburg, are as follows:

- Free or inexpensive
- Food and drink, while not essential, are important
- Highly accessible: proximate for many (walking distance)
- Involve regulars—those who habitually congregate there
- Welcoming and comfortable
- Both new friends and old should be found there

While Gettysburg does not strictly meet all the criteria Oldenburg sets forth, it comes damn close. And surely once it overtakes you, establishes feelings of a sense of place—it becomes something larger than itself. And yet it is impossible to truly define.

For example, many people I spoke with identified that what drew them to Gettysburg was something "intangible," something they really could not put into words. Yes, it's the history of the battle, but it is so much more than that. Yes, the town is unique, but it is more than that. Each of us must decide for ourselves the nature of that unusual attraction—that spell, if you will—that Gettysburg holds over us.

All good things must come to an end, and as they say in the movies, "Here endeth the lesson."

I do hope you've enjoyed it.

Select Bibliography

The main reading materials I used to help me write this book include the following five titles:

Bowden, Scott and Ward, Bill. *Last Chance For Victory*. Savas Publishing Company, 2000.
Coddington, Edwin B. *The Gettysburg Campaign: A Study in Commands*. Simon & Shuster, 1997.
Guelzo, Allen C., *Gettysburg: The Last Invasion*. Vintage Books, 2014.
Sears, Stephen W., *Gettysburg*. Mariner Books/Houghton Mifflin, 2004.
Trudeau, Noah Andrew, *Gettysburg: A Testing of Courage*. New York: HarperCollins, 2002.

I have read untold other titles on Gettysburg and the Civil War, and a few of my favorites (most of whom I dipped into while writing *Discovering Gettysburg*) are as follows:

Adkin, Mark, *The Gettysburg Companion: The Complete Guide to America's Most Famous Battle*. Stackpole Books, 2008.
Desjardin, Thomas S., *These Honored Dead: How the Story of Gettysburg Shaped American Memory*. Da Capo Press, 2003.
Gallagher, Gary W., Editor, *Three Days at Gettysburg: Essays on Confederate and Union Leadership*. The Kent State University Press, 1999.
Petruzzi, J. David and Stanley, Steven, *The Complete Guide to Gettysburg: Walking and Driving Tours of the Battlefield, Town, Cemeteries, Field Hospital Sites, and other Topics of Historical Interest*. Savas Beatie, 2009.
———, *The Gettysburg Campaign in Numbers and Losses: Synopses, Orders of Battle, Strengths, Casualties, and Maps, June 9-July 14, 1863*. El Dorado Hill, CA: Savas Beatie, 2012.

Books Providing Specific Information about the Battle of Gettysburg:

Artillery:
Cole, Philip M., *Civil War Artillery at Gettysburg*. Colecraft Industries, 2002.
Gottfried, Bradley M., Ph.D., *The Artillery of Gettysburg*. Cumberland House, 2008.
Newton, George, S*ilent Sentinels: A Reference Guide to the Artillery at Gettysburg*, Savas Beatie, 2005.

Cavalry:
Longacre, Edward G., *The Cavalry at Gettysburg*. Lincoln, NE: University of Nebraska Press (Bison Books), 1993.
Wittenberg, Eric J., *Gettysburg's Forgotten Cavalry Actions*. New York: Savas Beatie, 2011.
——, *Protecting the Flank at Gettysburg*. El Dorado Hills, CA: Savas Beatie, 2013.
Wittenberg, Eric J. and Petruzzi, J. David, *Plenty of Blame To Go Around: Jeb Stuart's Controversial Ride to Gettysburg*. New York: Savas Beatie, 2011.
Wittenberg, Eric J., Petruzzi, J. David, and Nugent, Michael F., *One Continuous Flight: The Retreat from Gettysburg and the Pursuit of Lee's Army of Northern Virginia, July 4-14, 1863*. New York: Savas Beatie, 2008.

Individuals:
Desjardin, Thomas A., *Joshua L. Chamberlain*. Van Nuys, CA: Greystone Communications, 1999.
Hessler, James A., *Sickles at Gettysburg*. New York: Savas Beatie, 2009, 2010.
Huntington, Tom, *Searching For George Gordon Meade: The Forgotten Victor of Gettysburg*. Mechanicsburg, PA: Stackpole Books.
Jordan, David M., *Winfield Scott Hancock*. Bloomington, IN: Indiana University Press, 1996.
Longacre, Edward G., *General Buford, A Military Biography*. Cambridge, MA: Da Capo Books, 1995.
Mingus, Scott L., Sr., *Confederate General William "Extra Billy" Smith: From Virginia's Statehouse to Gettysburg Scapegoat*. El Dorado Hills, CA: Savas Beatie, 2013.

Monuments:
Hartwig, D. Scott and Ann Marie, *Gettysburg: The Complete Pictorial of Battlefield Monuments*. Gettysburg: Thomas Publications, 1996.
Huntington, Tom, *Guide to Gettysburg Battlefield Monuments: Find Every Monument and Tablet in the Park*. Mechanicsburg, PA: Stackpole Books, 2013.
McLaughlin, Donald W., *Crossroads of the Conflict: Defining Hours for the Blue and Gray – A Guide to the Monuments of Gettysburg*. Denver: Outskirts Press, Inc., 1986.

Related Actions:
Mingus, Scott L., Sr., *Flames Beyond Gettysburg: The Confederate Expedition to the Susquehanna River, June 1863*. New York: Savas Beatie, 2012.

Specific Actions of the Battle of Gettysburg:
Adelman, Garry E., *Little Round Top: A Detailed Tour Guide*. Gettysburg; Thomas Publications, 2000.

Adelman, Garry E. and Smith, Timothy H., *Devil's Den: A History and Guide*. Gettysburg: Thomas Publications, 1997.

Archer, John M., *Fury on the Bliss Farm at Gettysburg*. Gettysburg: Ten Roads Publishing, 2012.

Cox, John D., *Culp's Hill: The Attack and Defense of the Union Flank July 2, 1863*. Cambridge, MA: Da Capo Press, 2003.

Hessler, James A. and Motts, Wayne and Stanley, Steven, *Pickett's Charge at Gettysburg: A Guide To The Most Famous Attack in American History*. El Dorado Hills, CA: Savas Beatie, 2014.

Jorgensen, Jay, *The Wheatfield at Gettysburg: A Walking Tour*. Gettysburg: Thomas Publications, 2002.

Norton, Oliver Wilcox, *The Attack and Defense of Little Round Top, Gettysburg, July 2, 1863 – 1913*. Ithaca, NY: Cornell University Library, The James Verner Scaife Collection – Civil War Literature, 1913.

Pfanz. Harry W., *Gettysburg: Culp's Hill and Cemetery Hill*. Chapel Hill, NC: The University of North Carolina Press, 1993.

——, Gettysburg: *The First Day*. Chapel Hill, NC: The University of North Carolina Press, 2001.

——, Gettysburg: *The Second Day*. Chapel Hill, NC: The University of North Carolina Press, 1987.

Shultz, David L. and Mingus, Scott L. Sr., *The Second Day at Gettysburg*. El Dorado Hills, CA: Savas Beatie LLC, 2015.

Thomas, James E., *The First Day at Gettysburg: A Walking Tour*. Gettysburg: Thomas Publications, 2005.

Specialty Guides:

Anonymous, *Cemetery Ridge Walking Trail*. Gettysburg: National Park Service, Gettysburg National Military Park, no copyright date listed.

National Park Service and Boy Scouts of America, *Gettysburg Heritage Trail Guide: Hiking the Billy Yank and Johnny Reb Trails*. Boy Scouts of America: York-Adams Area Council, 2008.

Paths of Heroes Series – Four Booklet Series Published by the Friends of the National Parks at Gettysburg: MacLachlan, Renae, *One — A Lion to the Last: Lt. William J. Fisher and the 10th U. S. Infantry*, 2003.

——, *Two – A Brave and Stubborn Resistance: The 73rd Pennsylvania and Cemetery Hill*, 2003.

——, *Three – Forward & On We Went: The 8th Louisiana's Twilight Assault on Cemetery Hill*, 2003.

——, *Four – A Feat of Arms: Freeman McGilvery and the Plum Run Artillery Line*, 2003.

Specific Places:

Gudmestad, Nancie W., *The Shriver's Story: Eyewitnesses To The Battle of Gettysburg*. Gettysburg: The Shriver House Museum, 2008.

Smith, Timothy H., Edited by Loeffel-Atkins, Bernadette, *"In The Eye Of The Storm" – The Farnsworth House and the Battle of Gettysburg*. Gettysburg: Farnsworth Military Impressions, 2008.

Specific Units:

Desjardin, Thomas A., *Stand Firm Ye Boys From Maine: The 20th Maine and the Gettysburg Campaign*. Oxford: Oxford University Press, 1995.

Herdegen, Lance J., *The Iron Brigade in Civil War and Memory: The Black Hats from Bull Run to Appomattox and Thereafter*. New York: Savas Beatie, 2012.

——, *Those Damned Black Hats!*. New York: Savas Beatie, 2008.

Nolan, Alan T., *The Iron Brigade: A Military History*. Bloomington, IN: Indiana University Press, 1994.

Mingus, Scott L., Sr., *The Louisiana Tigers in the Gettysburg Campaign: June-July 1863*. Baton Rouge: Louisiana State University Press, 2009.

Maps:

Gottfried, Bradley M., *The Maps of Gettysburg: An Atlas of the Gettysburg Campaign, June 3-July 13, 1863*. New York: Savas Beatie, 2007.

Interesting Sidelights:

Anonymous, Gettysburg National Military Park: *Official Guide Museum and Visitor Center*. Nashville, TN: Beckon Books, an imprint of FRP Books, 2011.

Brennerman, Chris and Boardman, Sue and Dowling, Bill, *The Gettysburg Cyclorama: The Turning Point of the Civil War on Canvas*, New York: Savas Beatie, 2015.

Drake, Kevin, *Test Your Knowledge On The Battle of Gettysburg*. Gettysburg: Xulon Press, 2010.

Finfrock, Barbara J., *Twenty Years On Six Thousand Acres: The History of the Friends of the National Parks at Gettysburg 1989-2009*. Gettysburg: Barbara J. Finfrock, 2009.

Nasby, Dolly, *Gettysburg: Then and Now*. Charleston, SC: Arcadia Publishing, 2008.

Riley, Johlene "Spooky", *Ghostly Encounters of Gettysburg*. Gettysburg: Arbor House, 2011.

Index

Acknowledgments

So many people have helped me in so many ways. Their contributions, in whatever form they took, have been invaluable. As they say, "Couldn't a dunnit without ya."

At the risk of belaboring the obvious I want to thank my wife Marilyn. From the outset, her constant encouragement and support and knowledge have been key to my pursuing this dream. Her tolerance as I put almost every other aspect of our life aside while writing this book, the numerous trips we have made to Gettysburg, the hours I have spent on the battlefield, were always met with a smile upon my return, and a "What did you learn today?" She is amazing.

Next, is my ever-so-talented partner in this endeavor, Tim Hartman. Tim is not only a brilliant artist but one of the most gracious and supportive people I have ever known. He contributed not only his wonderful caricatures, drawings, maps, and cartoons, but sound advice and encouragement whenever I needed it.

Thanks to Enis Koral (my best friend and fellow Civil War enthusiast—especially when it involves getting out and showing his stamina on those amazing battlefields!) who is a wonderful photographer who contributed greatly to the book; and to his wife Mimi—especially for her indulgence as her husband lent me some of his valuable time.

Simply put, Theodore P. Savas, Managing Director of Savas Beatie, made this book possible. He published it (of course!), but during the entire process offered endless guidance and advice on every aspect of it. I thank him for his inspiration, his wisdom, his patience, and his very good and discerning taste—and, of course, his brilliance as an editor and fact-checker! Editorial Director Steven Smith helped substantially in shaping my manuscript. He shared his knowledge of the subject, and forced me to "get me to the heart of the matter." Ted also had historian and award-winning Civil War author Tom Huntington read an early draft. Tom offered invaluable guidance during the preliminary stages by helping me shape my ridiculously long *magnum opus* into a manageable size. And, where would I be without the brilliant marketing and publicity skills of Sarah Keeney, my publisher's longstanding Marketing Director, the promotional acumen of Media Specialist Renee Morehouse, the guidance of Administrative Director Stephanie Ferro, and Donna Endacott, SB's astute Account Manager? I must also thank Ian Hughes of England for his beautiful dust jacket and, finally, Savas Beatie's Production Manager Lee Merideth for his own artistic sensibilities in laying-out the book.

Stephanie Lower Shaara, one-time manager of the James Gettys Hotel, helped me tremendously throughout, encouraging me to write this book, and helping me meet and connect with many valuable contributors, herself included. Her knowledge and love of Gettysburg is palpable and, I might add, wonderfully contagious. A word of thanks to her parents, George and Audrey Lower, for their support and hospitality. And, of course, I mustn't forget the staff at both the James Gettys Hotel and Lord Nelson's Gallery for that extra measure of care whenever we visited.

Over the last several years I have met so many historians and authors who have studied and written about all aspects of the Battle of Gettysburg. In every case, they have been helpful and generous in sharing their knowledge. I would be impossible to name them all, but you know who you are, and know that I am thankful. Still, I want to single out two individuals who went above and beyond. Prolific authors and historians themselves, they also share the distinction of being Savas Beatie authors: Scott L. Mingus, Sr. and J. David Petruzzi. My association with them began when they agreed to be interviewed for the book, but since then they have become my friends, and were among the first people to look at parts of this work during its development. I can't thank them enough for their countless contributions.

Dean Shultz and his wife Judy are the owners of a special farm near the Baltimore Pike that surrounds the famous "Lost Avenue," aka Neill Avenue, which perhaps less than one-in-ten-thousand visitors to Gettysburg ever get to see! Dean is universally recognized as one of the foremost experts on the Battle of Gettysburg. Understanding my interest in not only the battle but that special little corner of the battlefield that sits in the middle of his property, he generously spent numerous hours showing Enis, another group of friends, and me this unique place on the Gettysburg battlefield.

There is simply no way this book could have been written without the tremendous support and contributions of the folks at the new Gettysburg National Military Park Museum and Visitor Center. Without exception, National Park Service Rangers are an extraordinary group of people: knowledgeable, friendly, communicative, and always helpful. I owe them a great debt for their innumerable contributions. I would especially like to thank Ed Clark, Bob Kirby, Matt Atkinson, Clyde Bell, Christopher Gwinn, Scott Hartwig, John Heiser, John Nicholas, and the ever-helpful, Katie Lawhon. In addition, I want to add a word of thanks to non-Ranger NPS employees, as well: Toni Dufficy, Jo Sanders, Norma Lohman, and Lisa Kamps (the latter not actually a NPS employee but the manager of wonderful bookstore located in the Visitor Center).

The Licensed Battlefield Guides of the Gettysburg National Military Park are another very special "elite" group of people. Regulated by the NPS, these men and women are among the most knowledgeable and cordial representatives of the Gettysburg experience you will find. Having passed a test that I can only compare to a qualifying exam for a doctorate degree, they are an endless source of information about the battle and the Civil War. I thank them all, and especially those who have actively contributed to this book: Sue Boardman, Joanne Lewis, George Newton, Deb Novotny, James Hessler, George Symons, and the late Jim Tate.

And what a wonderful discovery it was finding the Gettysburg Foundation (GF) and their membership program known as the Friends of Gettysburg. Their unique private/public collaboration with the NPS has helped turn the Gettysburg National Military Park into the premiere historic park in the NPS system. Joanne Hanley, former President of the GF, is a treasure; she has been tremendously helpful and supportive throughout my entire project. In addition, Cindy Small, former employee Susan Bonser, and Warren Wilde went out of their way to help me. My thanks to them all.

Within the community were many wonderful individuals who helped me discover this special place, with many of their neighbors from nearby towns equally helpful. My thanks to: Rick Beamer, Susan Beck, Charles Bender, Krystle Brough, David Craine, John Fidler, Barbara Finfrock, Jim Glessner, Nancie Gudmestad, Marion Thomas Harbaugh, Eric Lindblade, Debbie March, Steve Mott, Jack and Maria Paladino, John Perry, Bonnie Riley, Johlene "Spooky" Riley, Guy Seiferd, Jane Sewell, Loring Shultz, Florence Tarbox, and Bill and Fran Wickham. And a tip of the hat to Mayor William "Bill" Troxell—a wonderful advocate for Gettysburg.

For my brief discussion of Gettysburg College, the Lutheran Theological Seminary, the new Seminary Ridge Museum, and the Adams County Historical Society, I want to extend my special thanks to: Janet Morgan Riggs, Cathy Bain, Peter Carmichael, Barbara Franco, Brian Jordan, Brian Douglas Johnson, Benjamin Neely, and the Reverend John R. Spangler.

And how much would we miss the reenactor community that pays so much attention to the Battle of Gettysburg? I want to thank Steve Alexander, Michael Krauss, Michael Wassuta, and Cindy Tutoli, for their invaluable help in understanding the special role these people play in the Gettysburg experience.

John A. Miller and R. Lee Royer of the new Monterrey Pass Museum and Battlefield for their contribution to our knowledge of the Gettysburg Campaign, and their help in bringing me up to date on this special new facility.

Among my many personal friends who have given me encouragement during the writing of this book, I would like to especially thank Brian Kellow, Susan Harris Smith, and Philip Smith, all published authors themselves, for those special insights into the world of publishing they so generously provided.

Terry Reimer, Director of Research at the National Museum of Civil War Medicine, Frederick, MD, clarified issues about hospitals in Frederick after the battle.

As I noted earlier, I am not a trained historian. I have relied heavily on three outstanding single-volume histories of the campaign and battle to fill in many of the facts. These are Stephen W. Sears' Gettysburg; Noah Andre Trudeau's Gettysburg: A Testing of Courage, and of course, what is still widely considered the best single volume of the battle, Edwin B. Coddington's masterful and timeless Gettysburg: A Study in Command. I must also mention Allen C. Guelzo and Scott Bowden and Bill Ward, latecomers on the scene for me but their work, too, provided me with invaluable insight. In addition, many other books have helped fill in any historical gaps in greater detail. (A Select Bibliography can be found at the end of this book.)

In sum, to the many other people who have helped in the preparation of this book, I offer a heartfelt "thank you." And to those of you I may have missed, I apologize, and please know my appreciation for your contributions has not diminished one bit.

About the Author

Stephen Coleman has spent most of his adult life as a professor of theater at the University of Pittsburgh. A specialist in Shakespeare, acting, directing, and stage combat, he taught for more than 30 years and practiced his craft on stage and screen, including roles in *Silence of the Lambs*, where he had the pleasure of being literally defaced by the epicurean Hannibal Lecter and in the PBS Series *The War That Made America*, where as the ill-fated General Braddock he was shot from the back of a horse. It was only after he retired that he discovered a new interest: the Civil War, and especially, Gettysburg.

About the Illustrator

Tim Hartman is a native of Pittsburgh, Pennsylvania, and has been professionally acting, singing, writing, cartooning, and storytelling since 1982. Though known primarily for his work on the stage, including nearly 300 plays and musicals, including appearances on Broadway in "A Tale of Two Cities" and the Tony nominated "Finian's Rainbow," Tim's favorite job is performing his own brand of stand-up comedy storytelling for children and family audiences. He is also an award-winning political cartoonist and illustrator whose work has appeared widely in newspapers.